"Fifty years ago, I became a Christian throu *ity.* Since then, Stott's books and sermons have been my closest companions. If we could be allowed but one mentor to grow us into Christlikeness, John Stott would be at the top of my list. I am so very grateful to Tim Chester for summarizing Stott's theological contributions in a manner that is exceptionally well done. Reading this book was a profoundly moving experience."

Derek W. H. Thomas, Senior Minister, First Presbyterian Church, Columbia, South Carolina; author, *Let's Study Revelation* and *Let's Study Galatians*

"John Stott was, of course, an inspiring leader and Christian disciple. But what made his legacy so powerful was that he was also a master of the distilled theological summary, the result of his deep wrestling with the Scriptures. His crystal clarity was always hard-won. Tim Chester has achieved the almost impossible by distilling a lifetime's ministry into a highly accessible and, above all, heartwarming book. We have so much to learn from Stott, and I am confident that this book will open up his legacy for a new generation. I am so grateful for Chester's work and this book, and I thoroughly recommend it."

Mark Meynell, Director (Europe and Caribbean), Langham Preaching; editor, *The Preacher's Notebook: The Collected Quotes, Illustrations, and Prayers of John Stott*

"Why should anyone read John Stott these days? Tim Chester's book provides abundant reason and motivation. While not a biography, it tracks the sources and maturing of Stott's thinking along the historic contours of his immense lifetime's ministry, and across the breadth of his spiritual passions and intellectual profundity. Thoroughly researched and meticulously documented, this is a superb introduction to one of the greatest yet most humble leaders God has ever gifted to his church—comprehensively worthy of the man himself while glorifying Christ, as he would have wanted. If you knew John Stott, relish the spiritual challenge and tonic of journeying with him through this book. If you didn't, start here! You will be enriched, informed, and inspired."

Christopher J. H. Wright, International Ministries Director, Langham Partnership

"John Stott towered over sixty years of global evangelicalism. This is the best examination of his theology of the Christian life, full of insight and practical helpfulness."

Julian Hardyman, Senior Pastor, Eden Baptist Church, Cambridge, United Kingdom

"This highly readable book invites us into the life and teaching of John Stott. It interprets for us the social, ecclesial, and theological contexts Stott navigated through the course of his ministry. Drawing on a broad range of Stott's writing, this book vibrantly conveys the central emphases and methods of his thinking, preaching, and institutional leadership—challenging readers to consider how the pursuit of Christlikeness takes visible shape in a life of service, obedience, and humility."

Laura S. Meitzner Yoder, Director and John Stott Chair of Human Needs and Global Resources, Professor of Environmental Studies, Wheaton College

STOTT

on the Christian Life

THEOLOGIANS ON THE CHRISTIAN LIFE

EDITED BY STEPHEN J. NICHOLS AND JUSTIN TAYLOR

Augustine on the Christian Life: Transformed by the Power of God, Gerald Bray

Bavinck on the Christian Life: Following Jesus in Faithful Service, John Bolt

Bonhoeffer on the Christian Life: From the Cross, for the World, Stephen J. Nichols

Calvin on the Christian Life: Glorifying and Enjoying God Forever, Michael Horton

Edwards on the Christian Life: Alive to the Beauty of God, Dane C. Ortlund

Lewis on the Christian Life: Becoming Truly Human in the Presence of God, Joe Rigney

Lloyd-Jones on the Christian Life: Doctrine and Life as Fuel and Fire, Jason Meyer

Luther on the Christian Life: Cross and Freedom, Carl R. Trueman

Newton on the Christian Life: To Live Is Christ, Tony Reinke

Owen on the Christian Life: Living for the Glory of God in Christ, Matthew Barrett and Michael A. G. Haykin

Packer on the Christian Life: Knowing God in Christ, Walking by the Spirit, Sam Storms

Schaeffer on the Christian Life: Countercultural Spirituality, William Edgar

Spurgeon on the Christian Life: Alive in Christ, Michael Reeves

Stott on the Christian Life: Between Two Worlds, Tim Chester

Warfield on the Christian Life: Living in Light of the Gospel, Fred G. Zaspel

Wesley on the Christian Life: The Heart Renewed in Love, Fred Sanders

STOTT

on the Christian Life

BETWEEN TWO WORLDS

TIM CHESTER

CROSSWAY®
WHEATON, ILLINOIS

Stott on the Christian Life: Between Two Worlds

Published by Crossway
1300 Crescent Street
Wheaton, Illinois 60187

Cover design: Josh Dennis

Portrait: Richard Solomon Artists, Mark Summers

First printing 2020

Printed in the United States of America

Trade paperback ISBN: 978-1-4335-6057-6
ePub ISBN: 978-1-4335-6060-6
PDF ISBN: 978-1-4335-6058-3
Mobipocket ISBN: 978-1-4335-6059-0

Library of Congress Cataloging-in-Publication Data

Names: Chester, Tim, author.
Title: Stott on the Christian life : between two worlds / Tim Chester.
Description: Wheaton, Illinois : Crossway, [2020] | Series: Theologians on the Christian life | Includes bibliographical references and index.
Identifiers: LCCN 2019059550 (print) | LCCN 2019059551 (ebook) | ISBN 9781433560576 (trade paperback) | ISBN 9781433560583 (pdf) | ISBN 9781433560590 (mobi) | ISBN 9781433560606 (epub)
Subjects: LCSH: Stott, John R. W. | Church of England—Clergy—Biography. | Anglican Communion—England—Clergy—Biography. | Evangelicalism—Church of England—Biography. | Christian life.
Classification: LCC BX5199.S8344 C47 2020 (print) | LCC BX5199.S8344 (ebook) | DDC 283.092 [B]—dc23
LC record available at https://lccn.loc.gov/2019059550
LC ebook record available at https://lccn.loc.gov/2019059551

Crossway is a publishing ministry of Good News Publishers.

VP 30 29 28 27 26 25 24 23 22 21 20
15 14 13 12 11 10 9 8 7 6 5 4 3 2 1

CONTENTS

SERIES PREFACE

Some might call us spoiled. We live in an era of significant and substantial resources for Christians on living the Christian life. We have ready access to books, DVD series, online material, seminars—all in the interest of encouraging us in our daily walk with Christ. The laity, the people in the pew, have access to more information than scholars dreamed of having in previous centuries.

Yet, for all our abundance of resources, we also lack something. We tend to lack the perspectives from the past, perspectives from a different time and place than our own. To put the matter differently, we have so many riches in our current horizon that we tend not to look to the horizons of the past.

That is unfortunate, especially when it comes to learning about and practicing discipleship. It's like owning a mansion and choosing to live in only one room. This series invites you to explore the other rooms.

As we go exploring, we will visit places and times different from our own. We will see different models, approaches, and emphases. This series does not intend for these models to be copied uncritically, and it certainly does not intend to put these figures from the past high upon a pedestal like some race of super-Christians. This series intends, however, to help us in the present listen to the past. We believe there is wisdom in the past twenty centuries of the church, wisdom for living the Christian life.

Stephen J. Nichols and Justin Taylor

INTRODUCTION

When I was nineteen, I attended a day conference where John Stott was the speaker. When we arrived, the friend with whom I had come went off to the restroom, and I was left alone and feeling a bit out of place. An older man noticed me, came over, and began talking to me, asking about me. When my friend returned, the man introduced himself, "Hello, I'm John Stott." My jaw nearly hit the floor. I had been chatting with the great John Stott without realizing it.

That brief encounter made a big impression on me. Stott—the only speaker that day—had seen an awkward-looking teenager standing alone and had taken it upon himself to make the young man feel welcome. I met him a few times thereafter, and he always remembered my name. The private John Stott was just as impressive as the public persona: gracious, humble, and without affectation.

To be asked to write a book on Stott's theology of the Christian life was an offer I could not refuse, and it has been a tremendous pleasure to spend an extended period of time with him through his writings in a concentrated way. At the same time, it has been a daunting prospect for a number for reasons. For one thing, I know many people who knew Stott well, far better than I did. I have comforted myself with the thought that I am not writing another biography.[1] I have not sought to unearth new material on Stott's life or to provide some kind of psychoanalytic study of his motives. I have written about his *theology*, primarily as presented in his published writings, though also as exemplified in his life.

[1] See Timothy Dudley-Smith, *John Stott*, vol. 1, *The Making of a Leader* (Leicester: Inter-Varsity Press, 1999); Dudley-Smith, *John Stott*, vol. 2, *A Global Ministry* (Leicester: Inter-Varsity Press, 2001); Roger Steer, *Inside Story: The Life of John Stott* (Nottingham: Inter-Varsity Press, 2009); and Alister Chapman, *Godly Ambition: John Stott and the Evangelical Movement* (New York: Oxford University Press, 2012).

Writing about a historical figure often involves presenting that person's thought in a more accessible way, simplifying the complexity of his or her ideas. But Stott is famous for the clarity of his thinking and the precision of his prose. There has been little scope for me to make him clearer than he already is! Instead I have presented a synthesis of his approach to the Christian life. In addition, I have attempted to identify something of the inner logic of his theology, locate his ideas in their historical content, and explore their abiding significance. I hope this book will encourage a new generation of evangelical Christians to benefit from Stott's thought.

One of my first thoughts on approaching the task was to wonder whether Stott had a distinctive perspective on the Christian life. Was he perhaps simply an articulate advocate of mainstream evangelical orthodoxy? But the more I have explored his theology in its historical context, the more I have realized that it has been Stott, perhaps more than anyone else, who has influenced the evangelical world I inhabit. So it is not just that Stott reflects evangelicalism; evangelicalism reflects Stott. A contemporary evangelical understanding of the Christian life was not simply something Stott regurgitated; it was also something he significantly shaped. This is one of the reasons why he is such an important figure to consider. We are looking at ourselves in the mirror when we look at Stott; we are exploring our own story.

Moreover, Stott was far from simply an echo of the consensus. On a number of issues, he fought for the positions he held, sometimes countering opposite extremes simultaneously. On the doctrine of Scripture, for example, he battled both liberalism and fundamentalism. On missions, he fought an ecumenical missiology that neglected evangelism and a narrow evangelical missiology that neglected social action. Instinctively irenic by temperament, he brought together divided evangelicals on many issues. But he was also ready and willing to stand his ground. Scripture was always his ultimate authority, and he was willing to follow wherever it led. One of his books was originally entitled *Christ the Controversialist*. In it he draws lessons from Christ's confrontations with the people of his day, making Christ's approach a model for a contemporary willingness to stand firm on the truth. "Certainly every right-thinking person will avoid unnecessary controversy, and we should steer clear of argument for argument's sake. . . . But we cannot avoid controversy itself. 'Defending and confirming the gospel' is part of what God calls us to do."[2] So, for example, Stott defended

[2] John Stott, *But I Say to You: Christ the Controversialist* (Nottingham: Inter-Varsity Press, 2013), 19–20.

substitutionary atonement at a moment when it might easily have been eclipsed, and he redirected evangelicalism away from a prevailing quietistic approach to sanctification.

Stott was a pastor-theologian, as am I. He was offered posts in academia on several occasions, but he chose to remain embedded in the local church. He took theology seriously and read widely. But he did not write like an academic theologian, nor did he engage in self-referential theological discussions. His theological work had to be squeezed around a full schedule of parish responsibilities, organizational commitments, and speaking engagements. But his theology is stronger rather than weaker as a result. He wrote *from* the church *for* the church—which is as it should be.[3]

Stott was also an expositor. This not only provided the foundation for his thought; it also ensured a balance in his ministry. He was not, and could not be, a man of limited theological interests. Inevitably, therefore, I have not covered everything Stott said about the Christian life. I have not included, for example, a sustained treatment of his teaching on prayer or the eschatological framework of the Christian life.[4] Instead I have focused on what I consider to be his key emphases and distinctive contributions.

The Sunday after Stott's death, I announced his passing to my congregation. I was aware that among them were people who had never heard of John Stott. So I tried in a few words to convey what he had contributed both to the wider church and to my own life. It was one of the few times I have broken down in tears on a Sunday morning.

I am grateful to Chris Wright and Ted Schroder, who both agreed to talk with me about this project; to Julian Hardyman and Mark Meynell, who both made constructive comments on the manuscript; and to the staff of the Church of England Record Centre for assisting me with access to the archive of Stott's papers. I have also made use of an interview I conducted with John Stott for my book *Awakening to a World of Need*.[5]

---

[3] For Stott's own comments on this, see John Stott, *The Epistles of John* (London: Tyndale Press, 1964), 11. For an example of the difference this creates, see the contrasting analyses of 1 Thessalonians Stott provides in *The Message of Thessalonians* (Leicester: Inter-Varsity Press; Downers Grove, IL: InterVarsity Press, 1991), 19–20.

[4] See, for example, the conclusion to John Stott, *The Contemporary Christian: An Urgent Plea for Double Listening* (Leicester: Inter-Varsity Press, 1992), 375–92.

[5] Tim Chester, *Awakening to a World of Need: The Recovery of Evangelical Social Concern* (Leicester: Inter-Varsity Press, 1993), 22–24.

CHAPTER 1

AN EVANGELICAL LIFE

John Stott was born on April 27, 1921, into a privileged home. His father, Arnold Stott, was a rising doctor who would go on to become physician to the royal household. Stott senior had served in the First World War and would serve again in the Second, rising to the rank of major general. John was the longed-for son with three older sisters. It was a home with servants, including a succession of nannies. The one who stuck was Nanny Golden, a devout Christian, who taught the children Christian choruses. The Stotts lived in Harley Street, the area of London traditionally associated with doctors. And, as a child, Stott was taken to the nearby church, All Souls, Langham Place.

Early in his childhood John acquired a love of the natural world, encouraged by his father. Together they would catch butterflies using traps baited with treacle and laced with beer to make their prey drowsy. But when a sibling squabble led to a cushion landing on John's butterfly box, John shifted his attentions to what became a lifelong fascination: bird-watching. Letters and diaries ever after switched easily between accounts of his work and birds he had seen.

School Days

Arnold Stott had been educated at Rugby, the elite private school that gave its name to the sport, and Rugby School is where John was destined. But first he spent a spell at Oakley Hall prep school. John was not always happy at Oakley Hall. Perhaps the ice that formed in the wash basins during cold winter days and the occasional canings from which Stott was not immune did not help. But it was not all hardship. John was not above a prank, a habit that continued throughout his life. His school friends referred to him as "the boy with disappearing eyes" because his eyes would narrow to a squint when he laughed.[1]

Boarding school was a well-worn track for the children of the English upper classes. It was a route designed to instill not only a top-class education but also a stiff upper lip, a suppression of the emotions that Stott would come to lament. The first time his mother came to see him at Oakley Hall, he met her in the headmaster's office, where he found her standing next to the headmaster and his wife. Without thinking, Stott advanced toward his mother, his hand outstretched, and said, "How do you do, Mrs. Stott?" The headmaster's wife burst out laughing, but Emily Stott had the presence of mind to cover her son's embarrassment by shaking his hand and replying, "How do you do, Johnny?"[2] It was an incident that encapsulated the confusion of a boy taken from a happy home to the stark surroundings of boarding school dorms. Nevertheless, Stott became head boy, the UK equivalent of class president, and won a scholarship to Rugby.

Conversion

Religion of a rather formal kind was part of the life at Rugby School. There was a brief service in the chapel each day as well as "house prayers" in dormitories at night. Stott later described feeling that "if there is a God, I was estranged from him. I tried to find him, but he seemed to be enveloped in a fog I could not penetrate." This estrangement was coupled with a sense of defeat. He could not be the person he knew he should be.[3] He would creep into the school chapel to read religious books and seek God, but to no avail.

What brought change was the testimony of another schoolboy. John Bridger, a year ahead of Stott, invited him to what today we would call the school "Christian Union," but which was simply known as "the meeting." It met each Sunday afternoon in one of the classrooms with Bridger leading and sometimes giving a talk (which astonished Stott, because his experi-

---

1 David Jones, in *John Stott: A Portrait by His Friends*, ed. Chris Wright (Nottingham: Inter-Varsity Press, 2011), 138.

2 Timothy Dudley-Smith, *John Stott*, vol. 1, *The Making of a Leader* (Leicester: Inter-Varsity Press, 1999), 57–58.

3 John Stott, *Why I Am a Christian* (Leicester: Inter-Varsity Press, 2003), 27.

ence of religion to date had always been clerical). Then on Sunday, February 13, 1938, a few weeks before Stott's seventeenth birthday, they had a visiting speaker, E. J. H. Nash, or "Bash," as he was known. A few years previously Nash had joined the staff of Scripture Union to work with schoolboys, somewhat controversially focusing on elite schools with the aim of evangelizing the future leaders of the nation. He had developed a ministry built around vacation camps supplemented by support of Christian Unions during term times. The camps became known colloquially as Iwerne Camps (after the Dorset village of Iwerne Minster, in which they were held), or simply "Bash" camps. Bridger had been converted at just such a camp two years before.

Stott later wrote of Nash's visit: "He was nothing to look at, and certainly no ambassador for muscular Christianity. Yet as he spoke I was riveted." Nash confronted the boys with a question posed by Pilate, "What shall I do with Jesus who is called Christ?" (Matt. 27:22), making clear that neutrality was not an option. "In a way I can't express," recalled Stott, "I was bowled over by this because it was an entirely new concept to me that one had to do anything with Jesus."[4] Stott would later write:

> I used to think that because Jesus has died on the cross, by some kind of rather mechanical transaction the whole world had been put right with God. I remember how puzzled, even indignant, I was when it was first suggested to me that I needed to appropriate Christ and his salvation for myself. I thank God that later he opened by eyes to see that I must do more than acknowledge I needed *a* Saviour, more even than acknowledge that Jesus Christ as *the* Saviour I needed; it was necessary to accept him as *my* Saviour.[5]

After the meeting Stott approached Nash, who took him for a drive in his car to answer his questions. "To my astonishment," says Stott, "his presentation of Christ crucified and risen exactly corresponded with the need of which I was aware."[6]

As was his custom, Nash did not push for an immediate decision. But that night Stott "made the experiment of faith, and 'opened the door' to Christ."

---

[4] John Stott, interview by Timothy Dudley-Smith, in Dudley-Smith, *John Stott*, 1:93.
[5] John Stott, *Basic Christianity*, rev. ed. (Leicester: Inter-Varsity Press, 1971), 121–22.
[6] John Stott, in John Eddison, ed., *Bash—A Study in Spiritual Power* (Basingstoke: Marshalls, 1983), 58, cited in Dudley-Smith, *John Stott*, 1:94.

> I saw no flash of lightening, heard no peals of thunder, felt no electric shock pass through my body, in fact I had no emotional experience at all. I just crept into bed and went to sleep. For weeks afterwards, even months, I was unsure what had happened to me. But gradually I grew . . . into a clearer understanding and a firmer assurance of the salvation and lordship of Jesus Christ.[7]

Stott's diary entry a couple of days later reads: "I really have felt an immense and new joy throughout today. It is the joy of being at peace with the world—and of being in touch with God. How well do I know now that He rules me—and that I never really knew Him before."[8]

Nash began to correspond with Stott, writing a letter once a week for at least the following seven or so years.[9] Some covered theological topics, others contained ethical exhortations, while others offered practical guidance on issues like prayer. Soon Stott was inviting other boys to the Scripture Union camps. A friend called Peter Melly accepted his invitation (much to Stott's surprise) and was converted at an Easter camp. By the summer of 1939 a dozen boys accompanied Stott from his school "house" to the camp. John became their de facto leader and pastor.

Meanwhile Stott had become head boy and also played the lead role in the school production of Shakespeare's *Richard II* to some acclaim. The following summer Stott accompanied Nash on a mission with a small rural church in Staffordshire before attending the Scripture Union camp for two weeks at the end of August along with sixteen others from Rugby School. Three days after the end of the camp, Britain was at war, and the Stotts moved from central London to a house in the countryside.

University Days

Stott went to Cambridge University in October 1940 to study modern languages. Numbers were lower than normal with so many young men entering the army. John joined the first aid squad.

He was extremely disciplined, working nine or ten hours a day. He set his alarm for 6:00 each morning (later in life it would become 5:00 a.m.) to allow time for an hour and a half of prayer and Bible study before breakfast

---

[7] John Stott, "The Four Questions," November 1979, JRWS manuscript, cited in Dudley-Smith, *John Stott*, 1:94.

[8] John Stott, diary entry, February 15, 1938, cited in Dudley-Smith, *John Stott*, 1:96.

[9] John Stott, *The Message of 2 Timothy: Guard the Gospel* (Leicester: Inter-Varsity Press; Downers Grove, IL: InterVarsity Press, 1973), 29.

at 8:00. He routinely left events at 9:30 p.m. to get to bed in time to keep up this routine.

Stott threw himself into the life of the Cambridge Inter-Collegiate Christian Union (CICCU). CICCU itself was founded in 1877 to nurture students in the evangelical faith and to evangelize their fellow students. Technically, Stott never joined CICCU, having promised his father (who described CICCU as "a lot of anaemic wets") that he would not do so.[10] But Stott was a member in all but name, making a regular donation in lieu of a subscription. He routinely invited people to CICCU's evangelistic "lectures," and in his first term two of his contacts were converted. He took a lead in discipling young Christians and organized Bible studies. "This is what we find in the passage, isn't it?" he would say.[11] Not all his attempts at evangelism were successful. Stott describes sharing the gospel with a fellow undergraduate. As he explained the free gift of salvation through Christ's finished work, the student suddenly shouted, "Horrible! Horrible! Horrible!"[12] These were hard times to be an evangelical. Each college had a chaplain, who without exception was a High Church Anglican steeped in liberal theology.

Stott continued to be involved in "Bash camps," quickly becoming Nash's right-hand man and, in the process, turning the camps "from a slightly amateur organisation into a well-oiled machine"[13]—a far-from-straightforward task during wartime rationing. The camp ministry not only filled his holidays; planning and preparation also involved daily tasks throughout each term. Nash demanded a high level of commitment from camp helpers, but it was also a great training ground, and many future evangelical leaders were shaped first as campers and then as leaders. Nash was not slow to give young men the opportunity to speak. Stott himself wrote, "Though I blush when I remember some of the naïve and even downright erroneous notions I taught, I can never be thankful enough that Bash pushed me into the deep end to sink or swim."[14] David Watson, who would later become a significant British evangelist and church leader, reckoned he attended more than thirty-five camps in total (two at Christmas, two at Easter, and three each summer), learning how to lead people to Christ,

10 John Stott, interview by Timothy Dudley-Smith, in Dudley-Smith, *John Stott*, 1:131.
11 John Sheldon, letter to Timothy Dudley-Smith, June 12, 1989, in Dudley-Smith, *John Stott*, 1:125.
12 John Stott, *Between Two Worlds: The Art of Preaching in the Twentieth Century* (Grand Rapids, MI: Eerdmans, 1982), 309–10.
13 Oliver Barclay, in Wright, *John Stott*, 30.
14 John Stott, in Eddison, *Bash*, 61, cited in Dudley-Smith, *John Stott*, 1:145.

answer common questions, disciple young converts, lead Bible studies, give talks, and so on.[15] Nash's high standards were more than matched by Stott's meticulous organization. He was still only nineteen and in his first year of university study. Yet, in 1941, Nash wrote a memo expressing his desire that, "if anything should happen to me," the work of the camps should be handed on to Stott.[16]

At the end of his second year, Stott got a first in French and a 2.1 in German.[17] Being used to doing well academically, he was disappointed with the 2.1. But by this point he had decided to switch tracks and study theology.

Ordination

A month into his final year at Rugby School, Stott and a group of other boys were taken to a recruiting office to "attest." Stott did not realize at the time that this was the equivalent of enlisting. Only later did he realize that he would be expected to report for duty on his twentieth birthday. Stott, though, was becoming a pacifist on the basis of his reading of the Sermon on the Mount. Nash, too, was a pacifist, and though it seems he did not shape Stott's initial instinctive pacifism, he was happy to affirm it. Later Stott would adopt the theory of "just war," a mainstay of Christian ethical reflection. But at the time, no one explained just war theory to him, and instead he was subjected to somewhat jingoistic propaganda that did little to convince him. Just as significantly, he was by now intent on ordination. Two obstacles stood in his way: his attestation and his father.

Arnold Stott was by now back in uniform. Despite being in his fifties, he had been recalled to the army and posted to France. Stott senior had been suspicious of his son's conversion but had assumed it would prove a passing phase. Ordination was another matter. Arnold had always nurtured the hope that John would enter the diplomatic service. Moreover, he believed it was John's duty to serve in the forces during this time of war. John, though, felt constrained by a higher duty toward God. What followed was a painful breach between father and son, conducted through letters and visits, sometimes mediated through Stott's mother. Arnold declared he could no longer fund John's university education, though he never quite

[15] David Watson, *You Are My God* (London: Hodder & Stoughton, 1983), 39, cited in Dudley-Smith, *John Stott*, 1:146–47.
[16] E. J. H. Nash, letter, March 30, 1941, cited in Dudley-Smith, *John Stott*, 1:143.
[17] Equivalent in the United States to an A in French and an A- or B+ in German.

carried through this threat. When John proved resolute, Arnold accepted his son's decision. "Am consenting but with great reluctance and unhappiness," Arnold wrote in a telegram. Nevertheless, as John wrote later, "for two years he found it virtually impossible to speak to me."[18]

In principle those training for Christian ministry could be exempted from the military service, but they had to prove ordination had been their intent before the outbreak of war. Stott had in fact told his headmaster he wanted to be ordained six months before hostilities commenced. But it was still a protracted process to secure exemption, especially given the opposition of his family. Eventually he received the backing of the bishop of Manchester to become an ordinand of the Church of England and switched to studying theology at Ridley Hall, Cambridge, in October 1942.

Stott spent most of his time at Ridley studying on his own. He did not attend a single lecture in his final year. With the assistance of the vice-principal, Cyril Bowles, he ranged beyond the normal set reading. Stott's intellectual development did not involve an unquestioning or simplistic acceptance of the orthodoxies in which his faith had initially been nurtured. "During my three years of reading theology at Cambridge," he would later write, "I wrestled painfully with the challenges of liberalism."[19] Oliver Barclay comments:

> I do not think others realized how acutely difficult John found this at times, just because he was so honest-minded. I well remember him sitting in my college room virtually in tears, saying that if he could not work his way through the liberal teaching, his ministry would be destroyed and he would be left with no ability to preach a word from God.[20]

These days Christian students have access to a plethora of academic works by evangelical scholars defending the authority of Scripture, but little of that existed in Stott's day. The New Testament scholar John Wenham, then a curate in Cambridge, introduced Stott to the writings of B. B. Warfield (1851–1921). Stott was also helped by attending meetings of the newly established Tyndale House, Cambridge, founded by the Inter-Varsity Fellowship (now Universities and Colleges Christian Fellowship) to bolster evangelical biblical scholarship.

---

[18] John Stott, in Eddison, *Bash*, 59, cited in Dudley-Smith, *John Stott*, 1:162.
[19] John Stott, in David L. Edwards with a response from John Stott, *Essentials: A Liberal-Evangelical Dialogue* (London: Hodder & Stoughton, 1988), 35.
[20] Oliver Barclay, in Wright, *John Stott*, 31–32.

Nash hoped Stott would continue his ministry with the Scripture Union camps. But Stott wanted to be involved in parish ministry. Harold Earnshaw-Smith, rector of All Souls, the church the Stotts had attended in London, was a regular visitor to CICCU. In 1945, he preached at its anniversary service, and Stott read the Bible passage. Afterward Earnshaw-Smith invited Stott to become his curate (assistant pastor), and Stott accepted. Stott's father declared it would be "a good place in which to begin." It would prove a "beginning" that lasted a lifetime.[21] Stott was ordained by the bishop of London on December 21, 1945, a few months after the end of the Second World War.

Geoffrey Fisher, the archbishop of Canterbury when Stott was ordained, described evangelicals at the time as a "cowed, beaten, depressed group."[22] Timothy Dudley-Smith says, "At the time of his ordination in 1945 it was difficult to see a future for evangelicalism, in the Church of England at least, as anything more than a faithful remnant, marginalized and all but excluded from the main stream of church life."[23] Here is Stott's own assessment:

> When I was ordained in 1945, soon after the end of World War II, there were few evangelicals in the Church of England. For over a century Anglo-Catholic thought had predominated, though weakened by liberal theology. . . . There were no evangelical bishops and no evangelical theological teachers in any university. The few evangelical clergy there were fought bravely, but had their backs to the wall. The evangelical movement was despised and rejected.[24]

Evangelicals were not just marginalized; they were also often backward looking. Michael Baughen writes, "There were all sorts of rules and shibboleths about liturgy (not a jot or tittle of the Prayer Book could be changed), clergy dress (even the size of collars!), negative commandments about the cinema, or dancing, or women wearing trousers, and the like." Any departure from these cultural norms might be enough to damn a young man as a "liberal" and lead to his marginalization. Evangelical church practice, says Baughen, was "stifling."[25] Stott was about to change this.

---

[21] Cited in Dudley-Smith, *John Stott*, 1:205.
[22] Edward Carpenter, *Archbisop Fisher: His Life and Times* (Norwich: Canterbury, 1991), 300, cited in Dudley-Smith, *John Stott*, 1:217.
[23] Dudley-Smith, *John Stott*, 1:9.
[24] John Stott, "Evangelicals in the Church of England," unpublished memorandum, August 1983, JRWS papers, cited in Dudley-Smith, *John Stott*, 1:217.
[25] Michael Baughen, in Wright, *John Stott*, 69.

All Souls Church

When Stott first become curate, the All Souls building was closed, having been damaged during the bombing of London. The congregation was meeting down the road at St Peter's, Vere Street. Earnshaw-Smith had reestablished All Souls as a clearly evangelical church. On his first Sunday he had found the communion table set for the celebrant to stand facing east with his back to the congregation (as if offering a sacrifice to God), as is customary in Anglo-Catholic churches. He pointedly moved to take his place on the north side of the table (so pastor and people were gathered *around* the communion table).

Along with regular preaching, Stott was involved in door-to-door parish visiting and took responsibility for the "Children's Church" (which later became the "Family Service") and the young people's work. While the parish of All Souls contained some of London's most expensive properties, it also encompassed poorer areas of what is now social housing. Stott took the youngsters away on camp, modeled in part on his experience of "Bash camps," albeit with children from very different backgrounds. He would wake the campers by parading round their tents playing an accordion.

During his curacy Stott spent two days living as a tramp on the streets of London. He let his stubble grow, dressed in old clothes, and spent a sleepless night under the arches of Charing Cross Bridge surrounded by the regular down-and-outers. His attempts to beg a cup of tea the next morning proved unsuccessful. The following night he queued for a bed in a Salvation Army hostel, for a moment forgetting his role and chiding the Salvation Army officer for his lack of compassion. The following morning he was outed when he attempted to get breakfast and was relieved to return to his normal life.

In Stott's first year at All Souls, Earnshaw-Smith, then aged fifty-five, suffered a heart attack. While the rector recovered, de facto leadership of the church fell to Stott. Invitations to other roles came. London Bible College invited him to be their New Testament tutor. He considered becoming the chaplain at Eton College and, at the other end of the social spectrum, chaplain of the Docklands Settlement. But Stott felt unable to leave the parish.

In 1950, Earnshaw-Smith died. The rector of All Souls is a Crown appointment, which in practice means the post is filled by the prime minister on the advice of a patronage secretary. A delegation from the

Parochial Parish Council, the body that represents the congregation, led by the senior church warden, Geoffrey Bles (the publisher of C. S. Lewis), made it clear they were interested in only one name. It seems the bishop of London, William Wand, agreed. So it was that in September 1950, Stott became the new rector. Though not entirely without precedent, it was unusual for a curate to move straight to the senior role in the same parish.

It made little sense to have a single man living in the thirteen-room rectory. So the curates and some students joined Stott along with a "house-mother." Far from vowing celibacy, Stott expected to marry. He had had schoolboy crushes on girls and remained somewhat dazzled by beautiful women throughout his life. He once wrote that there were two women who attracted him.

> It's difficult to explain what happened. All I can really say is that when I had to make up my mind whether to go forward to commitment, I lacked assurance that this was God's will for me. So I drew back. Having done it twice, I realise it was probably God calling me to be single. Looking back over my life, I think I know why God has called me to be single—because I could never have travelled or written as I have done if I had had the responsibilities of family. It has been lonely in some ways, but I'm grateful for a very large circle of friends.[26]

The centerpiece of parish evangelism was a new innovation, a regular "Guest Service." Throughout the 1950s the church grew steadily, much of that growth coming through new converts. Before the Second World War, around three hundred people were on the electoral roll (members of the church), but this grew to over seven hundred. Within the parish was Harley Street, the traditional home of leading doctors, and Oxford Street, the retail center of London. So Stott introduced an annual "Doctors' Service" and appointed a "Chaplain to the Stores." He also opened "the Clubhouse," modeled on a Victorian mission hall, to reach the poorer areas of the parish. Remarkably, 392 children and young people came on the opening day. Very few had ever attended the church, though Stott knew many by name. These early efforts at reaching the working-class areas of the parish were undoubtedly somewhat paternalistic, but such attitudes were universal

---

[26] Steve Turner, "Backing the Basics," *Church Times*, October 13, 1995, cited in Dudley-Smith, *John Stott*, 1:330.

among the upper classes in 1950s Britain, and Stott was unusual in his passion to reach beyond his own social class.

In the 1960s, All Souls started organizing church members into mid-week fellowship groups—a common enough practice today, but an innovation at the time. It also established "Care and Counsel," a Christian counseling center. "In those days," comments Myra Chave-Jones, the psychotherapist who led the work, "Care and Counsel was ahead of its time, breaking entirely new ground in the conventional evangelical world, where the usual attitude was that 'more prayer and Bible study would solve such problems.'"[27]

Stott was also heavily involved in hosting Billy Graham's mission in the Harringay Arena in 1954. Stott attended most evenings, and All Souls organized buses for people to travel from the parish to the arena. The campaign culminated in a closing meeting at Wembley Arena attended by 120,000 people. Not only were many people saved, but evangelicalism in Britain was given a much-needed confidence boost.

University Missions

In November 1952, Stott returned to Cambridge to be the main speaker at the triennial CICCU evangelistic campaign, known as a "mission." The speaker at the previous two missions had been the American Donald Grey Barnhouse. Barnhouse was a strong personality who connected well with many of the ex-servicemen returning to the university after the war, but he riled the senior fellows. Stott was a different prospect. He was polished, urbane, and one of their own, having graduated with a first in theology. Attendance was so great that at the final meeting, people had to be turned away. At the close of the mission the student committee presented him with a leather-bound Bible that became his pulpit Bible for many years to come.

It was a key moment in postwar student work. Stott himself recognized its value, and student missions became an important part of his work for the next twenty-five years. Mirroring Bash's commitment to reaching future leaders, Stott attached special importance to student evangelism because students would go on to make up the majority of the world's future leaders.[28]

[27] Myra Chave-Jones, in Wright, *John Stott*, 36.
[28] John Stott, "Evangelism in the Student World," *Christian Graduate*, March 1959, 1, cited in Alister Chapman, *Godly Ambition: John Stott and the Evangelical Movement* (New York: Oxford University Press, 2012), 34.

He led missions to Oxford University in 1954 and Durham University in 1955, as well as being assistant missioner when Billy Graham spoke at the 1955 CICCU mission. Stott spoke for a second time at missions in Oxford in 1957, Cambridge in 1958, and Durham in 1959. In 1956 and 1957, he led missions at several universities in Canada and the United States in the course of a four-month tour (during which he spent Christmas with the Graham family). The All Souls Church council agreed to release Stott for this extended period but added a stipulation: they required him to take a few days off for bird-watching before returning—a feature that became a regular part of Stott's travels. The trip to the United States was followed by similar tours of Australia (1958) and South Africa (1959).

Stott returned to Cambridge for his final university mission in 1977, twenty-five years after his first. The impact of this twenty-five-year ministry was enormous. Many people were converted through his talks, which combined clear Bible exposition, warm apologetical awareness, and an unambiguous call for response. His talks set a pattern many have followed, and the missions gave a generation of evangelicals confidence in the gospel. The substance of his addresses, honed in many different contexts, became his book *Basic Christianity*, first published in 1958. It has sold over 2.5 million copies and been translated into over fifty languages, becoming the standard evangelistic book for a generation of Christians.

While Stott was on a visit to Australia, his father died. The family had agreed beforehand that, should this happen, Stott should continue to fulfill his responsibilities. The funeral took place in his absence, but a memorial service was delayed until his return. It was a difficult time. Stott's voice was failing, and his thoughts were back in Britain. Before the final meeting in Sydney, he asked the mission committee to pray that God's power would be made perfect in weakness (2 Cor. 12:9). In the years that followed he often had people tell him they were converted on the night he lost his voice.[29] Before the Melbourne mission he locked himself in his room and prayed for strength. "Hour followed hour," he wrote later, until he sought to lay hold of the promise of Psalm 145:18:

> The LORD is near to all who call on him,
> to all who call on him in truth.

[29] Stott, *Between Two Worlds*, 333–34.

"All I can say is that as I sought to fulfil the conditions, he fulfilled the promise. I experienced nearness. I rejoiced in his presence. I was assured of his blessing, and was able to go forward into the mission."[30]

Hookses, Frances, and the Queen

In 1952, Stott was on holiday with friends in Pembrokeshire in South Wales, when they came across a deserted cottage. Stott took a fancy to it and asked if it might be bought. The following year a letter arrived saying The Hookses was on the market, but Stott was outbid. A few months later, however, the new owner found himself unexpectedly moving on. Stott had just received £750 for his first book, *Men with a Message*. So £750 is what he offered, and his offer was accepted. The Hookses became his much-loved holiday home and writer's retreat, a retreat he shared with friends and Christian groups. In 1960 a member of the congregation arranged for two outbuildings to be converted into what became known as The Hermitage, Stott's personal writing room. One of the rituals of Hookses was that Stott would insist on washing the dishes after the evening meal. This, though, could also be an occasion for mischief. For Stott would invite a new acquaintance to dry while he washed. There were two sinks, the second used to rinse off the soap suds. Stott would drop plates into the second sink in such a way as to splash water over his assistants, seeing how wet he could get them before they complained.

In late 1956, Frances Whitehead became first the church secretary and then Stott's personal secretary. She became affectionately known as "Frances the Omnicompetent" or "SOAK" (Source of All Knowledge). When he published *The Cross of Christ*, Stott included a dedication "to Frances Whitehead in gratitude for 30 years of outstanding loyal and efficient service." She would continue serving him for another twenty-five years, right up until his retirement.

On more than one occasion Stott was asked to consider becoming a bishop. But each time he chose to remain at All Souls. One appointment he did accept in 1959 (since it did not involve leaving the parish) was to be one of the chaplains to the queen, a largely honorary title that involved preaching occasionally at St James's Palace. In 1983, he preached at Sandringham House and joined the royal family for a barbeque on the beach. A few days

[30] John Stott, memorandum to Timothy Dudley-Smith, February 1996, cited in Dudley-Smith, *John Stott*, 1:407.

later a police motorcycle arrived at his London flat with a brace of pheasants, a present from the queen.

The Wider Church

In addition to his pastoral responsibilities, his travel, and his writing, Stott was actively involved in networks and organizations, both within the Anglican Church and beyond:

- He was the first chair of Frontier Youth Trust.
- He was the first chair and later president of Latimer House, the Anglican evangelical think tank.
- He reestablished the Eclectic Society for younger evangelical Anglican clergy.
- He served four terms as a chair of the UK Inter-Varsity Fellowship.
- He was a leading figure in the Evangelical Fellowship of the Anglican Communion (EFAC).
- He was one of the founders of the Church of England Evangelical Council (the English member group of the EFAC) and chair of the National Evangelical Anglican Congress (NEAC).
- He established the Evangelical Fellowship of the Anglican Communion Literature Committee and Bursary Fund, forerunners of Langham Literature and Langham Scholars.
- He was president of Tearfund, the evangelical development agency (akin to World Relief, the humanitarian arm of the National Association of Evangelicals).
- He was a founding trustee of the Shaftesbury Project, an evangelical think tank on social issues.
- He was the chair of the Evangelical Conference on Social Ethics.
- He was, at different points, involved in debates over the reform of the Anglican liturgy and canon law, and led criticism of the Anglican-Roman Catholic International Commission (ARCIC).

"In those days," comments Richard Bewes, "Stott seemed to be everywhere."[31]

When the then bishop of Durham, David Jenkins, reinterpreted the resurrection as a series of experiences involving the enduring personality of Jesus and poured doubt on the historicity of the virgin birth, Stott both met with him privately and refuted him publicly. Stott wrote an article in

[31] Richard Bewes, in Wright, *John Stott*, 76.

The Times, the UK newspaper of record, before developing his critique into a book entitled *The Authentic Jesus*.[32]

In 1970 Stott and All Souls perhaps bowed to the inevitable: Stott's wider role was growing, and the congregation needed a pastor who could focus on its needs. Stott continued as rector, but Michael Baughen came as vicar, and to all intents and purposes Baughen functioned as the church's leader. The Baughen family moved into the rectory, and a new flat was built for Stott over the garage. The transition was tough for Stott, but he remained resolutely loyal to Baughen and careful to submit to his leadership within the church. Five years later, Baughen became rector and Stott became rector emeritus.

In his book *Godly Ambition*, Alister Chapman presents Stott's career as a series of disappointments which propelled him in frustration from parish ministry to student work, to involvement in evangelical Anglicanism, to the global stage. No doubt there is some truth in this. Certainly not all Stott's hopes were realized (especially his hopes of reaching the working-class population of the parish). But by any comparative standards Stott saw considerable success in each of these spheres. Chapman's thesis appears stronger than it is, because he treats Stott's life thematically, masking the way these "stages" in Stott's career in fact overlapped. Stott was not seeking out new ministries to compensate for disappointments. A more natural reading is that success in one arena opened new opportunities in other areas.

In the 1970s, Stott made multiple visits to North America, three visits to Australia, almost annual visits to Asia, at least four visits to Africa, two visits to Latin America, and numerous visits across Europe. The core of what he did wherever he went was university missions and expository sermons. At the end of one trip to Latin America he told the All Souls congregation that he learned three valuable lessons: enjoying a siesta (Stott was already well known for his HHH—his "horizontal half hour"—after lunch), renouncing the English vice of punctuality, and kissing all the women when you enter a room. Then he added: "But alas! I shall have now to unlearn at least two of those lessons."[33]

In 1973, Stott realized a lifelong ambition of bird-watching within the Arctic Circle, staying at Bathurst Inlet Lodge in Canada. Canada's Dominion Day fell on a Sunday, and Stott offered to lead a service as a result of which

32 John Stott, *The Authentic Jesus: A Response to Current Scepticism in the Church* (Basingstoke: Marshall, Morgan and Scott, 1985).

33 Andrew Kirk, in Wright, *John Stott*, 177.

he found himself appointed as the "Honorary Chaplain" with an invitation to return the following year.

Stott was a key figure at the Lausanne Congress in 1974, which *Time* magazine described as "possibly the widest ranging meeting of Christians ever held."[34] The aim was to galvanize evangelicals toward the task of world evangelization, but Lausanne also did much to provide theological coherence to the evangelical movement, as well as placing social action on its agenda. Stott had gone to Lausanne "without any lively expectation of it being important." But "God met with us," he said, and the outcome surpassed anything he could have imagined.[35] David Wells describes it as "the high-water mark" in the "resurgence of biblical Christianity," adding, "The importance of the Lausanne Covenant remains undiminished for its evangelical cohesion, vision, and conviction, and no small part of this remarkable moment belonged to Stott."[36]

In 1968, Stott published a series of expositions under the title *The Message of Galatians*. The phrase "The Bible Speaks Today" was on the cover, but there was no further indication that this was the first in a series. Only in 1973 did a second volume appear, *Guard the Gospel: The Message of 2 Timothy*. From this emerged the Bible Speaks Today commentary series, with Stott as the New Testament series editor. Originally it was conceived as a ten-year project, though in the end it took thirty years to complete. Stott himself contributed the volumes on the Sermon on the Mount, Acts, Romans, Galatians, Ephesians, Thessalonians, 1 Timothy and Titus, and 2 Timothy. The series was called The Bible Speaks Today because "it is today's message we want our readers to hear and heed. . . . The application will sometimes be to the burning theological and moral issues of the day, and sometimes to our personal and social responsibilities as Christians."[37]

By the 1970s, Stott's books were selling in increasing numbers. At the same time, his travels made him acutely aware of the dearth of Christian literature available to most pastors of the Global South. "I remember a Christian youth worker in Soweto," he wrote, "whose eyes, when I presented him with a book, filled with tears. He said it was the first Christian

[34] "Religion: A Challenge from Evangelicals," *Time*, August 5, 1974, http://content.time.com/time/magazine/article/0,9171,879423,00.html.

[35] John Stott, interview by Timothy Dudley-Smith, in Dudley-Smith, *John Stott*, vol. 2, *A Global Ministry* (Leicester: Inter-Varsity Press, 2001), 217.

[36] David F. Wells, "Guardians of God's Word," *Christianity Today* 40, no. 10 (1996), cited in Dudley-Smith, *John Stott*, 2:228.

[37] John Stott, "The Bible Speaks Today (Memorandum to Authors)," August 1972, JRWS Papers, cited in Dudley-Smith, *John Stott*, 2:244.

book he ever possessed apart from the Bible."[38] So it was that the Evangelical Literature Trust was born in 1971 to channel Stott's royalties into providing free or subsidized books to pastors around the world. Later ELT was incorporated into the Langham Partnership, which also added a fund to support scholarships for Global South students.

Roy McCloughry became the first in a succession of study assistants in 1976. The role involved everything from summarizing books, compiling indices, and tracking down references, to chauffeuring, doing dishes after meetings, and running errands. Most found it impossible to keep pace with Stott's own regime. Frances Whitehead told one of the study assistants that being Stott's secretary was like driving in a small car with a fire engine behind you, sirens blaring and lights flashing. The assistant replied that being a study assistant was like riding a bicycle with the car and fire engine at full tilt on your back.

It was also in 1976 that Stott acquired the moniker "Uncle John." At a meeting of Christian Union leaders a student addressed him as "John." Stott graciously let it be known that he felt this showed a lack of respect for an older Christian. So John Wyatt, a member of All Souls and the chair of the meeting, asked how he would like to be addressed. This, it seems, threw Stott somewhat. Eventually Wyatt suggested "Uncle John." "Oh, yes!" replied Stott. "If you want to call me Uncle John, I won't protest at that." It was not long before Frances Whitehead became "Auntie Frances."[39]

In 1979, while Stott was in the United States, his sister Joy was rushed to the hospital, having taken an overdose. She had faithfully cared for her parents in their old age. But following her mother's death in 1966, she had gone downhill and was diagnosed with schizophrenia. She settled in Derbyshire, near her sisters. But the "voices" got worse, and medication had little effect. She lingered long enough for Stott to see her when he returned to England, but she died a few days later. The coroner returned an open verdict, refusing to decide whether it was a genuine suicide or a miscalculated cry for help. Her local vicar wrote to Stott after her death expressing his confidence that she died trusting "in the love of God." Stott used the small legacy he received from her estate to build an extension to Hookses, which he named "Joy's Room" in her honor.

[38] John Stott, "John Stott Speaks Out," interview by Michael G. Maudlin, *Christianity Today* 37, no. 2 (1993), cited in Dudley-Smith, *John Stott*, 2:232.

[39] Roy McCloughry, memoradum to Timothy Dudley-Smith, September 8, 1994, cited in Dudley-Smith, *John Stott*, 2:234.

Essentials

In 1986, Stott was invited to lunch by David Edwards, then the provost of Southwark Cathedral and a liberal church historian. Edwards pitched the idea of a book in which Edwards assessed Stott's theology and Stott wrote a response. Despite the prospect of intense scrutiny of his work, Stott agreed. What developed was subtitled *A Liberal-Evangelical Dialogue*. At the heart, *Essentials*, the book's main title, was a critique of Stott's evangelical theology of Scripture and the cross by Edwards, with a robust response by Stott.

But what garnered attention, especially in the United States, were Stott's comments on the future of the unregenerate. In the book Stott said he was open to "the possibility that Scripture points in the direction of annihilation, and that 'eternal conscious torment' is a tradition which has to yield to the supreme authority of Scripture."[40] Some thought Stott had "changed his mind" on hell, but in a private briefing document he said a tentative annihilationism had been his position "for over 50 years,"[41] and certainly in notes from 1962, Stott says we "cannot be dogmatic" on whether hell will be "conscious."[42] Though Stott was not the only evangelical taking this position (John Wenham and Philip Edgcumbe Hughes had come to the same conclusions), for some people this immediately placed Stott outside the camp. Stott refused to "dogmatise" about his position and asked people not to speak of his "endorsement of annihilationism." "'Endorsement' is too strong a word for what I hold only 'tentatively.'"[43] He called for a dialogue among evangelicals on the basis of Scripture.

The issue was not simply whether this view was correct but also whether it could be held by an evangelical. There are plenty of other issues on which evangelicals routinely agree to disagree without casting aspersions on one another's orthodoxy. But many assumed annihilationism involved a denial of the authority of Scripture. Stott, though, explicitly warned against asking what one's heart says rather than asking what God's word says. Responding to one scholar's description of him as "that erstwhile evangelical," Stott wrote, "The hallmark of authentic evangelicalism

---

[40] John Stott, in Edwards, *Essentials*, 315. See also Stott, *The Message of Thessalonians: Preparing for the Coming King* (Leicester: Inter-Varsity Press; Downers Grove, IL: InterVarsity Press, 1991), 149.

[41] John Stott, "A Statement about Eternal Punishment (For Private Circulation Only)," Church of England Record Centre, STOTT/5/3(1).

[42] John Stott, "Annual School 1962: Eschatology," Church of England Record Centre, STOTT/2/4.

[43] John Stott, letter to Donald Macleod, January 18, 1992; see also Stott, letter to Roger Nicole, June 13, 1991, Church of England Record Centre, STOTT/5/3(3).

is not that we repeat traditional beliefs, however ancient, but rather that we are always willing to submit them to fresh biblical scrutiny."[44]

Stott's position, he claimed, arose from his reading of Scripture. He argued that (1) the language of destruction suggests an end of existence; (2) the purpose of fire, the dominant image of hell, is to destroy rather than inflict pain; (3) justice demands a punishment commensurate with the crime, which suggests a punishment in time to match crimes committed in time; and (4) the eternal existence of the impenitent in hell is hard to reconcile with God's ultimate triumph over evil. "The debate," he was keen to emphasize, "concerns not the eternity but the *nature* of this punishment, whether the wicked will endure conscious torment for ever or will be annihilated for ever."[45] The respected evangelical New Testament scholar F. F. Bruce wrote to Stott to say that, while he himself remained agnostic on the issue, "annihilation is certainly an acceptable interpretation of the relevant New Testament passages."[46] Stott himself concluded: "I believe that the ultimate annihilation of the wicked should at least be accepted as a legitimate, biblically founded alternative to their eternal conscious torment."[47]

"Retirement" and Retirement

In his sixties, a time when most people are beginning their retirement, Stott visited over a hundred countries, including three extended trips to Latin America and at least twenty visits to the United States. The demands these visits made were huge. On his sixty-fifth birthday he set up AGE, his "Accountability (or Advisory) Group of Elders," which met three or four times a year under the benign chairmanship of Richard Bewes, by then the rector of All Souls, to help Stott manage his priorities. Often its purpose was to give Stott a guilt-free way of turning down requests. His study assistant wrote a briefing for hosts, often ignored, asking them to limit his schedule to two talks a day.

For his seventieth birthday some friends paid for him to go on a bird-watching trip to Antarctica (thus ensuring Stott had visited every continent). In 1998, while bird-watching in Lebanon, Stott handed his binoculars to a companion because they appeared to be faulty. But the fault lay with

44 John Stott, "A Statement about Eternal Punishment."
45 John Stott, "A Statement about Eternal Punishment."
46 F. F. Bruce, cited in John Stott, "A Statement about Eternal Punishment (For Private Circulation Only)," Church of England Record Centre, STOTT/5/3(1).
47 John Stott, in Edwards, *Essentials*, 320.

his vision. This was followed by abdominal pains, and his return had to be delayed. In London he was examined by his friend and doctor John Wyatt. Stott had suffered two embolisms, leaving permanent damage to his left eye and an irregular heartbeat. This meant he could no longer drive and required revised guidelines for hosts when he was traveling.

Stott began to reduce his wider organizational commitments to focus his attention on what would become his two legacy institutions: Langham Partnership, with its ministry to majority-world church leaders, and the London Institute for Contemporary Christianity. The LICC was founded by Stott in 1982 to give people from all walks of life a Christian worldview and a vision for integral mission. Stott was asked, as he had been previously, to put his name forward as archbishop of Sydney, and he declined, citing his commitment to the LICC as one of the reasons.

In his seventies he visited more than forty countries, many on multiple occasions, including China. Stott once told a group of English clergy, "One of the main burdens God has given me is for the rising Christian leadership of the Third World . . . the students and pastors of the Third World are my priority concern."[48] His success in this venture was in good measure due to his personal humility, along with his recognition of the past injustices of colonial history and the present injustice of global inequity. He was a celebrity, a natural leader, and the product of his elite background, but he used his influence to back emerging Global South leaders. Vinay Samuel said, "I do not know any context in Asia, Africa and Latin America where key evangelical leaders do not regard Dr Stott as a pastor, friend, and theological mentor."[49] Corey Widmer, one of his study assistants, wrote of a visit with Stott to Africa: "I have never seen him as I have seen him here—so vibrant, alive, strong, compassionate, and brimming with kindness and wisdom."[50] There is perhaps a sense in which being overseas allowed Stott to escape the emotional constraints of English upper-class culture.

In 1983, Robert Runcie, the then archbishop of Canterbury, bestowed on Stott an honorary doctorate. In 2006, Stott was awarded the honorary title of Commander of the Order of the British Empire (CBE) by the queen "for services to Christian scholarship and the Christian world." The following year, age finally caught up with him, and he stepped back from active

[48] John Stott, recording of interview by Gavin Reid, Church Society Recording C108, November 1978, cited in Dudley-Smith, *John Stott*, 2:326.
[49] Vinay Samuel to London Institute for Contemporary Christianity, July 19, 1996, cited in Dudley-Smith, *John Stott*, 2:432.
[50] Corey Widmer, personal journal, cited in Dudley-Smith, *John Stott*, 2:436

ministry, aged eighty-six, to live in the College of St Barnabas, a retirement home for Anglican clergy in Surrey.

The Reverend Dr. John Stott, CBE, died at 3:15 p.m. on July 27, 2011, aged ninety. Family and close friends were gathered around his bedside, where together they read from the Scriptures and listened to Handel's *Messiah*. After his death, many, many tributes were made to him. Billy Graham said, "The evangelical world has lost one of its greatest spokesmen, and I have lost one of my close personal friends and advisors."[51] Stott's funeral took place on August 8, 2011, with people queuing around All Souls to attend. Memorial services also took place around the globe. His ashes were interred at Dale Cemetery in South Wales, near his beloved Hookses.

Perhaps the last word on his life should go to Frances Whitehead, his secretary for over fifty years, and the person who saw both the public and private Stott more than anyone else:

> As I look back over the years, I can say without hesitation that my earliest impressions of John as a man of the utmost integrity have proved abundantly true. He was not only a brilliant Bible expositor, but also one who sought constantly to live out what he believed and taught. He was a man of deep convictions and total commitment, and there was no dichotomy between faith and practice. He lived to serve and please God, to bring glory to his name, and to boast in nothing but the cross of Jesus Christ. He rarely, if ever, talked about himself.[52]

[51] Cited in Wolfgang Saxon, "Rev. John Stott, Major Evangelical Figure, Dies at 90," *New York Times*, July 27, 2011, https://www.nytimes.com/2011/07/28/world/europe/28stott.html.
[52] Frances Whitehead, in Wright, *John Stott*, 58–59.

CHAPTER 2

A CHRISTIAN MIND

When it was announced that Billy Graham was to lead an evangelistic mission at Cambridge University in 1955, Canon H. K. Luce, the headmaster of Durham School, wrote a letter of concern to *The Times* newspaper in which he lamented "the recent increase of fundamentalism among university students." Fundamentalism, he maintained, had no place in an institution that existed for the advancement of learning. He concluded, "Is it not time that our religious leaders made it plain that while they respect, or even admire, Dr Graham's sincerity and personal power, they cannot regard fundamentalism as likely to issue in anything but disillusionment and disaster for educated men and women in this twentieth-century world?" This provoked a spate of follow-up letters. Michael Ramsey, then bishop of Durham and later archbishop of Canterbury, wrote in support of Luce, describing "the new fundamentalist movement" as "harmful."[1]

In a letter published on August 25, Stott himself weighed in. He expressed surprise that so far no one contributing to the debate had paused to define "fundamentalism." He noted the term's noble origins as a means to describe those who emphasized the fundamentals of biblical faith. Nevertheless, he recognized that in recent years it had become associated with "certain extremes and extravagances" so that it was almost a synonym for "obscurantism." "It is . . . in this sense that Dr Billy Graham and others associated with him," including Stott himself, "have repudiated it," he wrote.

[1] Michael Ramsey, letter to the editor of *The Times*, August 20, 1955, cited in Timothy Dudley-Smith, *John Stott*, vol. 1, *The Making of a Leader* (Leicester: Inter-Varsity Press, 1999), 345–46.

Stott nevertheless affirmed the necessity and authority of divine revelation. "The real point at issue in this controversy . . . seems to be the place of the mind in the perception of divine truth." He agreed with the statement made by Ramsey that "revelation is essentially reasonable." But, citing Isaiah 55:9, 1 Corinthians 1:21, and Matthew 11:25, he added, "It is often in conflict with the unenlightened reason of sinful men." As such, he concluded, conversion is not what Ramsey called "the stifling of the mind" but "the humble (and intelligent) submission of the mind to a divine revelation."[2]

Stott's courteous yet resolute defense of evangelical orthodoxy and biblical authority in the face of its cultural despisers was clear. But also striking was the careful way he distanced himself from an anti-intellectual fundamentalism that stood for "the bigoted rejection of all biblical criticism, a mechanical view of inspiration and an excessively literalistic interpretation of Scripture."[3] Stott actively encouraged other evangelicals to drop the term "fundamentalist"[4] and unambiguously aligned himself with "the new evangelicals," who had begun to distinguish themselves from fundamentalism. While wanting to remain true to traditional Protestant orthodoxy and the authority of Scripture, they rejected what they saw as fundamentalism's anti-intellectualism and separatism. Though still largely conservative in their politics, they nevertheless deplored fundamentalism's lack of cultural involvement and apathy over social issues. They spoke of themselves as new evangelicals or neoevangelicals, although, as their influence grew, they were soon thought of as the evangelicals, with fundamentalism becoming regarded as a subculture within orthodoxy.

A number of events helped give the group an identity and bring it to national prominence. In 1942 the National Association of Evangelicals (NAE) was established under the presidency of Harold J. Ockenga (1903–1985), pastor of Park Street Congregational Church in Boston. Ockenga then became the first president of Fuller Theological Seminary, founded in 1947 to provide evangelical scholarship of the highest standard and to encourage a more culturally engaged ministry.[5] The movement's leading spokesman was Carl F. H. Henry (1913–2003), who lectured at Fuller

---

[2] John Stott, letter to the editor of *The Times*, August 25, 1955, Church of England Record Centre, STOTT/5/15.

[3] John Stott, letter to the editor of *The Times*, August 25, 1955.

[4] Michael P. Jensen, *Sydney Anglicanism: An Apology* (Eugene, OR: Wipf & Stock, 2012), 15.

[5] See George M. Marsden, *Reforming Fundamentalism: Fuller Seminary and the New Evangelicalism* (Grand Rapids, MI: Eerdmans, 1987).

Seminary from its beginning and was a founding member of the NAE, as well as an advisor to Billy Graham. In 1956, Henry left Fuller to become the first editor of the new magazine *Christianity Today*, which became the mouthpiece of the new evangelicals.[6] It was avowedly scholarly and orthodox, and yet also popular. Billy Graham aligned himself with the new evangelicals from an early stage, and his growing prominence brought the new evangelicals to the attention of the wider public. The growing confidence of the new evangelicals also marked them off from the more pessimistic fundamentalists. The advent of liberalism and the questioning of orthodoxy had tended to place orthodox believers on the defensive, giving them a separatist, survivalist mentality. Now they were growing in number and producing able scholars capable of defending the faith. Stott shared the perspective of the new evangelicals, including their concern for an intellectually robust Christianity.

A Christian Mind

In the early 1960s, John Stott was asked by James Houston to speak at Regent College in Vancouver, Canada. Stott returned to Regent on a number of occasions and was impressed by its attempts to develop a distinctive Christian approach to a range of secular issues and to train laypeople.[7] He was also influenced by Harry Blamires, an Anglican theologian and literary critic who had been mentored by C. S. Lewis. In his book *The Christian Mind*, Blamires had called for the development of a Christian response to secularism,[8] and its influence on Stott is clear from the extensive use he makes of it in his own work. Blamires defines a Christian mind as "a mind trained, informed, equipped to handle data of secular controversy within a framework of reference which is constructed of Christian presuppositions."[9] A Christian thinker, says Blamires, "challenges current prejudices," "disturbs the complacent," "obstructs the busy pragmatists," "questions the foundations of all about him," and "is a nuisance."[10] Blamires deplores the lack of "a Christian mind" in the contemporary

6 See William Martin, *The Billy Graham Story: A Prophet with Honour* (London: Hutchinson, 1991), 211–17.
7 See John Stott, *Issues Facing Christians Today*, 2nd ed. (Basingstoke: Marshall, Morgan and Scott, 1990), xii.
8 Harry Blamires, *The Christian Mind: How Should a Christian Think?* (London: SPCK, 1963).
9 Blamires, *The Christian Mind*, 43, cited in John Stott, *Your Mind Matters: The Place of the Mind in the Christian Life*, 2nd ed. (Downers Grove, IL: InterVarsity Press, 2006), 33–34. See also Stott, *Focus on Christ: An Enquiry into the Theology of Prepositions* (Eastbourne: Kingsway, 1979), 76–77; and Stott, *Christian Basics: An Invitation to Discipleship* (London: Hodder, 1991), 44–45.
10 Blamires, *The Christian Mind*, 50, cited in Stott, *Your Mind Matters*, 34.

church. "It is difficult to do justice in words to the complete loss of intellectual morale in the twentieth-century Church. One cannot characterize it without having recourse to language which will sound hysterical and melodramatic."[11]

Blamires's approach contrasted with the "simple gospel" espoused by Nash, who was wary of apologetics and doctrine. Oliver Barclay says, "Bash was always frightened of the danger of going 'intellectual.'"[12] Stott never lost his appreciation of Nash's involvement in his life, but in this respect his own sharp mind and his exposure to other influences reshaped his outlook. And soon he set about reshaping the outlook of British evangelicalism.

In 1972, Stott gave the presidential address at the UK Inter-Varsity Fellowship annual conference and used the occasion to structure his thinking on the place of the mind in the Christian life. His address was later published as *Your Mind Matters* and is the clearest statement of his concern for a Christian mind, a concern that runs throughout his work.[13] His intention was to warn against what he called "the misery and menace of mindless Christianity."[14] Ideas rule the world, he says. So, if we want to win the world for Christ, then we must "destroy arguments and every lofty opinion raised against the knowledge of God, and take every thought captive to obey Christ" (2 Cor. 10:5).

Stott begins by expressing his fear that what Paul said about the Jews of his day is true of contemporary Christians: "They have a zeal for God, but not according to knowledge" (Rom. 10:2). Too often, says Stott, evangelicals are "keen but clueless."[15] He also laments a widespread anti-intellectualism in the wider culture of his day. The world no longer asks, "Is it true?" but "Does it work?" Today we might add the question "How does it make me feel?" But the same anti-intellectualism, argues Stott, is in the church. As examples, he cites Catholic ritualism, which substitutes mere performance for intelligent worship; ecumenical social action, which opts for joint activism over a search for doctrinal agreement; and Pentecostal Christianity, which makes "experience the major criterion of truth . . . putting our subjective experience above the revealed truth of God."[16]

[11] Blamires, *The Christian Mind*, 3, cited in Stott, *Your Mind Matters*, 34.
[12] Oliver Barclay, *Evangelicalism in Britain 1935–1995: A Personal Sketch* (Leicester, Inter-Varsity Press, 1997), 27.
[13] John Stott, *Your Mind Matters* (London: Inter-Varsity Press, 1973); subsequent citations of this title are from the second edition (2006). See also chap. 2 of Stott, *Issues Facing Christians Today*, 29–44.
[14] Stott, *Your Mind Matters*, 17.
[15] Stott, *Your Mind Matters*, 13.
[16] Stott, *Your Mind Matters*, 16–17.

Stott recognizes the need for both intellect and emotion in Christianity, but, clearly for him, "the greater danger is anti-intellectualism and a surrender to emotionalism."[17] It is a danger he sees in evangelistic preaching that "consists of nothing, but an appeal for decision."[18] It is a danger he sees in "the contemporary hunger for vivid, first-hand, emotional experiences, and in the enthronement of experience as the criterion of truth."[19] It is a danger that, if anything, is more acute now than it was in Stott's day.

We need to remember that Stott's emphasis on the mind is largely addressed to evangelical Christians, with a view to correcting their anti-intellectualism. In his dialogue with liberal theology he hits a different (albeit consistent) note. Liberalism is characterized by the priority it gives to human reason, effectively making reason the judge of Scripture. In this context Stott recognizes the limits of reason: "Reason had a vital role in the understanding and application of revelation, but it can never be a substitute for it. Without revelation reason gropes in the dark and flounders in the deep."[20]

Addressing evangelicals, however, in *Your Mind Matters* Stott identifies four reasons why Christians should use their minds based on the doctrines of creation, revelation, redemption, and judgment.

First, *God created humanity with a capacity to think.* This is one factor that distinguishes us from other animals. Indeed, unthinking people are rebuked in the Scriptures for behaving in a bestial way (Pss. 32:9; 73:22). "God expects man to co-operate with him, consciously and intelligently."[21] It is true that humanity's reason is now corrupted by sin, but this does not allow us to retreat from reason, not least because our instincts and emotions are also corrupted by sin. In spite of our fallenness, God still commands people to think and to interpret the world around them (Isa. 1:18; Matt. 16:1–4; Luke 12:54–57).

Second, *God's self-revelation indicates the importance of the mind, for God's revelation is rational revelation*, both his general revelation in nature and his special revelation in Scripture. God himself is "a rational God, who made us in his own image rational beings, has given us in nature and in

---

17 John Stott, *Balanced Christianity: A Call to Avoid Unnecessary Polarisation*, 2nd ed. (Nottingham: Inter-Varsity Press, 2014), 21.
18 Stott, *Balanced Christianity*, 21.
19 Stott, *Balanced Christianity*, 21.
20 John Stott, in David L. Edwards with John Stott, *Essentials: A Liberal-Evangelical Dialogue* (London: Hodder & Stoughton, 1988), 56.
21 Stott, *Your Mind Matters*, 23.

Scripture a double, rational revelation, and expects us to use our minds to explore what he has revealed."[22] "The assumed ability of man to read what God has written in the universe is extremely important," says Stott.[23] In *The Contemporary Christian* he explains, "All scientific research is based on the convictions that the universe is an intelligible, even meaningful, system; that there is a fundamental correspondence between the mind of the investigator and the data being investigated; and that this correspondence is rationality."[24] In other words, God has made a rational world with predictable patterns in nature, *and* God has made humanity with rational minds that can discern these patterns in nature.

So Stott refuses to view science as an enemy.[25] He critiques the god-of-gaps approach, in which the notion of God is employed merely to explain whatever is otherwise inexplicable. The problem with this is that the space left for God has been increasingly squeezed as scientific understanding has advanced so that now there is no need for God in a modernist worldview. But it is wrong to conceive science and Scripture as parallel or competing approaches. The real parallels are between nature and Scripture (complementary sources of information), and science and theology (our complementary attempts to make sense of this information).[26]

Third, Christians need to use their minds because *salvation is applied through the proclamation of the gospel—words addressed to minds*. Human rationality is key to redemption. "Communication in words presupposes a mind which can understand and interpret them."[27]

What about Paul's words in 1 Corinthians 1:21: "For since, in the wisdom of God, the world did not know God through wisdom, it pleased God through the folly of what we preach to save those who believe"? The contrast here, says Stott, is not between a rational and irrational presentation. The limitation of human wisdom does not mean God has dispensed with rationality. Instead, the contrast is between human wisdom (which, blinded by human pride, is in fact ignorance) and divine revelation (rationally presented in gospel proclamation). Not only does the gospel address the mind; it also renews the mind (Eph. 4:23; Col. 3:10).

[22] John Stott, *The Contemporary Christian: An Urgent Plea for Double Listening* (Leicester: Inter-Varsity Press, 1992), 115.
[23] Stott, *Your Mind Matters*, 28.
[24] Stott, *The Contemporary Christian*, 115.
[25] Stott, *Balanced Christianity*, 14.
[26] Stott, in Edwards, *Essentials*, 334–35.
[27] Stott, *Your Mind Matters*, 29.

Indeed, a spiritual person can be said to possess "the mind of Christ" (1 Cor. 2:15–16). In *The Living Church*, Stott adds, "I do not hesitate to say that anti-intellectualism and the fullness of the Spirit are mutually incompatible."[28]

The fourth reason Christians should use their minds is that *the doctrine of judgment assumes the importance of the mind.* "For if one thing is clear about biblical teaching on the judgment of God, it is that God will judge us by our knowledge, by our response (or lack of response) to his revelation."[29] Stott cites Jeremiah's warnings of judgment because the people had failed to listen to revelation (Jer. 7:25–26; 11:4, 7–8; 25:3–4; 32:33; 44:4–5) and Paul's assertion that all people are guilty before God because everyone has received revelation in some form or other (Rom. 1–2). Jesus himself says, "The one who rejects me and does not receive my words has a judge; the word that I have spoken will judge him on the last day" (John 12:48).

These four reasons explain why the Scriptures exhort us to acquire knowledge and wisdom (Prov. 1:22; 3:13–15; Isa. 5:13; Jer. 4:22; Hos. 4:6; 1 Cor. 2:6; 3:1–2; Heb. 5:11–6:3; 2 Pet. 1:5). They explain, too, why so many of Paul's prayers focus on growth in knowledge (Eph. 1:17–19; 3:14–19; Phil. 1:9–11; Col. 1:9–10). Stott concludes:

> Perhaps the current mood (cultivated in some Christian groups) of anti-intellectualism begins now to be seen as the serious evil it is. It is not true piety at all but part of the fashion of the world and therefore a form of worldliness. To denigrate the mind is to undermine foundational Christian doctrines. Has God created us rational beings, and shall we deny our humanity which he has given us? Has God spoken to us, and shall we not listen to his words? Has God renewed our mind through Christ, and shall we not think with it? Is God going to judge us by his Word, and shall we not be wise and build our house upon this rock?[30]

Pursuing a Christian Mind

Stott then turns to the practical implications of pursuing a Christian mind (or not pursuing one) for Christian worship, faith, holiness, guidance, evangelism, and ministry.

---

[28] John Stott, *The Living Church: Convictions of a Lifelong Pastor* (Leicester: Inter-Varsity Press, 2007), 23.
[29] Stott, *Your Mind Matters*, 35.
[30] Stott, *Your Mind Matters*, 38–39.

Worship

Unlike the Athenians, Christians do not worship "the unknown god" (Acts 17:23). The only worship acceptable to God is intelligent worship, or, as Jesus puts it, worship "in truth" (John 4:24). We are to praise the name of the Lord, but that requires an understanding of what is meant by God's name. The Psalms are full of the fruit of rational inquiry. Psalm 104, for example, finds reasons to praise God through the study of nature, while Psalm 77 finds reasons to praise God through the study of history. "All Christian worship, public and private, should be an intelligent response to God's self-revelation in his words and works recorded in Scripture."[31]

Stott elaborates on the need for the mind in worship in *Christ the Controversialist*. His starting point is Jesus's quotation of Isaiah 29:13 as recorded in Mark 7:6:

> This people honors me with their lips,
> but their heart is far from me.

"The first characteristic of heart-worship is that it is based on reason; the mind is fully involved."[32] The "heart" in the Bible does not simply refer to the seat of the emotions, as it does in Western culture. In the Bible, the "heart" is the center of our whole personality—hence, talk of "the thoughts . . . of the heart" (Heb. 4:12). "It is often used in a way that emphasizes the intellect more than the emotions."[33] Stott's point is that we must know God before we can worship him. "Christian worship could be defined as 'a response to revelation.'"[34]

Stott goes on to speak of the importance of worshiping God in spirit and through moral conduct. True worship consists not in outward forms (on which we should respect the preferences of our different temperaments) but in inward devotion empowered by the Holy Spirit. Nevertheless, the emphasis on the mind is striking.

> If the worshippers whom God is seeking are those who draw near to him with their heart and worship him in truth, we must be careful, when we go to church, not to leave our minds behind. We must beware of all forms of worship which appeal to the senses and the emotions but which do

[31] Stott, *Your Mind Matters*, 47–48.
[32] John Stott, *But I Say to You: Christ the Controversialist* (Nottingham: Inter-Varsity Press, 2013), 155.
[33] Stott, *But I Say to You*, 155.
[34] Stott, *The Living Church*, 37.

not fully engage the mind, especially those which even claim that they are superior forms of worship. No, the only worship that pleases God is heart-worship and heart-worship is worship based on reason. It is the worship of a rational God who has made us rational beings and given us a rational revelation so that we may worship him rationally, that is to say "with all our mind."[35]

Faith

Stott anticipates a false antithesis between faith and reason. "Faith," he says, "is not credulity."[36] Faith and sight are set in opposition in Scripture, but not faith and reason. "On the contrary, true faith is essentially reasonable because it trusts in the character and the promises of God. A believing Christian is one whose mind reflects and rests on these certitudes."[37] Nor is faith mere optimism. Stott rejects any connection between biblical faith and the power of positive thinking. It is not faith itself that brings change. What matters is the *object* of faith. "Faith is a reasoning trust, a trust which reckons thoughtfully and confidently upon the trustworthiness of God."[38]

Holiness

Stott regards the place of the mind a neglected aspect of the pursuit of holiness, despite Jesus's emphasis that the truth sets us free (John 8:32). "The major secret of holy living," Stott says elsewhere, "is the mind."[39] The first and most obvious way in which we need the mind to develop holiness is our need to know what God requires of us. Stott cites the Puritan John Owen: "That good which the mind cannot discover, the will cannot choose nor the affections cleave unto." Therefore, says Owen, "in Scripture the deceit of the mind is commonly laid down as the principle of all sin."[40] Referring to Romans 12:2 ("Do not be conformed to this world, but be transformed by the renewal of your mind"), Stott says in *Issues Facing Christians Today*: "The sequence is compelling. If we want to live straight, we have to think straight. If we want to think straight, we have to have renewed minds."[41] But

---

[35] Stott, *But I Say to You*, 158
[36] Stott, *Your Mind Matters*, 49.
[37] Stott, *Your Mind Matters*, 49.
[38] Stott, *Your Mind Matters*, 52.
[39] John Stott, *The Message of Romans: God's Good News for the World* (Leicester: Inter-Varsity Press; Downers Grove, IL: InterVarsity Press, 1994), 180.
[40] John Owen, *Pneumatologia* or *A Discourse concerning the Holy Spirit*, vol. 3 of *The Works of John Owen*, ed. William Goold (London: Banner of Truth, 1965), 281, cited in Stott, *Your Mind Matters*, 57.
[41] Stott, *Issues Facing Christians Today*, 32.

knowing what we should do is not the same as doing it. So, Stott says, "we must go further and set our minds upon it."[42] Here again he gives priority to the mind: "The battle is nearly always won in the mind. It is by the renewal of our mind that our character and behaviour become transformed. . . . Self-control is primarily mind-control."[43]

But we are changed through a focus not simply on what we should do for God but also on what God has done for us. That requires a second kind of mental discipline: "We are to consider not only what we should be but what by God's grace we already are."[44] We are to recall our new identity in Christ as children of God, temples of the Holy Spirit, heirs of glory, and so on. "Don't you know?" Paul keeps saying to the Romans and Corinthians, not to shame their ignorance but to bring them back to the truth of who they are in Christ. In conclusion: "Growth in knowledge is indispensable to growth in holiness."[45]

Guidance

Stott distinguishes between God's general will (applicable to all believers) and his particular will (specific to each believer). While his general will is revealed in Scripture, his particular will is not (although it is shaped by God's revealed will). How then does a person determine God's specific will for his or her life? "There is only one possible answer," says Stott, "namely by using the mind and the common sense which God has given you . . . trusting that God will guide you through your own mental processes."[46] It is a serious mistake to rely on "some irrational impulse or hunch" instead of using our God-given minds.[47]

People often point to verses like Psalm 32:8 ("I will instruct you and teach you in the way you should go; / I will counsel you with my eye upon you") to justify a "hotline" from heaven through which God directly tells us what to do. But Stott points out that this verse is immediately followed by

> Be not like a horse or a mule, without understanding,
> which must be curbed with bit and bridle,
> or it will not stay near you. (Ps. 32:9)

---

[42] Stott, *Your Mind Matters*, 57.
[43] Stott, *Your Mind Matters*, 58.
[44] Stott, *Your Mind Matters*, 59.
[45] John Stott, *The Message of Ephesians: God's New Society* (Leicester: Inter-Varsity Press, 1979), 54.
[46] Stott, *Your Mind Matters*, 64.
[47] Stott, *Your Mind Matters*, 65.

We should not expect God to guide us in the same manner we guide animals "without understanding." Human beings are *with* understanding, and therefore God guides us *through* understanding.

Evangelism

People are saved when they call on the name of the Lord. But this presupposes that people have heard of Christ. "Faith comes from hearing, and hearing through the word of Christ" (Rom. 10:17). So the proclamation of Christ cannot rely on emotional or anti-intellectual appeals for decisions. People need to understand who Christ is if they are to call on him. To support this contention, Stott points first to Paul's commitment to "persuading" people (Acts 17:2–4; 19:8–10; 2 Cor. 5:11), "to marshal arguments in order to prevail on people to change their mind."[48] Second, he highlights the way that, in the New Testament, "conversion is not infrequently described in terms of a person's response not to Christ himself but to 'the truth'" (Rom. 6:17; 2 Thess. 2:13; 1 Tim. 2:4; 4:3; Titus 1:1; 1 Pet. 1:22; 2 John 1–4).[49]

> There is an urgent need for more Christian thinkers who will dedicate their minds to Christ, not only as lecturers, but also as authors, journalists, dramatists and broadcasters, as television script-writers, producers and personalities, and as artists and actors who use a variety of art forms in which to communicate the gospel.[50]

In *The Contemporary Christian*, Stott tackles Paul's rejection of "lofty speech or wisdom" and "plausible words of wisdom" in 1 Corinthians 2:1–5. "There is no possible justification here either for a gospel without content or for a style without form. What Paul was renouncing was neither doctrinal substance, nor rational argument, but only the wisdom and the rhetoric of the world."[51] In his ministry in Corinth, says Luke, Paul "reasoned in the synagogue every Sabbath, and tried to persuade Jews and Greeks" (Acts 18:4), and Paul himself would later tell the Corinthians that "we persuade others" (2 Cor. 5:11). Says Stott: "We have no liberty, then, to invite people to come to Christ by closing, stifling or suspending their

[48] Stott, *Your Mind Matters*, 66–67. See also Stott, *The Message of Acts: To the Ends of the Earth* (Leicester: Inter-Varsity Press; Downers Grove, IL: InterVarsity Press, 1990), 312–13.
[49] Stott, *Your Mind Matters*, 69.
[50] Stott, *The Message of Acts*, 281.
[51] Stott, *The Contemporary Christian*, 58.

minds. No. Since God has made them rational beings, he expects them to use their minds."[52]

What then did Paul mean when he repudiated human wisdom and eloquence? Stott rejects the reconstruction that suggests Paul had decided the more intellectual approach he had taken in Athens had failed and so instead resolved, when he moved on to Corinth, to stick to the cross, plain and simple.[53] For one thing, Paul's approach in Athens did not fail (Acts 17:34), and in Acts, Luke presents Paul's address to the Areopagus as a model. What then lies behind Paul's determination to preach only Christ and him crucified? Stott identifies five characteristics of Corinth that made the cross offensive, though they are present everywhere to a greater or lesser extent:

> He knew that his message of Christ crucified would be regarded as intellectually foolish (incompatible with wisdom), religiously exclusive (incompatible with tolerance), personally humiliating (incompatible with self-esteem), morally demanding (incompatible with freedom) and politically subversive (incompatible with patriotism). No wonder Paul felt "weak . . . nervous and shaking with fear" [1 Cor. 2:3 NEB], and recognized that he had to make a decision . . . to proclaim nothing but Jesus Christ, and especially his cross.[54]

This emphasis on reason in evangelism does not mean Christianity is only for educated people.[55] Stott is advocating a rational presentation of the gospel rather than an academic presentation. Nor does it undermine the vital role of the Spirit.[56] Stott cites J. Gresham Machen. Without the mysterious work of the Spirit of God in regeneration "all our arguments are quite useless," says Machen. "But because argument is insufficient, it does not follow that it is unnecessary."[57] New birth by the Spirit does not make someone a Christian in the face of contrary evidence but opens the person's eyes to see the evidence clearly. Stott concludes: "In our evangelistic proclamation we must address the whole person (mind, heart and will) with the whole

---

[52] Stott, *The Contemporary Christian*, 59; see also Stott, *The Message of Acts*, 314.
[53] See Stott, *The Message of Acts*, 289–90.
[54] Stott, *The Contemporary Christian*, 67.
[55] Stott, *Your Mind Matters*, 70–71; see also Stott, *The Contemporary Christian*, 118–19; and Stott, *Between Two Worlds: The Art of Preaching in the Twentieth Century* (Grand Rapids, MI: Eerdmans, 1982), 146.
[56] See John Stott, *Our Guilty Silence: The Church, the Gospel and the World* (London: Hodder & Stoughton, 1967), 93–118; and Stott, *The Message of Thessalonians: Preparing for the Coming King* (Leicester: Inter-Varsity Press; Downers Grove, IL: InterVarsity Press, 1991), 33–35.
[57] J. Gresham Machen, *The Christian Faith in the Modern World* (Grand Rapids, MI: Eerdmans, 1947), 63, cited in Stott, *Your Mind Matters*, 72.

gospel. . . . Our objective is to win a total man for a total Christ."[58] In *The Contemporary Christian* he says:

> So much modern evangelism is an assault on the emotions and the will, without any comparable recognition of the mind. But our evangelistic appeal should never ask people to close or suspend their minds. The gospel requires us to humble our minds, indeed, but also to open them to God's truth.[59]

Ministry

When Stott turns to pastoral ministry, his aim is to elevate the centrality of preaching. He writes at a time of renewed interest in spiritual gifts, especially the more supernatural gifts. He accepts the validity of a wider range of gifts, as long as they are used for the common good. But "the gifts most to be coveted and prized are the teaching gifts, since it is by these that the church is most 'edified' or built up."[60] This is why teaching is the one ability required of potential elders.

Stott recognizes the danger of overreacting to the extreme of anti-intellectualism with the opposite extreme of an arid hyper-intellectualism. "We shall easily avoid this danger if we remember just one thing: God never intends knowledge to be an end in itself but always to be a means to some other end."[61] Then he flips his previous applications around. If we need knowledge to pursue true worship, faith, holiness, guidance, evangelism, and ministry, then it is equally true that true knowledge must lead worship, faith, holiness, obedience, evangelism, and ministry. "Knowledge carries with it the solemn responsibility to act on the knowledge we have, to translate knowledge into appropriate behaviour."[62]

Stott returned to the importance of the mind in 2006 when, then aged eighty-five, he addressed the International Fellowship of Evangelical Students (IFES) Graduate Conference for Europe and Eurasia. Stott gave the students three reasons why the mind matters: a responsible use of our minds (1) glorifies our Creator, (2) enriches our Christian life, and (3) strengthens

[58] Stott, *Your Mind Matters*, 73.
[59] Stott, *The Contemporary Christian*, 117–18.
[60] Stott, *Your Mind Matters*, 75.
[61] Stott, *Your Mind Matters*, 79.
[62] Stott, *Your Mind Matters*, 80.

our evangelistic witness.[63] Stott went on to explore what a Christian mind looks like in practice and commended thinking through issues from the perspective of the four key moments in the Bible story—creation, fall, redemption, and the end.[64] This generates a God-centered vision. "It insists that human beings can be defined only in relation to God, that without God they have ceased to be truly human."[65] It also involves viewing human beings as creatures with great dignity, worthy of respect, and capable of goodness and, at the same time, fallen beings, twisted by self—what he calls "the paradox of humanity."[66] In his lay training program at All Souls, Stott spoke of humanity's "dignity" and "degradation."[67] To give just one example of how this shapes a Christian approach to politics, it means a preference for democracy, since this accords people the dignity of participation in the political process while ensuring power is not concentrated in one person or institution.[68]

Mind, Emotions, and Affections

Stott makes the case for the emotions in spiritual experience, public worship, gospel preaching, and social and pastoral ministry.[69] "God has made us . . . both rational and emotional."[70] This, Stott confesses, is something he has had to learn, having been brought up in the rather repressed atmosphere of an English private school, with its emphasis on "the stiff upper lip."[71]

Nevertheless, his language is interesting. He does not say, "There should be . . . ," but says, "There is a place for emotion."[72] It is more permitted rather than required. The hierarchy is clear: "The mind exercises the primary role."[73] What does this mean? "First and negatively, *the mind controls the emotions*, or should do so."[74] Stott rejects those who advocate unfettered self-expression. Emotion in principle is good, but we are fallen

---

63 John Stott, *Students of the Word: Engaging with Scripture to Impact Our World* (Oxford: IFES, 2013), 27. See also Stott, "IFES Graduate Conference in Austria—Summer 2006: Lectures Outlines," Church of England Record Centre, STOTT/2/3; and Stott, *The Contemporary Christian*, 114–19.

64 Stott, *Issues Facing Christians Today*, 34–36; see also Stott, *Students of the Word*, 27.

65 Stott, *Issues Facing Christians Today*, 36–38.

66 Stott, *Students of the Word*, 46. See also Stott, *The Incomparable Christ* (Leicester: Inter-Varsity Press, 2001), 164–65; Stott, *Favourite Psalms: Growing Closer to God* (London: Monarch, 2003), 10; and Stott, *Why I Am a Christian* (Leicester: Inter-Varsity Press, 2003), 68–81.

67 John Stott, *Parochial Evangelism by the Laity* (Westminster: Church Information Board/London Diocese, 1952), 10.

68 Stott, *Issues Facing Christians Today*, 40–41.

69 Stott, *The Contemporary Christian*, 120–27.

70 Stott, *The Contemporary Christian*, 125.

71 Stott, *The Contemporary Christian*, 120; see also Stott, *Balanced Christianity*, 25.

72 Stott, *The Contemporary Christian*, 121.

73 Stott, *The Contemporary Christian*, 125.

74 Stott, *The Contemporary Christian*, 125.

human beings, and so emotions are fallen and therefore disordered. "They are ambiguous because we are ambiguous. Some are good, but others evil, and we have to learn to discriminate between them." Stott cites anger as an example. In fallen human beings, anger can be a right response to injustice (in *The Message of Ephesians*, he says we need more anger at sin),[75] but it can also be a wrong response to injured pride. "Secondly and positively, the *mind stimulates the emotions*. It is when we reflect on the truth that our heart catches fire."[76]

"It is important, then," Stott concludes, "to keep our mind and our emotions together, allowing our mind both to control and to stimulate our emotions."[77] Fair enough. But consider Stott's statement: "I begin with our mind because it is the central citadel of our personality and effectively rules our lives."[78] Is this true? Proverbs 4:23 says,

> Keep your heart with all vigilance,
> for from it flow the springs of life.

To be sure, the "heart" includes reason, but it also includes our motivations. "Christians cannot possibly," says Stott, "give free rein to our emotions. For our whole human being has been tainted and twisted by inherited sin, and that includes our emotions."[79] Therefore, he concludes, we need reason to control and shape our emotions. True. But we also need to recognize that our reason has been "tainted and twisted by inherited sin."

A third category that might have supplemented the dichotomy that Stott presents between mind and emotions is affections. Our affections are the things that motivate us—our desires, loves, hopes, and fears. They are not the same as emotions. I feel happy (an emotion) when my fears (affections) are allayed or my desires (affections) fulfilled. Emotions are the result of our deep-seated affections interacting with our circumstances. So it is not simply the mind that controls our emotions (and our will). The affections are also involved. And the link between the mind and the affections is complex. Sometimes the Bible speaks of the mind as the lead (such as in Rom. 12:2, a text often quoted by Stott), but sometimes it speaks of the affections as the lead. Romans 1:21, for example, says, "For although

75 Stott, *The Message of Ephesians*, 186.
76 Stott, *The Contemporary Christian*, 126.
77 Stott, *The Contemporary Christian*, 127.
78 Stott, *The Contemporary Christian*, 90.
79 Stott, *The Contemporary Christian*, 126.

they knew God, they did not honor him as God or give thanks to him, but they became futile in their thinking, and their foolish hearts were darkened." Here our affections (what we honor or desire) corrupt our minds. Our minds find ways to justify what our hearts desire. Or, as Ashley Null summarizes Thomas Cranmer's anthropology, "What the heart loves, the will chooses and the mind justifies."[80] So perhaps a more rounded view, one that reflects the biblical witness as a whole, is that our minds and affections are in dynamic interplay. Our reason shapes our affections, and our affections shape our reason.

Double Listening

One Monday morning in the late 1960s, at an All Souls Church staff team meeting, Ted Schroder, one of Stott's curates, blurted out, "John, you're not listening!" Stott recalled blushing because "he was quite right."[81] Stott saw it as a formative moment in more ways than one.[82] It was the beginning of the recognition that his wider interests meant he could no longer give All Souls the attention it required. But it was also part of a movement in Stott's thinking. Schroder was a New Zealander who broke the mold of previous curates, all of whom had shared Stott's social background, and all of whom had been somewhat in awe of him. Schroder felt Stott was not really addressing the concerns of the younger generation and so encouraged Stott to engage more with the wider culture. Stott started going to the theater and cinema—practices he had initially renounced as worldly after his conversion. Whereas previously Stott had turned to contemporary culture merely to illustrate sermon points, he now began to engage more deeply with its assumptions and address its concerns. His sympathy with the radical movements of the 1960s and 1970s (along with his critique) is evident in his commentary on the Sermon on the Mount. "Christians find this search for a cultural alternative," he writes, "one of the most hopeful, even exciting, signs of the times."[83] He subtitled the book *Christian Counter-Culture* in a deliberate echo of the counterculture movement.

It was the beginning of what became a central characteristic of Stott's theological approach: double listening. Here is the idea in Stott's own words:

---

80 Ashley Null, foreword to Winfield Bevins, *Our Common Prayer: A Field Guide to the Book of Common Prayer* (Hanover, NH: Simeon, 2013), 13.
81 Stott, *The Contemporary Christian*, 103.
82 See Dudley-Smith, *John Stott*, 2:28; and Stott, *Between Two Worlds*, 12.
83 John Stott, *The Message of the Sermon on the Mount: Christian Counter-Culture* (Leicester: Inter-Varsity Press; Downers Grove, IL: InterVarsity Press, 1978), 16.

> Double listening . . . is the faculty of listening to two voices at the same time, the voice of God through Scripture and the voices of men and women around us. These voices will often contradict one another, but our purpose in listening to them both is to discover how they relate to each other. Double listening is indispensable to Christian discipleship and Christian mission.[84]

> I believe we are called to the difficult and even painful task of "double listening." That is, we are to listen carefully (although of course with differing degrees of respect) both to the ancient Word and to the modern world, in order to relate the one to the other with a combination of fidelity and sensitivity.[85]

> We have to begin with a double refusal. We refuse to become either so absorbed in the Word, that we *escape* into it and fail to let it confront the world, or so absorbed in the world, that we *conform* to it and fail to subject it to the judgment of the Word. Escapism and conformity are opposite mistakes, but neither is a Christian option.[86]

Double listening is an approach to preaching, as the US title of Stott's book on preaching, *Between Two Worlds*, makes clear.[87] The preacher engages in a process of listening to the world and the Word with a view to bridging the gap "between two worlds." As early as 1952, Stott's notes for lay training included an exhortation to "know your audience as well as your Bible"—an early expression of double listening.[88]

But double listening is bigger than a homiletical process. It describes an orientation of the Christian life. "Double listening is indispensable to Christian discipleship and Christian mission. It is only through the discipline of double listening that it is possible to become a 'contemporary Christian.'"[89] In *The Authentic Jesus*, he says it is "essential to Christian maturity."[90]

Nowhere is double listening modeled more clearly than in *The Contemporary Christian*. Again and again Stott presents a secular standpoint or

---

84 Stott, *The Contemporary Christian*, 29.
85 Stott, *The Contemporary Christian*, 13.
86 Stott, *The Contemporary Christian*, 27.
87 The UK edition is entitled *I Believe in Preaching* (London: Hodder, 1982).
88 Stott, *Parochial Evangelism by the Laity*, 15.
89 Stott, *The Contemporary Christian*, 29.
90 John Stott, *The Authentic Jesus: A Response to Current Scepticism in the Church* (Basingstoke: Marshall, Morgan and Scott, 1985), 15.

issue in the best possible light, even though he may reject it. He looks for what is good in it. He particularly hears its challenge to Christianity. Only then does he move to critique and biblical reconstruction.

In chapter 14, for example, on secular challenges to the church, he outlines with great depth and sensitivity the contemporary quest for transcendence, significance, and community.[91] It is clear Stott believes modern people are looking for these things in the wrong place. But there is no sense of dismissal or scorn. Instead the overriding tone is empathy. There is also a humility, for Stott recognizes that while it might be assumed that transcendence, significance, and community would readily be found in the church, we have weakness in each area.[92]

In chapter 21, where Stott commends incarnational mission, he suggests that adopting a lifestyle that identifies with the poor may go too far and become inauthentic. He commends, instead, getting inside the thought-world of those we aim to reach.[93] It is what we might call an "incarnation of the mind" on which he focuses.

In the prelude to a resolute defense of the uniqueness of Christ, Stott first asks, "What is it about 'pluralism' that many find attractive?" "We shall not be in a position to respond to them until we have listened to them and struggled to understand and feel the appeal of their arguments."[94] Stott then outlines a number of reasons why people find pluralism attractive. He describes each case as accurately as he can and expresses sympathy for certain aspects of what is being said before finally offering a gospel response.[95]

It is important to recognize that for Stott the purpose of double listening is not to make the gospel more palatable to modern ears, still less to adapt it to modern sensibilities. Quite the opposite. While it is true that double listening enables us to connect the gospel to people's deepest longings, it also enables us to bring clarity to the call to repentance. So double listening is an asymmetrical process.

> I am not suggesting that we should listen to God and to our fellow human beings in the same way or with the same degree of deference. We listen to

[91] Stott, *The Contemporary Christian*, 222–38; see also Stott, *The Living Church*, 45; and Stott, *Why I Am a Christian*, 104–19.
[92] Stott, *The Contemporary Christian*, 236.
[93] Stott, *The Contemporary Christian*, 357–60.
[94] Stott, *The Contemporary Christian*, 298.
[95] Stott, *The Contemporary Christian*, 304.

> the Word with humble reverence, anxious to understand it, and resolved to believe and obey what we come to understand. We listen to the world with critical alertness, anxious to understand it too, and resolved not necessarily to believe and obey it, but to sympathize with it and to seek grace to discover how the gospel relates to it.[96]

At an IFES European Conference on Evangelism in 1988, Stott told a thousand students:

> We are fooling ourselves if we imagine that we can ever make the authentic gospel popular. . . . It's too simple in an age of rationalism; too narrow in an age of pluralism; too humiliating in an age of self-confidence; too demanding in an age of permissiveness; and too unpatriotic in an age of blind nationalism. . . . What are we going to share with friends? The authentic gospel or a gospel that has been corrupted in order to suit human pride?[97]

One way Stott put the discipline of double listening into practice throughout his ministry was by convening a reading group of young professionals. Every six weeks for over twenty years, they met to discuss a contemporary book or film. He explains, "Then we ask ourselves, (1) What are the main issues which this raises for Christians? and (2) How does the gospel relate to people who think and live like this?"[98] David Turner, a lawyer who went on to become a circuit judge, was a member of the reading group.

> We read novels, watched films, scanned magazines and tried to unpick their assumptions and world views. We read Castenada and Fowles, Pirsig and Potok, Golding, Roszak, and dozens of others. We wrestled with *Cosmopolitan* magazine. We found ourselves cringing with embarrassment at some risqué film, and standing baffled at the Tate gallery while one of our number enthused about Mark Rothko's "Black on Maroon."[99]

Later Turner joined another one of Stott's double-listening groups, a group known as "Christian debate," for more senior figures including Christian

---

96 Stott, *The Contemporary Christian*, 28.
97 John Stott, "The Crucial Decision," *IFES Overview, 1988/1989*, cited in Dudley-Smith, *John Stott*, 2:267.
98 Stott, *The Contemporary Christian*, 215; see also Stott, *The Living Church*, 107; and Stott, *Between Two Worlds*, 194–99.
99 David Turner, in *John Stott: A Portrait by His Friends*, ed. Chris Wright (Nottingham: Inter-Varsity Press, 2011), 83.

politicians, church leaders, and academics. "Again, papers were read, books discussed, contemporary and theological themes and authors occasionally interrogated in person."[100]

Balanced Christianity

Double listening is a discipline not just in relation to the world but also within the church. "Thank God," says Stott, "that he has given us two ears, so that we may engage in double listening, and may pay careful attention to both sides of every question."[101] Stott concludes *The Contemporary Christian* with an appeal for what he calls "Balanced Biblical Christianity."[102]

> I do not claim any close personal acquaintance with the devil. . . . But what I do know is that he is a fanatic, and the enemy of all common sense, moderation and balance. One of his favourite pastimes is to upset our equilibrium, and tip Christians (especially evangelical Christians) off balance. If he cannot induce us to deny Christ, he will get us to distort Christ instead. In consequence lopsided Christianity is widespread, in which we over-emphasise one aspect of a truth, while under-emphasising another.[103]

We need to develop this balanced, biblical Christianity, Stott says, "by combining truths which complement one another and not separating what God has joined."[104]

In part, this concern for balance is driven by a commitment to Christian unity. Too often "we push other people over to one pole while keeping the opposite pole as our preserve."[105] Stott is not thinking here of the big theological fault lines between evangelicalism and Catholicism or evangelicalism and liberalism. His focus is on the divisions among Bible-believing Christians with a shared commitment to the supremacy of Scripture. He cites the charismatic divide as one example. Today, thankfully, this is perhaps not the source of acrimony it was in Stott's day. But it has been replaced by other challenges. Indeed, perhaps this

100 Turner, in Wright, *John Stott*, 84.
101 Stott, *The Contemporary Christian*, 375.
102 Stott, *The Contemporary Christian*, 375, 643; see also chap. 6 of John Stott, *The Radical Disciple: Wholehearted Christian Living* (Leicester: Inter-Varsity Press, 2010), 87–102.
103 Stott, *The Contemporary Christian*, 375; see also Stott, *The Living Church*, 117.
104 Stott, *The Living Church*, 116–17.
105 Stott, *Balanced Christianity*, 16.

big divide has been replaced with a dozen smaller ones. We are as fragmented as ever.

Dialectic

But the focus on balance is not just driven by a concern for unity. It represents a key methodological principle for Stott. This is how his mind works. It is the logic underlying much of his reasoning.

In effect, Stott is posing a thesis along with an opposing antithesis before moving toward a synthesis. As such, his methodology resembles dialectical thinking. *Dialectic* is a potentially problematic term. It has been used to describe a theological position (what is now more often know as neoorthodoxy, or simply Barthianism, after the Swiss theologian Karl Barth). The term has also been used to describe a philosophy of history or historical determinism (most commonly associated with the German philosopher Hegel but employed more famously by Karl Marx). I am not suggesting Stott is adopting either of these approaches! Instead, I am using the term more narrowly to describe a methodology that arrives at truth by bringing together apparently conflicting ideas. "Dialectical" is a term Stott himself occasionally uses, but not often—just half a dozen times in *The Contemporary Christian*, for example. More often he refers to "balance" and, particularly in his later writings, "paradox."[106]

It is all too easy for balance to be neither one thing nor the other—a rather weak attempt to conciliate both sides of a debate with a bit of this and a bit of that, a kind of halfway house that leaves you always wondering whether the balance is in the right place. But Stott is doing something different. His approach is consistently both–and rather than fifty-fifty. "If we could straddle both poles simultaneously," Stott says, "we would exhibit a healthy biblical balance."[107]

So, for example, Stott says, "Escapism and conformity are opposite mistakes, but neither is a Christian option."[108] This is a classic piece of Stott-like reasoning. He identifies two extremes and then rejects both. Nor does he quite land somewhere in the middle with a bit of this and a bit of that.

---

[106] See, for example, "Preaching: Five Paradoxes," chap. 6 of Stott, *The Living Church*, 103–17; and Stott, "The Paradoxes of Preaching: A Lecture by John Stott at the Hookses on 28 November 2005," Church of England Record Centre, STOTT/2/3.

[107] Stott, *Balanced Christianity*, 16; see also Stott, "Charles Simeon: A Personal Appreciation," in *Evangelical Preaching: An Anthology of Sermons by Charles Simeon*, ed. James M. Houston (Portland, OR: Multnomah, 1986), xxxv.

[108] Stott, *The Contemporary Christian*, 27.

Instead, it is both–and. He is a *dialectical* thinker in the technical sense of the word.

Double listening is itself an example of this approach. Do we listen to the contemporary world? Yes, says Stott. But he also cites Peter Berger's warning not to "dance around the golden calves of modernity."[109] We face constant pressure to conform, comments Stott, while the Bible constantly calls us away from worldliness toward "vigorous non-conformity."[110] Do we therefore ignore the voices of the world around us? No, he says. We listen attentively. He is just as concerned to warn against obscurantism. It is not that we listen sometimes to the world and sometimes to God's word. Instead, we listen to both, bringing the world under the authority of the word.

Stott seems to have learned this dialectical both–and approach from Charles Simeon, the vicar of Trinity Church in Cambridge at the beginning of the nineteenth century and the key influence on much of Stott's understanding of Christian ministry. In *Balanced Christianity*, Stott includes a long quotation from a letter in which Simeon explicitly rejects an Aristotelian golden mean where truth resides in the middle ground. Instead, Simeon says, "The truth is not in the middle, and not in one extreme, but in both extremes."[111] Simeon disclaims adherence to parties or schools of thought, aspiring instead always to let Scripture speak for itself, even if that means that in his preaching "there will be found sentiments, not really opposite, but apparently of an opposite tendency, according to the subject."[112] Speaking of himself in the third person (as the author), Simeon explains:

> The author . . . is no friend to systematizers in theology. He has endeavoured to derive from the Scriptures alone his view of religion; and to them it is his wish to adhere, with scrupulous fidelity; never wrestling any portion of the Word of God to favour a particular opinion, but giving to every part of it that sense which it seems to him to have been designed by its Author to convey.[113]

Simeon's repeated example is the Calvinist-Arminian division, though Stott would apply the same principles to many other issues. "Why then

---

109 Stott, *The Contemporary Christian*, 25.
110 Stott, *The Contemporary Christian*, 25.
111 William Carus, ed., *Memoirs of the Life of the Rev. Charles Simeon* (New York: Robert Carter, 1847), 352, cited in Stott, *Balanced Christianity*, 17.
112 Charles Simeon, *Horae Homileticae*, 2nd ed., vol. 1 (London: Holdsworth & Ball, 1832), xiv.
113 Charles Simeon, *Horae Homileticae*, vol. 1 (London: Richard Watts, 1819), 4–5, cited in Stott, *Between Two Worlds*, 129, and in Stott, "Charles Simeon," xxxiii.

must these things be put in opposition to each other," asks Simeon, "so that every advocate for one of these points must of necessity controvert and explode the other?"[114] Simeon likens it to the wheels in a clock mechanism, apparently moving in opposite directions yet working together to achieve a common end.[115] Stott expresses his appreciation for the way Simeon has embraced "the biblical paradoxes (containing a contradiction which is apparent, not real), and even more the biblical antinomies (in which the contradiction seems real enough and cannot be logically resolved)."[116]

Stott's comments on Simeon are instructive: "His favourite example was again the Calvinist-Arminian controversy between divine sovereignty and human responsibility. Simeon (like Calvin himself) was convinced that we do not have to choose between these, since Scripture teaches both."[117]

Stott clearly shares Simeon's distaste for identifying himself closely with one "system" for fear this will cramp his ability to faithfully expound Scripture. Scripture rather than a theological system will be his guide. It is an approach Oliver Barclay describes as "inductively biblical."[118] One might question whether this is itself faithful to the breadth of Scripture and the Reformation principle of interpreting Scripture with Scripture. "The danger for Stott's preaching," Michael Jensen observes, "was that it became atomistic . . . better at explaining the parts than relating the parts to the whole."[119] But Simeon and Stott were unmoved by such accusations. They seemed happy to live with the discrepancies, letting them find resolution in an overall ministry.

But it is also significant that Stott adds the caveat "like Calvin himself." There is every reason to suppose that, while Stott may have avoided the term "Calvinist," his thought was consistent with that of the Reformed tradition. It is wrong to suppose Calvinists believe in divine sovereignty and not in human responsibility—that position represents the fatalism of hyper-Calvinism. Calvinists believe in both divine sovereignty and human responsibility (an approach known as "compatibilism"). By adding "like Calvin," Stott implicitly aligns himself with this position—one that matches

---

114 Simeon, *Horae Homileticae* (1832), 1:xvii.
115 Simeon, *Horae Homileticae* (1819), 1:5.
116 Stott, "Charles Simeon," xxxiv; see also Stott, *The Incomparable Christ*, 85; and Stott, *The Message of Romans*, 278.
117 Stott, "Charles Simeon," xxxiv.
118 Oliver R. Barclay, *Charles Simeon and the Evangelical Tradition* (Lewes: Focus Christian, 1986), 18.
119 Jensen, *Sydney Anglicanism*, 61.

his concern to stress all that Scripture stresses without reservation. Elsewhere Simeon, too, describes himself as "a moderate Calvinist."[120] But for both, this position was subservient to the text before them.

So, again and again in his theology, Stott states two opposing positions, identifying their strengths and weaknesses, before synthesizing them into a third position. On the doctrine of Scripture, for example, he works hard to hold the two authorships of Scripture together. He emphasizes *inspiration* with its affirmation of divine authorship while rejecting *dictation* with its denial of human authorship.

> In our doctrine of Scripture we must neither affirm that it is the Word of God in such a way as to deny that it is the words of human beings (which is fundamentalism), nor affirm that it is the words of human beings in such a way as to deny that it is the Word of God (which is liberalism), but rather affirm both equally, refusing to allow either to contradict the other.[121]

A few pages later Stott uses the same approach when talking about the church's message.

> The first extreme I will call *total fixity.* Some Christian people seem to be in bondage to words and formulae, and so become prisoners of a gospel stereotype. They wrap up their message in a nice, neat package. . . . The opposite extreme is *total fluidity* [in which] . . . you have to enter the situation first, and then you discover the gospel when you're there.[122]

Is there a middle way? Yes, says Stott in a passage in which he himself uses the term "dialectic":

> Both the extremes which I have described express important concerns which need to be preserved. . . . Somehow, then, we have to learn to combine these two proper concerns. We have to wrestle with the dialectic between the ancient Word and the modern world, between what has been given and what has been left open, between content and context, Scripture and culture, revelation and contextualization. We need more fidelity to Scripture and more sensitivity to people. Not one without the other, but both.[123]

---

120 Carus, *Memoirs of the Life of the Rev. Charles Simeon*, 242.
121 Stott, *The Contemporary Christian*, 169.
122 Stott, *The Contemporary Christian*, 252.
123 Stott, *The Contemporary Christian*, 253.

Or consider what Stott calls "holy worldliness."[124] He first identifies two false images of the church:

> The first false image is *the religious club* (or *introverted Christianity*). According to this view, the local church somewhat resembles the local golf club, except that the common interest of its members happens to be God rather than golf. . . . At the opposite extreme to the religious club is *the secular mission* (or *religionless Christianity*) . . . a "religionless Christianity" in which they reinterpreted worship as mission, love for God as love for neighbour, and prayer to God as encounter with people.[125]

Elsewhere he warns against "identification without proclamation" and "proclamation without identification."[126] Stott's constructive proposal characteristically combines what is true in both the extremes he rejects:

> There is a third way to understand the church, which combines what is true in both false images, and which recognizes that we have a responsibility both to worship God and to serve the world. This is *the double identity of the church* (or *incarnational Christianity*). By its "double identity" I mean that the church is a people who have been both called out of the world to worship God and sent back into the world to witness and serve.

Notice this is a solution "which combines what is true in both false images." Two opposites are explored. We identify what is right in both. We combine this to create a third option, which is not simply a midpoint between the two poles. We are not left balancing precariously, always in danger of veering off in one wrong direction or another. The exhortation is not to avoid too much of this and too much of that. We do not have to worry about over-affirming something as long as we do not let go of its complementary truth. So we have two strong truths which we affirm with all our might. In this case, this involves the call to worship and the call to witness, to come together as a congregation and to disperse into the world.

Stott's writings abound with examples of this both–and approach. Christianity is both historical and contemporary.[127] "Divine illumination

124 Stott, *The Contemporary Christian*, 242–45; see also Stott, *Our Guilty Silence*, 70.
125 Stott, *The Contemporary Christian*, 242–43.
126 Stott, *Our Guilty Silence*, 68–69.
127 Stott, *The Contemporary Christian*, 15–19.

and human thought belong together."[128] Human beings are characterized by both dignity and depravity.[129] We do not pursue new blessings from God because he has already blessed us with every spiritual blessing in Christ, but neither do we complacently settle for a shallow experience of those blessings.[130] We neither deify nor exploit nature but partner with God in its care.[131] Preaching requires faithfulness to the historical authors and sensitivity to the modern world.[132] We recognize both the now and the not yet of salvation.[133] In *The Living Church*, Stott identifies what he calls the five "paradoxes" of Christian preaching. It is to be

- both biblical and contemporary (relating the ancient text to the modern context);
- both authoritative and tentative (distinguishing between the infallible word and its fallible interpreters);
- both prophetic and pastoral (combining faithfulness with gentleness);
- both gifted and studied (necessitating a divine gift and human self-discipline);
- both thoughtful and passionate (letting the heart burn as Christ opens to us the Scriptures).[134]

Stott often says, "On the one hand . . . on the other hand." It is a logical construction loved as well by Simeon, who, for example, uses it seven times in the preface to *Horae Homileticae*, his collected sermons.[135] Here is just a selection of examples from Stott:

> On the one hand we are to live, serve and witness in the world. On the other hand we are to avoid becoming contaminated.[136]

> On the one hand, the New Testament writers lay considerable stress on our obligations to the state, to our employer, to our family and to society as a whole. . . . On the other hand, some New Testament authors remind us that we are "aliens and exiles" on earth.[137]

---

128 Stott, *The Message of Ephesians*, 67.
129 Stott, *The Contemporary Christian*, 33–45.
130 Stott, *The Message of Ephesians*, 52.
131 Stott, *The Radical Disciple*, 58–59.
132 Stott, *The Contemporary Christian*, 207–18.
133 Stott, *The Contemporary Christian*, 389–90.
134 Stott, *The Living Church*, 116; see also Stott, "The Paradoxes of Preaching"; and Stott, *The Contemporary Christian*, 207–18.
135 Simeon, *Horae Homileticae* (1832), 1:xi, xii, xvi, xvii, xviii, xix (twice).
136 Stott, *The Radical Disciple*, 19.
137 Stott, *Balanced Christianity*, 142.

> On the one hand, to turn the pulpit into a confessional would be inappropriate, unseemly, and helpful to nobody. Yet, on the other, to masquerade as perfect would be both dishonest in us and discouraging to the congregation.[138]

The material principle of Stott's theology—its heartbeat, as it were—is in essence, as we shall see, simply this: *the person of Christ*. And the ultimate source of his theology is always *Scripture*. But this dialectical approach was often the formal principle or shape of Stott's theology. The word "often" is also important. Stott was not some slavish advocate of a certain theological method. His mind was too expansive. Yet this was how he often approached topics. In part, his approach may have been driven by an irenic desire to unite divided groups. In part, it may have been driven by the humble generosity that so characterized his life. Because he was committed to understanding before he critiqued, he inevitably spotted the good in different positions. He was then well placed to synthesize what was valuable in contrasting positions.

[138] Stott, *Between Two Worlds*, 264.

CHAPTER 3

PREACHING THE WORD

A central feature of Stott's spirituality was his unwavering commitment to the Bible. It is God's word that, in the power of the Spirit, creates spiritual life and sustains spiritual life. "God's word is as essential to us spiritually as food is to us physically. Both life and health are—quite literally—impossible without it. It is by His word that God implants spiritual life within us. It is by the same word that He instructs, reforms, nourishes, encourages and strengthens us."[1] The secret of progress in the Christian life, says Stott, is a "healthy, hearty spiritual appetite."[2] The word is "the way of mature discipleship."[3] In his 1964 book *Confess Your Sins*, Stott argues against auricular confession, and it is striking how he focuses on the instrumentality of the Bible to counter the argument that auricular confession fosters repentance, assurance, and sanctification.[4]

> The greatest single secret of spiritual development lies in the personal, humble, believing, obedient response to the Word of God. It is as God speaks to us through his Word that His warnings can bring us to conviction of sin, His promises to assurance of forgiveness, and His commands to amendment of life. We live and grow by His Word.[5]

---

1 John Stott, *Understanding the Bible* (London: Scripture Union, 1972), 252–53; see also Stott, *The Bible: Book for Today* (Leicester: Inter-Varsity Press, 1982), 55–60, 65.
2 John Stott, *The Message of the Sermon on the Mount: Christian Counter-Culture* (Leicester: Inter-Varsity Press; Downers Grove, IL: InterVarsity Press, 1978), 45.
3 John Stott, *The Contemporary Christian: An Urgent Plea for Double Listening* (Leicester: Inter-Varsity Press, 1992), 173.
4 John Stott, *Confess Your Sins: The Way of Reconciliation* (London: Hodder, 1964), 72, 76, 81.
5 Stott, *Confess Your Sins*, 82.

Preaching the Word: Stott's Theology of Preaching

Central to this Word-centered vision is preaching: "It stands to reason that every recovery of confidence in the Word of God, and so in a living God who spoke and speaks, however this truth may be defined, is bound to result in a recovery of preaching."[6]

What is the secret of effective preaching? "Not mastering certain techniques but being mastered by certain convictions."[7] Theology is more important than methodology. Stott accepts that some homiletical principles are helpful to learn. But this is not where our confidence should lie. "Techniques can only make us orators; if we want to be preachers, theology is what we need."[8] This means holding certain key convictions. Above all, preaching requires a conviction that the Scriptures are divine revelation with divine intent. If God has not spoken, then the preacher is left sharing his own thoughts about God, and this is no basis for confident proclamation. We can preach only because we believe God has revealed himself in his word. God desires to be known, and therefore "we must speak and cannot remain silent."[9]

Stott acknowledges "the widespread disillusion with preaching."[10] "People are drugged by television, hostile to authority, weary and wary of words."[11] In the twentieth century, he claims, the tide of preaching ebbed, and "the ebb is still low today."[12] People are disenchanted with words. Words proliferate throughout our multiple media platforms, yet in the process they lose their currency. We no longer trust what we hear. All the more reason, says Stott, why we need to be convinced that "Scripture is God's Word written"[13] and that "God's Word is powerful," achieving what God purposes for it to achieve.[14]

We also need to be convinced that the Scriptures are the church's great need. "Churches live, grow and flourish by the Word of God; they wilt and wither without it. . . . Nothing, it seems to me, is more important for the life and growth, health and depth of the contemporary church than a recovery of serious biblical preaching."[15] Stott shows how again and again in the Bible

---

6 John Stott, *Between Two Worlds: The Art of Preaching in the Twentieth Century* (Grand Rapids, MI: Eerdmans, 1982), 41.
7 Stott, *Between Two Worlds*, 92; see also 10.
8 Stott, *Between Two Worlds*, 92.
9 Stott, *Between Two Worlds*, 96.
10 Stott, *The Contemporary Christian*, 207.
11 John Stott, *The Living Church: Convictions of a Lifelong Pastor* (Leicester: Inter-Varsity Press, 2007), 103.
12 Stott, *Between Two Worlds*, 43.
13 Stott, *Between Two Worlds*, 96.
14 Stott, *Between Two Worlds*, 103.
15 Stott, *The Contemporary Christian*, 208.

story the welfare of God's people hinges on hearing God's voice, trusting his word, and obeying his commands.[16] "A deaf church is a dead church."[17] Stott argues that church leaders should be seen not as priests but as pastors who protect and nurture the flock through the preaching of God's word.[18]

There are those who refuse to link the Spirit and the word, and therefore refuse to speak of God's word as being instrumental in the renewal of the church, for fear of constraining the sovereignty of God or misunderstanding of the "unction" of the Spirit.[19] But Stott is more than happy to link the two. "To be sure, it is the Holy Spirit who renews the church, but the Spirit's sword is the Word of God."[20]

Expounding the Word: Stott's Approach to Preaching

Evangelical preaching in the first half of the twentieth century was typically thematic, often strong on exhortation, but weak on exegetical and theological content. Stott's early experience of preaching was in "Bash" camps (see p. 17), where the camp talk was topical, perhaps beginning with a text but then launching off along thematic lines into wider exhortation, often involving the basic steps required to come to Christ. This was what Stott would have heard and learned from E. J. H. Nash. A common form of Bible preaching, it involved commenting on each verse in turn without any real attempt to grapple with the overall message of the passage.

Seven years later, when Stott arrived at All Souls in 1945, his preaching was transformed. He quickly gained a wider reputation. His approach was fresh, captivating, invigorating. There were no histrionics and no great rhetorical flourishes (though words were used with great care). Yet generations of listeners found his preaching mesmerizing. On hearing Stott at the 1964 Urbana Missionary Convention, one minister said: "God helping me, I am never going to enter the pulpit unprepared again and, God help me, I am going to do biblical exposition. I want to let people hear the Word of God like Stott did this morning. I never realized how fascinating and instructive that kind of preaching is."[21]

---

16 Stott, *Between Two Worlds*, 113.
17 Stott, *Between Two Worlds*, 113–14.
18 Stott, *Between Two Worlds*, 116–25.
19 See Ralph Cunnington, *Preaching with Spiritual Power: Calvin's Understanding of Word and Spirit in Preaching* (Fearn, Ross-shire: Mentor, 2015).
20 Stott, *The Contemporary Christian*, 208.
21 Keith Hunt and Gladys Hunt, *For Christ and the University* (Downers Grove, IL: InterVarsity Press, 1991), 437n2, cited in Timothy Dudley-Smith, *John Stott*, vol. 2, *A Global Ministry* (Leicester: Inter-Varsity Press, 2001), 119.

Stott had a name for this approach: "expository preaching": "All true Christian preaching is expository preaching. . . . To expound Scripture is to bring out of the text what is there and expose it to view. The expositor pries open what appears to be closed, makes plain what is obscure, unravels what is knotted and unfolds what is tightly packed."[22]

How did this transformation take place? From whom did Stott learn to preach in this way? The answer can be found on the wall of his London apartment. He had pictures of All Souls, his Cambridge college, and The Hookses, along with one portrait: Charles Simeon, the nineteenth-century vicar of Holy Trinity, Cambridge. In an introduction to a collection of Simeon's sermons, Stott describes how he was introduced to Simeon during his time at the university. "Simeon's uncompromising commitment to Scripture," he wrote, "captured my imagination and has held it ever since."[23] What Simeon described as "the practice of expounding the Scriptures" became Stott's practice.[24] In *Essentials* (about which, see p. 32), Stott describes Simeon as "one of my heroes."[25]

In many ways Stott is a twentieth-century mirror of Simeon. Sir Marcus Loane, the former archbishop of Sydney, writes: "John Stott was for our generation all that Charles Simeon had been for his generation. Stott at All Souls in London, like Simeon at Holy Trinity at Cambridge—each for more than fifty years, reaching out to touch the ends of the earth for God."[26] Gary Jenkins sums up the parallels:

> Two men, both bachelors, both Cambridge-educated, both from upper-middle-class homes. . . . Neither was married, neither was promoted to high office, and neither moved from their initial parochial base. Both were the undisputed leaders of the Anglican evangelicals of their day, both were accomplished preachers, and both sought to help, encourage and train a new generation of preachers in the art of preaching a certain kind of sermon.[27]

To this list we might add that both were converted as they entered adulthood. When Simeon first went to Cambridge, he discovered he was

[22] Stott, *Between Two Worlds*, 125–26; see Stott, *The Living Church*, 1–4.
[23] John Stott, "Charles Simeon: A Personal Appreciation," in *Evangelical Preaching: An Anthology of Sermons by Charles Simeon*, ed. James H. Houston (Portland OR: Multnomah, 1986), xxvii.
[24] Charles Simeon, *Horae Homileticae*, vol. 1 (London: Richard Watts, 1819), 8.
[25] John Stott, in David L. Edwards with John Stott, *Essentials: A Liberal-Evangelical Dialogue* (London: Hodder & Stoughton, 1988), 37.
[26] Marcus Loane, in *John Stott: A Portrait by His Friends*, ed. Chris Wright (Nottingham: Inter-Varsity Press, 2011), 91.
[27] Gary Jenkins, *A Tale of Two Preachers: Preaching in the Simeon-Stott Tradition* (Cambridge: Grove, 2012), 3.

required to attend the college communion service. The anticipation of this threw him into an agony of conviction until he read of the Israelites' transferring their sins onto the head of the sacrificial offering. "What?" he wrote later, describing his response: "May I transfer all my guilt to Another? Has God provided an offering for me that I may lay my sins on his head? Then, God willing, I will not bear them on my soul one moment longer." And so he laid his sins on Jesus and found that "peace flowed in rich abundance into my soul."[28]

Three years after his conversion, Simeon was ordained and began his ministry at St Edward's Church in Cambridge, where the Reformer and martyr Hugh Latimer had once preached. Within a year he had moved to Holy Trinity, the church of the Puritans Richard Sibbes and Thomas Goodwin. At first, however, he was met with fierce hostility. At that time, it was common for wealthy people to rent pews. The seat-holders in Simeon's church were so opposed to his evangelical preaching that, not only did they absent themselves, but they also locked their pews so no one else could sit in them.[29] When Simeon placed benches down the aisles, the church wardens dragged them out into the street. So, for the first ten years of his ministry, Simeon's congregation had to stand. Often rowdy students would disrupt the meetings, and on more than one occasion Simeon received a face-full of rotten eggs as he left the church.

But Simeon persevered, gradually winning respect. He remained for fifty-four years, exercising an influential ministry not only on the town but across the world. His memorial stone in the church's chancel reads, "To know nothing among you except Jesus Christ and him crucified" (1 Cor. 2:2). When Simeon died, the shops closed and university lectures were suspended as a mark of respect.

Since there was no ministerial training for ordination candidates, Simeon ran a kind of informal training college in his home. Charles Smyth notes that "Simeon was almost the first man in the history of the English pulpit since the Middle Ages to appreciate that it is perfectly possible to teach men how to preach, and to discover how to do so."[30] Each Sunday he would offer sermon classes in which the students would produce a sermon "skeleton" or outline, with Simeon giving feedback. And each Friday

---

28 Cited in Stott, "Charles Simeon," xxviii–xxix.

29 For a full account, see Ian Chapman, "Charles Simeon of Cambridge," *Churchman* 109, no. 4 (1995): 333–60.

30 Charles Smyth, *The Art of Preaching: A Practical Survey of Preaching in the Church of England 747–1939* (London: SPCK, 1940), 175.

he opened his home, inviting students to ask whatever questions they wished. Simeon is thought to have trained 1,100 clergy in this way.[31] He also published 2,636 sermon outlines in twenty-one volumes of his *Horae Homileticae.*

Simeon's imprint can be seen throughout Stott's ministry. We have already noted his influence on Stott's commitment to balance. Like Stott, Simeon was a pioneer in lay mobilization.[32] Like Stott, Simeon was influential in keeping evangelicals within the Church of England.[33] Like Stott, Simeon was an enthusiastic supporter of global mission (he was, for example, a founder of the Church Missionary Society).[34] Like Stott, Simeon was an advocate of social action.[35] But perhaps the most significant influence of Simeon was on Stott's preaching.

Twentieth-century preaching in Britain was dominated by two giants: Martyn Lloyd-Jones (1899–1981) and Stott. Lloyd-Jones preached like a sixteenth-century Puritan. He often focused on one verse, teasing out the theological truths it reflected and the uses to which it could legitimately be put. Often, in his famous Friday night expositions (which my mother attended in the 1960s), he would consider one verse over two or three weeks. It was a style not easily imitated, though many tried. Stott, in contrast, preached like a nineteenth-century evangelical. His book on preaching often cites Charles H. Spurgeon, the other great nineteenth-century British preacher. When Richard Bewes became vicar of All Souls, Stott gave him a bust of Spurgeon as a welcome gift. But it was Simeon to whom Stott primarily looked for his model.

Text-Led Preaching

Charles Simeon exhorted his students, "Be solicitous to ascertain from the original and from the context the true, faithful and primary meaning of every text."[36] Introducing *Horae Homileticae*, Simeon said, "The author has endeavoured without prejudice or partiality, to give to every text its just meaning, its natural bearing and its legitimate use."[37]

---

31 Jenkins, *A Tale of Two Preachers*, 4.

32 See Max Warren, "Charles Simeon: His Methods in the Local Church, the Church of England and the Nation," *Churchman* 92, no. 2 (1978): 112–24.

33 Paul A. Carr, "Are the Priorities and Concerns of Charles Simeon Relevant for Today?," *Churchman* 114, no. 2 (2000): 160.

34 John C. Bennett, "The Legacy of Charles Simeon," *International Bulletin of Missionary Research* 18, no. 2 (1994): 419.

35 See Carr, "Priorities and Concerns of Charles Simeon," 156.

36 Charles Simeon, in Smyth, *The Art of Preaching*, 176, cited in Stott, *Between Two Worlds*, 128.

37 Simeon, *Horae Homileticae* (1819), 1:12, cited in Stott, *Between Two Worlds*, 129.

Stott uses very similar language. We should look, he says, for "the plain, obvious, natural meaning of the text."[38] Our hermeneutical principles "arise logically from the kind of book the Bible is, and from the kind of God it declares him to be."[39] God's intent to be understood means the Bible is not a book of riddles. While not everything is equally plain (as 2 Pet. 3:16 acknowledges), God has communicated to us because he wants to be known. The natural meaning of the text does not necessarily mean the "literal" meaning, since the authors use figurative language. Jesus himself rebukes Nicodemus and the Samaritan woman for taking his figurative words too literally (John 3:3–8; 4:10–15). The key point is that we start with the *intention* of the author. "A text means what its author originally meant."[40] At the same time, we recognize that revelation is progressive. A fuller, richer, deeper picture emerges as the Bible story unfolds. "God's revelation has been cumulative—not in the sense that he later contradicted what he had earlier taught, but rather that he has amplified it."[41] So we need to interpret each passage in the light of the whole of Scripture. We are not at liberty to dip into Scripture at random, nor to proof text.[42] Preaching is not a conjuring trick in which insights are mysteriously brought out of the text like rabbits out of a hat. It is an exercise in making plain.

In a letter to his publishers, Simeon wrote: "My endeavour is to bring out of Scripture what is there, and not to thrust in what I think might be there. I have great jealousy on this head: never to speak more or less than I believe to be the mind of the Spirit in the passage I am expounding."[43] Stott quoted this in the brief he gave to authors of the Bible Speaks Today series. Simeon's nothing-more-and-nothing-less fidelity to Scripture was fundamental to his approach to preaching. Elsewhere he warns of "imposition," imposing on the text what is not there.[44] Simeon, comments Stott, "tried to divest himself of all preconceptions and to listen to God's Word with an open, unprejudiced, and impartial mind."[45] Stott himself says:

> We must do our utmost to ensure that . . . [the word] speaks to our time, but not bowdlerize it in order to secure a fake relevance. . . . Our

---

38 John Stott, *Students of the Word: Engaging with Scripture to Impact Our World* (Oxford: IFES, 2013), 27; see also Stott, *Understanding the Bible*, 217–24.
39 Stott, *Students of the Word*, 25.
40 Stott, *Students of the Word*, 31; see also Stott, *Understanding the Bible*, 224–30.
41 Stott, *Students of the Word*, 32.
42 Stott, *Students of the Word*, 34; see also Stott, *Understanding the Bible*, 230–37.
43 Cited in Stott, *Between Two Worlds*, 129.
44 Stott, *Between Two Worlds*, 125–26.
45 Stott, "Charles Simeon," xxxii.

> responsibility as expositors is to open it up in such a way that it speaks its message clearly, plainly, accurately, relevantly, without addition, subtraction or falsification.[46]

Recall that Simeon described himself as "no friend to systematizers in theology." "It is an invariable rule with him to endeavour," he said, speaking of himself in the third person, "to give to every portion of the word of God its full and proper force, without considering one moment what scheme it favours, or whose system it is likely to advance."[47] Simeon, for example, laments those of what he calls an "ultra-Evangelical taste," who find Christ and his salvation in every passage, ignoring the "practical lessons" and "lessons in morality" those passages were intended to convey.[48]

Stott, too, believes "exposition sets us limits."[49] We cannot make the text fit our theological system or meet a pastoral need it is not intended to address. "Exposition demands integrity."[50] "In expository preaching the biblical text is neither a conventional introduction to a sermon on a largely different theme, nor a convenient peg on which to hang a ragbag of miscellaneous thoughts, but a master which dictates and controls what is said."[51]

Is this expository preaching just for the educated? Gary Jenkins thinks not. "At its heart [Simeon's and Stott's] tradition stands not so much for a particular *style* of preaching—indeed each had their own quite different style—but rather for a particular attitude to Scripture and its place in the homiletical task."[52] In other words, the style of delivery may vary, but what is unwavering is a commitment to the integrity of the text.

Expository preaching therefore requires hard work. "The higher our view of the Bible, the more painstaking and conscientious our study of it should be. If this book is indeed the Word of God, then away with slovenly, slipshod exegesis!"[53] The first step Stott recommends in sermon preparation is to meditate on the text: "Read the text, re-read it, re-read it, and read it again. . . . Probe your text, like a bee with a spring blossom, or like a hummingbird probing a hibiscus flower for its nectar. Worry at it like a dog with a bone. Suck it as a child sucks an orange. Chew it as a cow chews the cud."[54]

---

[46] Stott, *Between Two Worlds*, 125–26.
[47] Simeon, *Horae Homileticae* (1819), 1:5.
[48] Simeon, *Horae Homileticae* (1819), 1:8.
[49] Stott, *Between Two Worlds*, 125.
[50] Stott, *Between Two Worlds*, 126.
[51] Stott, *Between Two Worlds*, 125–26.
[52] Jenkins, *A Tale of Two Preachers*, 21–22.
[53] Stott, *Between Two Worlds*, 182.
[54] Stott, *Between Two Worlds*, 220.

Presenting the Dominant Thought from the Text

Simeon said, "Every sermon should have like a telescope but one object in the field."[55] Introducing *Horae Homileticae*, he gives us a window onto his sermon preparation. "The first inquiry," he says, "is *What is the principal scope and meaning of the text?*"[56] Then he adds (in capital letters), "I BEG EVERY YOUNG MINISTER ESPECIALLY TO REMEMBER THIS."[57] Simeon's next step was to express this principal meaning in "a categorical proposition," what today might be called a "theme sentence" or "big idea." This, says Simeon, "is *the great secret* of all composition for the pulpit."[58]

Like Simeon, Stott emphasizes the need to isolate what Stott calls "the dominant thought" and express this in a single, clear, vivid sentence. This emphasis is not born simply of utility; it is not simply that Stott has found through trial and error that this produces better sermons. It arises from his convictions about the nature of Scripture. If God has intent in revealing himself in his Word, our focus must be on that intent. "If God speaks through what he had spoken, then it is essential to ask ourselves, 'What is he saying? Where does his emphasis lie?'" There may be a number of legitimate ways of handling a text and a number of legitimate lessons within a text. Nevertheless, "every text has an overriding thrust."[59]

The dominant thought of the passage then becomes the dominant thought of the sermon. Simeon's advice to young ministers was this: "that the leading point of the whole passage be the point mainly regarded; and the subordinate parts only so far noticed, as to throw additional light upon that."[60] In other words, everything in the sermon must reinforce the single, central message of the passage. If preachers do not follow this maxim, then people "are likely to be distracted with the diversity and incoherence of the matter brought before them."[61] "But if an unity of subject be preserved, the discourse will come with tenfold weight to the minds of the audience."[62]

This exactly describes "the great secret," to use Simeon's words, of Stott's approach to preaching. It is what person after person who heard him commented on. Neither Simeon nor Stott worked through a passage

55 William Carus, ed., *Memoirs of the Rev. Charles Simeon* (London: Hatchard, 1847), 418, cited in Stott, *Between Two Worlds*, 225.
56 Charles Simeon, *Horae Homileticae*, 2nd ed., vol. 1 (London: Holdsworth & Ball, 1832), vi.
57 Simeon, *Horae Homileticae* (1819), 1:vi–vii, cited in Stott, *Between Two Worlds*, 225.
58 Simeon, *Horae Homileticae* (1819), 1:xxi, cited in Stott, *Between Two Worlds*, 226.
59 Stott, *Between Two Worlds*, 224.
60 Simeon, *Horae Homileticae* (1819), 1:8–9.
61 Simeon, *Horae Homileticae* (1819), 1:9.
62 Simeon, *Horae Homileticae* (1819), 1:9.

verse by verse, making a sequence of unrelated comments on successive verses (a common misunderstanding of expository preaching). Rather they preached the big idea of the passage. All the details of the sermon were marshaled to help people grasp this central message and feel its power. Instead of thinking simply of the *meaning* of the text, we do well to think of the *intent* of the author(s). The preacher's task is not to offer a few thoughts, loosely related to the passage, but instead to identify the aim of the original authors—human and divine—and then replicate that aim in his preaching.

With Supporting Content and Structure from the Text

According to Simeon, "the next inquiry is, *Of what parts does the text consist, or into what parts may it be most easily and naturally resolved?*"[63] In other words, a sermon does not merely *start* with Scripture; it also continues with Scripture. The passage being preached controls not only the main theme but also the supporting content, structure, and application. Scripture is not being used simply to support or illustrate points being made. "The Scriptures themselves are to be the dominating presence in the sermon."[64] In other words, Simeon's concern is not simply to identify some key truths from the passage that he then expands, using his own wisdom, knowledge, and experience. Instead, his concern is to use words, ideas, and images *from the passage itself.* In this way, says Simeon, "an hackneyed way of treating texts will be avoided," "the observations will be more appropriate," and "the attention of the audience will be fixed more on the word of God."[65] In an 1821 article in the *Christian Observer*, Simeon wrote, "Reduce your text to a simple proposition, and lay that down as the warp; and then make use of the text itself as the woof; illustrating the main idea by the various terms in which it is contained. Screw the word into the minds of your hearers."[66]

Again, this is the pattern we see in Stott's preaching. Having identified the dominant thought *in* the text itself, Stott preaches the big idea *from* the text. This is what gives Stott's preaching such power. First, preaching is not simply imparting a series of ideas. There is one big idea and therefore one big aim. Second, the power behind that big aim is not the rhetoric of the

---

63 Simeon, *Horae Homileticae* (1832), 1:vi.
64 Jenkins, *A Tale of Two Preachers*, 12.
65 Simeon, *Horae Homileticae* (1832), 1:viii.
66 Hugh Evan Hopkins, *Charles Simeon of Cambridge* (London: Hodder & Stoughton, 1977), 59, cited in Stott, *Between Two Worlds*, 226.

preacher (though no one who has heard or read Stott would minimize that) but the word of God. By the end of the sermon we are convinced this is what the passage is saying and, therefore, this is what God is saying.

So Stott urges preachers, "Arrange your material to serve the dominant thought." All the material generated through the process of study now has to be knocked into shape, and the key is to ensure it serves the dominant thought. This will involve ruthlessly discarding anything irrelevant. "We have to subordinate our material to our theme in such a way as to illumine and enforce it."[67] This includes both content and structure. "The golden rule for sermon outlines is that each text must be allowed to supply its own structure."[68]

Stott warns against outlines that do violence to the text.[69] Nevertheless, he himself was famous for the clarity of his headings and perhaps the clarity they appeared to bring to a text. Reviewing *The Message of Galatians*, Michael Green wrote wryly, "St Paul might be pleasantly surprised to see how neatly he had subdivided his material when writing this Epistle."[70]

"Simeon," writes Stott, "cultivated a direct and simple style."[71] The preachers of his day were either academic in style or given to flowery rhetoric. But, introducing *Horae Homileticae*, Simeon wrote, "The author has invariably proposed to himself three things as indispensably necessary in every discourse; UNITY in the design, PERSPICUITY in the arrangement, and SIMPLICITY in the diction."[72] The prose of his sermons, comments Stott, "is straightforward and fluent"—a comment that could equally be made of Stott's own sermons.[73] "In order to communicate clearly," writes Stott, "we have to clothe our thoughts in words . . . so it is worth taking trouble over our words."[74] Words need to be simple, clear, and vivid. Illustrations (which Stott identifies as a weakness in his own preaching) need to illumine the topic appropriately without distracting from it. In *The Cross of Christ*, Stott says, "One of the greatest arts or gifts in gospel-preaching is to turn people's ears into eyes, to make them see what we are talking about."[75]

---

67 Stott, *Between Two Worlds*, 228.
68 Stott, *Between Two Worlds*, 229.
69 Stott, *Between Two Worlds*, 230.
70 Cited in Roger Steer, *Inside Story: The Life of John Stott* (Nottingham: Inter-Varsity Press, 2009), 144.
71 Stott, "Charles Simeon," xxxvii.
72 Simeon, *Horae Homileticae* (1832), 1:vi.
73 Stott, "Charles Simeon," xxxvii.
74 Stott, *Between Two Worlds*, 231.
75 John Stott, *The Cross of Christ*, 2nd ed. (Leicester: Inter-Varsity Press, 1989), 343.

Concluding with an Appeal

Simeon's sermons, according to Stott's analysis of them, end with "an 'Address,' 'Application,' or 'Entreaty,' which drives the message home by calling on the congregation to make precise and practical responses (usually two at a time)."[76] This is the model Stott found in Simeon, and this is the model he himself adopted and commended to others. Conclusions should recapitulate, says Stott. "A true conclusion, however, goes beyond recapitulation to personal application."[77] Citing a nineteenth-century manual of preaching, Stott says, "If there is no summons, there is no sermon."[78] He himself says, "It is not enough to expound a thoroughly orthodox doctrine of reconciliation if we never beg people to come to Christ."[79]

Stott encourages preachers to anticipate the "filters" people adopt to evade the import of the sermon.[80] "You might say to me . . ." was a common phrase in his sermons.[81]

"The main objective of preaching," says Stott, "is to expound Scripture so faithfully and relevantly that Jesus Christ is perceived in all his adequacy to meet human need."[82] Again, this echoes Simeon. Simeon ends his addition to the preface of his 1832 edition of *Horae Homileticae* with this test for every sermon: "Does it uniformly tend to humble the sinner? to exalt the Saviour? to promote holiness?"[83]

Delivered with Conviction in Dependence on God

The reason Simeon's ministry created a stir, says Stott, was that he "began preaching his expository sermons with much emotion."[84] Preachers, says Stott, need to *mean* what they say, *do* what they say, and *feel* what they say.[85]

> It seems to me that one might well single out freshness of spiritual experience as the first indispensable quality of the effective preacher. No amount of homiletical technique can compensate for the absence of a

---

76 Stott, "Charles Simeon," xxxviii.
77 Stott, *Between Two Worlds*, 246.
78 Stott, *Between Two Worlds*, 246.
79 Stott, *The Cross of Christ*, 201.
80 Stott, *Between Two Worlds*, 253–54; and Stott, *The Message of Romans: God's Good News for the World* (Leicester: Inter-Varsity Press; Downers Grove, IL: InterVarsity Press, 1994), 98.
81 Jonathan Hustler, "The Late Greats: John Stott," *Preach* 14 (2018): 27.
82 Stott, *Between Two Worlds*, 325.
83 Simeon, *Horae Homileticae* (1819), 1:xxi, cited in Stott, *Between Two Worlds*, 251.
84 Stott, *Between Two Worlds*, 281.
85 Stott, *Between Two Worlds*, 262.

> close personal walk with God. Unless he puts a new song in our mouth, even the most polished sermons will lack the sparkle of authenticity.[86]

Stott recognizes that the way a person expresses feelings is often a reflection of that individual's natural temperament. So preachers will express their passion for the truth they are proclaiming in ways that match their character. Nevertheless, citing Jesus in Matthew 23:37 and Paul in Philippians 3:18, along with the examples of George Whitefield and D. L. Moody, Stott adds, "I constantly find myself wishing that we twentieth-century preachers could learn to weep again."[87]

Having begun by saying that what the preacher believes matters more than methodology, Stott ends by saying that the way the preacher lives likewise matters more than methodology. "Preaching can never be degraded into the learning of a few rhetorical techniques. A whole theology lies beneath it, and a whole lifestyle behind it. The practice of preaching cannot be divorced from the person of the preacher."[88]

Because God's word inevitably offends human pride and confronts contemporary immorality, "there is an urgent need for courageous preachers in the pulpits of the world today."[89] It is always tempting to flatter people and tell them what they want to hear. But we can be faithful to God's word only if we speak of sin, guilt, judgment, and the cross. "I doubt very much if it is possible to be faithful and popular at the same time."[90]

Stott balances this call for courage with a call to humility. Courage can all too easily turn into arrogance. "Pride is without doubt the chief occupational hazard of the preacher" since in that moment you are the center of the congregation's attention. Again, Stott is following Simeon, who once wrote, "The three lessons which a minister has to learn are (1) Humility, (2) Humility, (3) Humility."[91] To counter this tendency toward pride, Stott invites preachers to submit to God's word rather than airing their own opinions, pursue Christ's glory rather than their own, and preach with a sense of dependence on God. Stott says, "Speaking personally, I have always

---

86 John Stott, *Authentic Christianity: From the Writings of John Stott*, ed. Timothy Dudley-Smith (Downers Grove, IL: InterVarsity Press, 1995), 273.

87 Stott, *Between Two Worlds*, 275–76.

88 Stott, *Between Two Worlds*, 265.

89 Stott, *Between Two Worlds*, 299.

90 John Stott, *Evangelical Truth: A Personal Plea for Unity, Integrity and Faithfulness*, rev. ed. (Nottingham: Inter-Varsity Press, 2015), 95.

91 A. W. Brown, *Recollections of the Conversation Parties of the Rev Charles Simeon* (London: Hamilton, Adams & Co, 1863), 17, cited in Carr, "Priorities and Concerns of Charles Simeon," 156; see also Arthur Bennett, "Charles Simeon: Prince of Evangelicals," *Churchman* 102, no. 2 (1988): 134–35.

found it helpful to do as much of my sermon preparation as possible on my knees, with the Bible open before me, in prayerful study."[92] He would also pray over a sermon before delivering it, even when delivering the same message several times on a preaching tour.[93] "We need to pray until our text comes freshly alive to us, the glory shines forth from it, the fire burns in our heart, and we begin to experience the explosive power of God's Word within us."[94]

That the Voice of God Might Be Heard

All the key elements in Stott's approach to preaching were designed to ensure that the text of Scripture was to the fore:

- a dominant idea based on the intent of the author,
- supported by content from the text,
- in a structure derived from the text,
- in a style focused on making the text clear.

And with this focus on the text, the authority of God in his word was also to the fore. This is what people experienced listening to Stott. He did not convey authority through force of personality; his style was in many ways subdued. The focus was on making the text clear.

Theologian Kenneth Kantzer, sometime editor of *Christianity Today*, summed up the impact of hearing Stott in a way that captures the goal of his preaching: "When I hear him expound a text, invariably I exclaim to myself, 'That's exactly what it means! Why didn't I see it before?'"[95] Likewise, Greg Scharf says of Stott's preaching: "I remember hearing a number of those messages when the clarity of it, just as clear as crystal, stood out so dramatically I found myself wondering, *Could it be any clearer than this? Could the text of Scripture be more powerfully spoken than this?*"[96]

It would be hard to exaggerate Stott's impact on evangelical preaching. The Australian evangelist John Chapman once said he tore up all his old sermons after the first time he heard Stott preach![97] Michael Jensen comments, "The rise of the expository sermon model in Sydney Anglican

---

[92] Stott, *Between Two Worlds*, 222.
[93] René Padilla, in Wright, *John Stott*, 121.
[94] Stott, *Between Two Worlds*, 257.
[95] Kenneth Kantzer, editorial, *Christianity Today* 25, no. 11 (1981).
[96] Greg Scharf, "Lessons from John Stott," Preaching Today, accessed https://www.preachingtoday.com/skills/themes/bedrockpreaching/200303.25.html.
[97] Michael P. Jensen, *Sydney Anglicanism: An Apology* (Eugene, OR: Wipf & Stock, 2012), 59.

Churches received particular impetus from the visit of the great English preacher John Stott to Sydney in 1958."

> Stott's sermons were models of engagement with the text in its context. . . . He preached immaculately prepared sermons with an English coolness of manner that were, in their way, aesthetically pleasing in their plainness of style and reserve of emotion and in their directness towards their purposes—a bit like modernist architecture, all clean lines and balance.[98]

If there is a criticism to be made of Stott's preaching, it is that throughout his ministry he preached relatively rarely on the Old Testament.[99] An analysis of his recorded sermons on the All Souls website shows that only 14 percent were on Old Testament passages, and most of these were ad hoc sermons rather than expository series.[100] Perhaps the avoidance of "systematizers" that Stott had learned from Simeon left him with an inadequate framework to appropriate the Old Testament in a Christ-centered way. One mitigating factor was Stott's resolution not to publish exposition he had not first preached, which, since he was the New Testament editor of the Bible Speaks Today series, led to a focus on New Testament material. Nevertheless, people have confirmed anecdotally the impression given in these figures. Stott is not alone in this. Only 8 percent of Martyn Lloyd-Jones's online sermons are on the Old Testament.[101] It is worth reflecting what effect this imbalance creates in a ministry.

Living the Word: Radical Obedience and Bridge Building

Stott dislikes the adjective "conservative" to modify the noun "evangelical," as it implies someone who is resistant to change. So, if a qualification of "evangelical" must be made, he says (somewhat tongue in cheek), let it be "radical conservative evangelical."[102] His point is that, like Jesus, we have a conservative view of Scripture, but, like Jesus, we are to be radically committed to following wherever it leads, even if that means sacrificing our sacred cows.

98 Jensen, *Sydney Anglicanism*, 59–60.
99 Hustler, "The Late Greats," 27.
100 See Online Sermon Library, All Souls, https://www.allsouls.org/Media/AllMedia.aspx.
101 See MLJ Trust, https://www.mljtrust.org/sermons.
102 Stott, in Edwards, *Essentials*, 88; see also Stott, "That Word 'Radical,'" *Church of England Newspaper*, February 24, 1967, 7.

> The hallmark of Evangelicals is not so much an impeccable set of words as a submissive spirit, namely their *a priori* resolve to believe and obey whatever Scripture may be shown to teach. They are committed to Scripture in advance, whatever it may later be found to say. They claim no liberty to lay down their own terms for belief and behaviour. They see this humble and obedient stance as an essential implication of Christ's lordship over them.[103]

Again, notice that Stott's doctrine of Scripture is tied tightly to his Christology. We cannot have Christ without his word. "We must allow the word of God to confront us, to disturb our security, to undermine our complacency, and to overthrow our patterns of thoughts and behaviour."[104]

In more than one place in his writings, Stott tells the story of two brothers who had grown up in a Christian home. To Stott's astonishment, they told him they were interested not in whether Christianity was *true* but in whether it was *relevant*. What they struggled to see was why they should pay any attention to someone who lived two thousand years ago in a completely different culture. Stott comments, "Nothing has brought home to me more forcefully the gulf which people perceive between the Bible and themselves, and so the challenge which confronts Christian preachers today."[105] In *Between Two Worlds*, Stott confesses, "Although I hope that in recent years I have begun to mend my ways, yet previously both my theory and my practice were to expound the biblical text and leave the application largely to the Holy Spirit."[106]

Stott began to view preaching as not simply opening up the text of Scripture but also bridge building. It is a phrase he had first used in 1961,[107] but he developed it in more detail in *Between Two Worlds*. There he describes a chasm between the biblical world and the modern world. Conservatives live primarily on the Bible side of the gulf, while liberals live primarily on the side of modern culture. But faithful preaching is a bridge that spans the gap. Through preaching, the world of the Bible should be brought into the modern world so that modern hearers are confronted with the Bible's claims. The preacher must show the relevance of the Scriptures and their demands on our lives. This conviction does not

103 Stott, in Edwards, *Essentials*, 104.
104 John Stott, *Culture and the Bible* (Downers Grove, IL: InterVarsity Press, 1979), 33.
105 Stott, *Between Two Worlds*, 138–39.
106 Stott, *Between Two Worlds*, 141.
107 John Stott, *The Preacher's Portrait* (London: Tyndale Press; Grand Rapids, MI: Eerdmans, 1961), 25.

simply arise out of necessity. It is, Stott argues, implicit in the nature of revelation. In both the person of Christ and the text of Scripture, God accommodated to the specifics of human language and culture. So the doctrines of both incarnation and inspiration establish a divine precedent for this bridge building.

Preaching as bridge building means we must speak to the day-to-day realities of people's lives: work, marriage, parenting, sex, and so on. We must address the personal and social issues of our day. This does not mean outlining political programs in the pulpit. Instead, Stott urges preachers to outline a Christian worldview and show how biblical principles apply to contemporary issues so that Christian opinion formers and policy makers can be salt and light in their spheres of influence. When it comes to controversial issues, Stott says we should neither avoid such topics nor take a partisan line. Instead, preachers should expound biblical principles, summarize alternative positions, perhaps indicate their own preference, and then leave the congregation free to decide.[108] "Such preaching will be authoritative in expounding biblical principles, but tentative in applying them to the complex issues of the day."[109]

We must address the questions and longings of modern people. "Jesus Christ either has the answers to these questions or—in the case of intractable mysteries like pain and evil—he throws more light on them than can be gathered from any other sources."[110] But we will effectively show how Christ is the fulfilment of human aspirations only if we have carefully understood those aspirations. "The One we preach is not Christ-in-a-vacuum, nor a mystical Christ unrelated to the real world, nor even only the Jesus of ancient history, but rather the contemporary Christ who once lived and died, and now lives to meet human need in all its variety today."[111]

Bridge building therefore requires double listening. Preachers must be men of the word and men of the world, preparing their sermons with a Bible in one hand and a newspaper in the other. "Our bridges . . . must be firmly anchored on both sides of the chasm, by refusing either to compromise the divine content of the message or to ignore the human context in which it has to be spoken."[112] Citing David Read, Stott illustrates this by saying the

---

108 Stott, *Between Two Worlds*, 168–73.
109 Stott, *Between Two Worlds*, 178.
110 Stott, *Between Two Worlds*, 151.
111 Stott, *Between Two Worlds*, 154.
112 Stott, *Between Two Worlds*, 145.

preacher cannot walk directly from the study to the pulpit; he must make the journey via the street, in and out of homes, hospitals, farms, factories, cinemas. So, while biblical and theological studies are indispensable, they are not enough. They need to be "supplemented by contemporary studies."[113] This kind of study begins with listening to people. "We need, then, to ask people questions and get them talking."[114]

So, biblical fidelity involves not only thinking ourselves back into the situation of the biblical authors but also thinking our way into the minds of contemporary people. Otherwise, we cannot ensure that the word hits home. Again, this arises from a recognition of divine intent in revelation. God intends his word to bring change, and we are faithful to that divine intent only if we accurately identify how God's word comforts and confronts those who hear. The word is not simply to be heard; it is to be lived. So the true purpose of contextualization—or "transposition," as Stott calls it—is not to compromise or to accommodate the preferences of the contemporary world. Quite the opposite. True contextualization is important precisely so the word of God can confront us where it matters. Cultural transposition "is not a conveniently respectable way to dodge awkward passages of Scripture by declaring them to be culturally relative." Instead, it is the only way of ensuring that "obedience becomes contemporary."[115]

There are those today who decry contextualization in the name of fidelity to the timeless message of Scripture. In reality, of course, they themselves inevitably contextualize whenever they apply the word, even if they do not own the terminology. The danger, though, is that such unreflective contextualization leaves the hearers unchallenged. The Bible is applied to the issues of yesterday and not the issues of today.

Reading Stott's works, one is struck by the way he always had the unbeliever in mind. Many of his books, of course, started life as addresses to a wider audience. But even those which address debates within the evangelical world are couched in a language that reflects an awareness of the watching world. It is clear he did his theology in conversation with the wider culture. The language he used, the way he formulated his arguments, and the applications he made all reflect this. He was attuned to those outside the church.

---

113 Stott, *Between Two Worlds*, 190.
114 Stott, *Between Two Worlds*, 192.
115 Stott, *The Contemporary Christian*, 206.

Trusting the Word: Stott's Theology of Scripture

Stott's commitment to preaching rests on strong convictions about the authority and reliability of Scripture. He pities the preacher who enters the pulpit with no Bible in his hands. The empty-handed preacher cannot speak with confidence "for he has nothing worth saying."

> But to enter the pulpit with the confidence that God has spoken, that he has caused what he has spoken to be written, and that we have this inspired text in our hands—ah! then our head begins to swim, our heart to beat, our blood to flow, and our eyes to sparkle, with the sheer glory of having God's Word in our hands and on our lips.[116]

When Stott was ordained in 1945, those who shared this confidence in the Bible were few and far between. Evangelicals were, in his words, "a small and despised minority."[117]

Stott spent much of his ministry mapping out the territory between liberalism and fundamentalism. He made a repeated and robust defense of the authority of Scripture. But he was also concerned to say what a commitment to biblical authority meant and—just as importantly—what it did not mean. As we have noted already, Stott, along with Carl Henry and Billy Graham, distanced himself from fundamentalism without going over to liberalism, instead carving out a middle ground for evangelicalism. Stott's second book, *Fundamentalism and Evangelism*, was an explicit attempt to do this.[118] After James Barr published a 1978 attack on fundamentalism in his book entitled *Fundamentalism*, Stott had an exchange of letters with him in which he complained that Barr had inaccurately lumped evangelicals and fundamentalist together. Stott defended evangelicalism from liberalism and distanced evangelicalism from fundamentalism.

One of the key ways Stott did this was to emphasize the dual authorship of Scripture.[119] A choice between fundamentalism, which stresses the divine authorship to the effective exclusion of human input, and liberalism, which stresses the human authorship to the extent that Scripture becomes a fallible product, is a false choice. Stott cites Packer: this false choice "assumes that God and man stand in such a relation to each other

---

116 Stott, *The Contemporary Christian*, 210.

117 Stott, in Edwards, *Essentials*, 35.

118 John Stott, *Fundamentalism and Evangelism* (London: Crusade Booklet, 1956; published in book form, Grand Rapids, MI: Eerdmans, 1959).

119 See, for example, Stott, *Evangelical Truth*, 52–61.

than they cannot both be free agents in the same action. . . . But the affinities of this are with Deism, not Christian Theism."[120]

Typically, Stott employs a both–and argument. The Bible is neither exclusively divine nor exclusively human, nor is it a bit of both. Rather, it is fully divine and fully human.

> The same Scripture which says "the mouth of the LORD has spoken" [Isa. 1:20] also says that God spoke "by the mouth of his holy prophets" [Acts 3:18, 21]. Out of whose mouth did Scripture come, then? God's or man's? The only biblical answer is "both." Indeed, God spoke through the human authors in such a way that his words were simultaneously their words, and their words were simultaneously his. This is the double authorship of the Bible. Scripture is equally the Word of God and the words of human beings. Better, it is the Word of God through the words of human beings.[121]

We read the Bible well when we take both authors seriously. Good hermeneutics is not simply the way of reading the Bible that has proved most useful or effective. Nor is it the product of trial and error. True hermeneutics arises from the doctrine of Scripture.

> The way we understand Scripture will affect the way we read it. . . . Because Scripture is the Word of God, we should read it as we read no other book—on our knees, humbly, reverently, prayerfully, looking to the Holy Spirit for illumination. But because Scripture is also the words of human beings, we should read it as we read *every* other book, using our minds, thinking, pondering and reflecting, and paying close attention to its literary, historical, cultural and linguistic characteristics. This combination of humble reverence and critical reflection is not only not impossible; it is indispensable.[122]

Christ Endorsed the Old Testament

Central to Stott's confidence in the authority of Scripture is not a case-by-case refutation of the supposed discrepancies but a Christocentric argument that we should treat the Scriptures as Christ treated them.[123] "The

---

120 J. I. Packer, *Fundamentalism and the Word of God* (London: Inter-Varsity Press, 1958), 81, cited by Stott, in Edwards, *Essentials*, 92, and in Stott, *Evangelical Truth*, 56.
121 Stott, *The Contemporary Christian*, 168–69.
122 Stott, *The Contemporary Christian*, 170; and Stott, *Evangelical Truth*, 57; see also Stott, *Understanding the Bible*, 207, 209; and Stott, *The Bible*, 18.
123 Stott took his lead from R. T. France, *Jesus and the Old Testament* (London: Tyndale Press, 1971); and John W. Wenham, *Christ and the Bible* (London: Tyndale Press, 1972).

major reason why we desire to submit to the authority of the Bible is that Jesus Christ authenticated it as possessing the authority of God."[124] In other words, Stott starts not with the inerrancy of Scripture but with *the inerrancy of Jesus*. "We claim that he was inerrant, that all his teaching was true, including his endorsement of the authority of Scripture."[125] As a result, "his view of Scripture must become ours."[126]

Stott makes much of the fact that Jesus everywhere assumed the Scriptures to be God's reliable and authoritative word. "We find it extremely impressive that our incarnate Lord, whose own authority amazed his contemporaries, should have subordinated himself to the authority of the Old Testament Scriptures as he did, regarding them as his Father's written word."[127] Stott points to the way Jesus described the Old Testament Scriptures as "the word of God" and attributed its words to the Holy Spirit (Mark 7:13; 12:36). Stott provides a whole raft of texts to show that "Jesus Christ endorsed the authority of the Old Testament. There is no occasion on which he contradicted it, or gave the slightest hint that he questioned its divine origin."[128]

Stott's point is not simply that this confirms the authority of Scripture. It is also that following Christ means submitting to the word. We cannot be Christlike without also being word-centered. (He could, perhaps, have made more of Christ-the-Word recorded in Scripture-the-word rather than simply focusing on the example of Christ.) "Submission to Scripture is for us evangelicals a sign of our submission to Christ, a test of our loyalty to him."[129]

David Edwards counters by citing Jesus's words "But I say to you . . ." in the Sermon on the Mount as examples of Jesus rejecting the Old Testament. It was an argument Stott had already met. When he started his theological studies at Ridley Hall, his tutor was John Burnaby, later Regius Professor of Divinity. Burnaby, too, had claimed Jesus was contradicting Moses. But Stott points out that the six "But I say to you" statements in Matthew 5 are preceded by a strong declaration of the abiding authority of the Old Testament in verses 17–20. "What Jesus was rejecting, then, was not the law itself but interpretations of it which were either too literal, or too superficial, or thoroughly perverted."[130]

124 Stott, *The Bible*, 27; see also Stott, *Students of the Word*, 15–18; and Stott, *Understanding the Bible*, 190–201.
125 Stott, *Understanding the Bible*, 153.
126 Stott, *The Bible*, 29.
127 Stott, in Edwards, *Essentials*, 85.
128 John Stott, *But I Say to You: Christ the Controversialist* (Nottingham: Inter-Varsity Press, 2013), 86.
129 Stott, in Edwards, *Essentials*, 85.
130 Stott, in Edwards, *Essentials*, 88; see also Stott, *The Message of the Sermon on the Mount*, 76–79.

Stott's response to Edwards goes further. The point is not simply that Jesus is correcting misinterpretations. He is also fulfilling the law, and fulfillment is not the same as repudiation. Quite the opposite. It is an affirmation of what has gone before. The types and promises of the Old Testament are affirmed when they are fulfilled in Christ even as they themselves thus fall away. We no longer offer sacrifices, because Christ has died once for all. But that reality does not mean the Old Testament call for sacrifices was mistaken. It simply means it has served its purpose and been confirmed in its fulfillment. Stott concludes, "Jesus went *beyond* the Old Testament, but he did not go *against* it."[131] He was "deepening not destroying the demands of the law."[132]

What Stott is countering is a liberal Christianity that claims to be committed to Christ but rejects the authority of Scripture. Edwards talks about "the gospel revealed in the Bible,"[133] which sounds innocuous enough but actually implies a canon within the canon—a canon, moreover, that is determined in good measure by what seems reasonable to the modern world. What results is, in fact, a variety of "christs" as—without the controlling influence of Scripture—people project onto the person of Christ their own presuppositions and predilections. Stott's point, in contrast, is that to accept Christ is to accept the Scriptures. In *Focus on Christ*, he puts it even more starkly: "Will the church listen humbly and obediently to Jesus Christ, or will it behave like the brash adolescent it often seems to be, contradicting its master and putting him right where he has gone wrong? Is the church 'over' or 'under' Christ?"[134]

The same logic applies to those Christians who privilege the words of Jesus over the rest of Scripture. The problem is that this does not treat Scripture as Christ treated it. Commenting on John 5:39–40, Stott says, first, that Christ regarded all Scripture as the word of God and, second, that Christ taught that all Scripture points to him—not just his words in the Gospels.[135]

Christ Commissioned the New Testament

Christ's acceptance of the Scriptures provides the basis on which we accept the authority of the Old Testament. But what about the Scriptures that, from

131 Stott, in Edwards, *Essentials*, 87.
132 Stott, in Edwards, *Essentials*, 82.
133 Stott, in Edwards, *Essentials*, 30.
134 John Stott, *Focus on Christ: An Enquiry into the Theology of Prepositions* (Eastbourne: Kingsway, 1979), 83.
135 Stott, *The Contemporary Christian*, 167.

the perspective of Christ's ministry, were yet to be written? What about the New Testament? Here again Stott applies a Christocentric approach, arguing this time that Christ made provision for the New Testament by commissioning the apostles and empowering them with the Holy Spirit. The word "apostle" means "sent one," and Stott highlights how the language of "sending" is routinely used of Old Testament prophets. His point is that New Testament apostles are in the same tradition as Old Testament prophets, with both groups providing divine revelation through the Holy Spirit. Jesus commissioned the apostles to be eyewitnesses of his life, death, and resurrection. Moreover, he promised that the Holy Spirit would enable them to record their eyewitness testimony accurately and to confirm their authority through miracles.[136] Contra the Roman Catholic Church, which claims authority through apostolic succession, the true apostolic succession is to submit to the apostolic testimony recorded in the New Testament. This argument—from Christ to the apostolic testimony to the New Testament—has become commonplace.[137] But that is due to the legacy of Stott and his generation.

A second line to Stott's Christocentric apologetic for biblical authority focuses on God's intent. In *The Contemporary Christian*, Stott develops a theology of Scripture that examines the terms "revelation," "inspiration," and "providence." "Revelation" highlights God's initiative to unveil or disclose himself. "Inspiration" describes the means he chose to disclose himself, namely, through human authors. "Providence" describes "the loving foresight and provision of God by which he arranged for the words he had spoken first to be written, to form what we call 'Scripture,' and then to be preserved across the centuries so as to be available to all people in all places at all times, for their salvation and enrichment."[138] The point is that inspiration and providence ensure that God's revelation is heard. God has not revealed himself in vain. He achieves what he purposes, and therefore he has ensured that his revelation is received accurately, first by inspiring the human authors to record it accurately and then by seeing that their record is preserved. If God has revealed himself in Christ, then we should expect him to do so in a way that continues to be effective.

---

136 Stott, *Students of the Word*, 18–23; and Stott, in Edwards, *Essentials*, 89.
137 See Stott, *The Bible*, 29–32; Stott, *The Living Church*, 26; Stott, *Calling Christian Leaders: Biblical Models of Church, Gospel and Ministry* (Leicester: Inter-Varsity Press, 2002), 19–20, 68; Stott, *Evangelical Truth*, 44; and Stott, *The Message of Acts: To the Ends of the Earth* (Leicester: Inter-Varsity Press; Downers Grove, IL: InterVarsity Press, 1990), 34–37.
138 Stott, *The Contemporary Christian*, 210.

> Is it not inconceivable, therefore, that God should first have spoken and acted in Christ and then have allowed his saving word and deed to be lost in the mists of antiquity? If God's good news was meant for everybody, which it was and is, then he would have made provision for its reliable preservation, so that all people in all places at all times could have beneficial access to it. This is an *a priori* deduction from our basic Christian beliefs about God, Christ and salvation.[139]

Inconsistencies

What about the alleged inconsistencies in the Bible, apparent contradictions that liberals believe make inerrancy untenable? Stott recognizes the problem ("We don't read the Bible with our eyes shut or our minds inert!"[140]), and he rejects any approach that ignores it or pretends it is not there.[141] He cites a large body of evangelical scholarship that provides plausible explanations for the supposed discrepancies.[142] Much of this involves avoiding overliteral readings by clarifying what the author(s) did and did not intend. We should allow that they paraphrased speeches, translated into different cultural idioms, subordinated chronology to theology, rounded figures, and so on.[143]

"But then, in spite of those which remain, we should retain our belief about Scripture on the ground that Jesus himself taught and exhibited it."[144] It does sound somewhat as if Stott is saying in the end you just have to put up with some discrepancies. His argument would have benefited from a more presuppositional approach, which recognizes the limitations of human knowledge and reason (though he does highlight the need for "illumination" in *Evangelical Truth*).[145] We are limited because we are finite—our knowledge is small. And we are limited because we are sinful—our reason is twisted. No one stands on neutral ground in these debates. The Christian is "biased" because, as Stott puts it, we "retain our belief about Scripture on the ground that Jesus himself taught and exhibited it."[146] But the skeptic is equally biased by his or her presuppositions.

---

139 Stott, in Edwards, *Essentials*, 83–84.
140 Stott, in Edwards, *Essentials*, 95.
141 Stott, *The Contemporary Christian*, 179–80.
142 Stott, in Edwards, *Essentials*, 99. For examples of this in Stott's own work, see Stott, *The Message of Acts*, 45–49, 55–56, and 379–82.
143 Stott, in Edwards, *Essentials*, 100.
144 Stott, *The Contemporary Christian*, 180; see also Stott, *Understanding the Bible*, 202–3.
145 Stott, *Evangelical Truth*, 48–49.
146 Stott, *The Contemporary Christian*, 180.

Inerrancy

There are two approaches to inerrancy within evangelicalism. Some accept minor factual errors on matters that do not pertain to the central message of the text. In other words, they accept that there are some errors in matters of history and geography, but not in theology and ethics. This could be called "limited inerrancy." Others do not make this concession. Instead, they hold the Bible to be inerrant in all that it affirms. The phrase "all that it affirms" allows for poetic metaphors or clear exaggeration for effect. There are two further qualifications: the Scriptures are inerrant as (1) originally given and (2) correctly interpreted. "These additions are not evasions," says Stott, "but common-sense explanations of what we mean by inerrancy."[147] Inerrancy does not validate "every weird and wonderful interpretation which Bible students produce."[148]

Stott is not greatly enamored of the word "inerrancy," because it describes Scripture negatively, as what it is not. He prefers positive statements like "true" or "trustworthy."[149] Nevertheless, he concedes that negatives are important and identifies himself as belonging to the second group, believing the Bible is inerrant in all that it affirms. "The distinction between different spheres of inerrancy (theology and ethics versus history and science), though understandable, is nevertheless arbitrary. Neither Jesus nor the apostles made it."[150] But there is also a positive theological reason for his preference for inerrancy:

> Our theological *a priori* that the Bible is God's word through human words carries with it the conviction that the God who has spoken does not in the process contradict himself. That is why patient attempts at harmonisation seem to me more Christian than either a premature declaration of error or a resort to artificial manipulation.[151]

"Evangelical faith," he concludes, "is historic, mainline, trinitarian Christianity, not an eccentric deviation from it."[152] What is striking is the way, for Stott, these discussions inevitably circle back to two complementary dimensions: the need for humility and the authority of Christ:

---

147 Stott, in Edwards, *Essentials*, 101; see also Stott, *Understanding the Bible*, 184–85.
148 Stott, in Edwards, *Essentials*, 101.
149 Stott, in Edwards, *Essentials*, 95.
150 Stott, in Edwards, *Essentials*, 103.
151 Stott, in Edwards, *Essentials*, 102.
152 Stott, in Edwards, *Essentials*, 39.

> The acceptance of inerrancy is more conducive to an attitude of reverent humility before God's word, than a belief in limited inerrancy, let alone errancy. . . . [Limited inerrancy] fosters more a critical than a humble spirit.[153]

> We shall not behave as if we thought the New Testament were a collection of fallible opinions of fallible human beings. We shall rather put ourselves humbly under its authority, and listen attentively to what God has to say to us through his Word.[154]

> But is not this submission of our minds to the mind of Christ an intellectual imprisonment? No more so than the submission of our wills to the will of Christ is moral bondage. Certainly it is a surrender of liberty, for no Christian can be a "free thinker." Yet it is that kind of surrender which is true freedom—freedom from our own miserable subjectivity, and freedom from bondage to the current whims and fancies of the world.[155]

It is worth rehearsing these arguments even if some readers are unaware of the debates in their classic liberal-versus-evangelical form. For we can be sure they will come round again in some new guise. We can be sure of it because it is already happening. Today's evangelical "innovators" are merely yesterday's liberals reheated. Addressing the National Evangelical Anglican Congress at Keele in 1967, Stott said, "The greatest need of the Church in this as in every age is humbly to submit to the authority of the Word and prayerfully to seek the illumination of the Spirit." It is a point easily overlooked that whenever Stott wrote something along the lines of "David says" or "Paul writes," we can be sure Stott meant that this is what God says, and therefore what we should believe or obey. And it is a conviction voiced in the prayer John Stott routinely used before preaching:

> Heavenly Father, we bow in your presence.
> May your word be our rule,
> your Spirit our teacher,
> and your greater glory our supreme concern,
> through Jesus Christ our Lord.[156]

---

153 Stott, in Edwards, *Essentials*, 103–4.
154 Stott, *Calling Christian Leaders*, 29.
155 Cited in Dudley-Smith, *John Stott*, 2:89–90.
156 Stott, *Between Two Worlds*, 340.

CHAPTER 4

SATISFACTION THROUGH SUBSTITUTION

"The gospel is not good news primarily of a baby in a manger, a young man at a carpenter's bench, a preacher in the fields of Galilee, or even an empty tomb. The gospel concerns Christ upon his cross."[1] Given this conviction, it is perhaps no surprise to find that Stott regarded his book on the atonement, *The Cross of Christ*, his greatest achievement. "More of my own heart and mind went into it," he once said, "than into anything else I have written."[2] It is often regarded as his magnum opus.[3] Yet, unusually, the idea for the book came not from Stott himself but at the suggestion of the publishers.[4] Its impact was immediate, for it had to be reprinted within a week of publication.

The nature of the atonement has been one of the key fault lines, alongside the authority of Scripture, between evangelicals and liberals. This was perhaps the key context in which Stott wrote *The Cross of Christ*. There he engages with Catholicism in a chapter on the Eucharist and a section on justification, but the most constant "conversation partner" is liberal Christianity.

This fault line was epitomized in the division within UK Christian student work, and Stott himself begins the book by retelling the story.[5] In

---

1 John Stott, *The Message of Galatians: Only One Way* (Leicester: Inter-Varsity Press; Downers Grove, IL: InterVarsity Press, 1968), 74.
2 Cited in Roger Steer, *Inside Story: The Life of John Stott* (Nottingham: Inter-Varsity Press, 2009), 216.
3 See, for example, Dick Lucas in *John Stott: A Portrait by His Friends*, ed. Chris Wright (Nottingham: Inter-Varsity Press, 2011), 46.
4 Frank Entwistle in Wright, *John Stott*, 94.
5 John Stott, *The Cross of Christ*, 2nd ed. (Leicester: Inter-Varsity Press, 1989), 8–9; see also David Goodhew, "The Rise of the Cambridge Inter-Collegiate Christian Union, 1910–1971," *Journal of Ecclesiastical History*

March 1910 the Cambridge Inter-Collegiate Christian Union (CICCU) disaffiliated from the Student Christian Movement (SCM) over concern about the latter's view of the authority of Scripture and the nature of the atonement. After the First World War, SCM approached the leaders of CICCU in an attempt to persuade them to rejoin. After an hour or so of talking, Norman Grubb, the secretary of CICCU, asked the SCM representative a direct question: "Does the SCM put the atoning blood of Jesus Christ central?" As Grubb relates it, "He hesitated, and then said, 'Well, we acknowledge it, but not necessarily central.'" That settled the matter for the leaders of CICCU: "We could never join something that did not maintain the atoning blood of Jesus Christ as its centre; and we parted company."[6] Over the coming months, the CICCU leaders realized other universities needed Christian Unions with the same convictions, and so in 1919 the Inter-Varsity Fellowship was born (now the Universities and Colleges Christian Fellowship). In time this spawned similar bodies across the world, linked together under the umbrella of the International Fellowship of Evangelical Students (IFES), another body close to Stott's heart.

Stott was himself all too aware of the challenge of doing theology in a context hostile to evangelical convictions. "One of the difficulties in reading theology" at Cambridge University, he once wrote, "was not so much the individual liberal arguments but just looking round that room of 200 students drinking in every word of the great Professor C. H. Dodd and saying to myself, 'I'm the only person who doesn't agree with him.'"[7] As we will see, in *The Cross of Christ*, Stott would take on Dodd's rejection of propitiation.

The scandal of the atonement is not, of course, unique to the modern era.[8] From the beginning of the church a crucified Savior was an object of scorn. Stott says, therefore, that the tenacity of early Christians to adopt the cross as their central symbol makes sense only if this reflects the centrality of the cross in the mind of Jesus himself. Jesus repeatedly foretold his violent death, which he saw as a fulfillment of the Scriptures, and to which he headed by his own deliberate choice. Exploring the Last Supper, Gethsemane, and the cry of dereliction, Stott concludes that Jesus saw his death

---

54, no. 1 (2003): 62–88; and David M. Thompson, *Same Difference? Liberals and Conservatives in the Student Movement* (Birmingham: Student Christian Movement, 1990).

[6] Norman P. Grubb, *Once Caught, No Escape* (London: Lutterworth, 1969), 56, cited in Stott, *The Cross of Christ*, 8–9.

[7] John Stott, interview by Timothy Dudley-Smith, in Dudley-Smith, *John Stott*, vol. 1, *The Making of a Leader* (Leicester: Inter-Varsity Press, 1999), 182–83.

[8] John Stott, *Our Guilty Silence: The Church, the Gospel and the World* (London: Hodder & Stoughton, 1967), 40–41.

as central, necessary, and purposeful. It was a sacrifice offered to God in which Jesus experienced the judgment of God on our behalf. The apostles, too, attributed Jesus's death not only to the actions of wicked men but also to the purpose of God. The cross is the most offensive feature of Christianity to its opponents, yet to its adherents it is precious. "Where faith sees glory, unbelief sees only disgrace."[9]

Atonement Is Multifaceted

Stott says there are "several pictures" of salvation in the New Testament and highlights propitiation, redemption, justification, and reconciliation.[10] In *The Contemporary Christian*, he leads with the idea of freedom.[11] Typically, this choice is the result of double listening: freedom both echoes the aspirations of the contemporary world and unites key biblical motifs.[12] Stott starts with freedom from guilt but also speaks of freedom from self and fear. He then goes on to speak of freedom *for* love. Elsewhere Stott says, "Salvation is not just another word for forgiveness. It is much bigger and broader than that. It presents God's total plan for humanity."[13] He then unfolds this in three stages: first, forgiveness, reconciliation, and adoption; second, progressive liberation from sin; and, third, final deliverance, transformed bodies, and a new creation.

Stott warns against formulaic or reductionistic understandings of the gospel, especially any that reduce it to forgiveness of sin alone. He talks about those who "seem to be in bondage to words and formulae," who "wrap up their message in a nice, neat package; and they tape, label and price-tag it as if it were destined for the supermarket."[14] They then complain if their favorite phrases are not used. What such people miss is the rich diversity of biblical language to describe salvation. This diversity allows us to focus on whatever "image" is most appropriate in a given context.

At the other extreme, though, are quasi-evangelicals who attempt to use the diversity of salvation imagery to realign or refocus the doctrine of salvation. Often this is done to divert the focus from substitutionary atonement. Substitutionary atonement is just one image among many, we are

---

[9] Stott, *The Cross of Christ*, 40.
[10] Stott, *The Cross of Christ*, 167.
[11] John Stott, *The Contemporary Christian: An Urgent Plea for Double Listening* (Leicester: Inter-Varsity Press, 1992), 46–56; see also Stott, *Why I Am a Christian* (Leicester: Inter-Varsity Press, 2003), 85–97.
[12] Stott, *The Contemporary Christian*, 46–47.
[13] John Stott, *But I Say to You: Christ the Controversialist* (Nottingham: Inter-Varsity Press, 2013), 101.
[14] Stott, *The Contemporary Christian*, 252.

told, so why make it central? Substitutionary atonement is portrayed as an evangelical obsession, perhaps reflecting a morbid and unhealthy preoccupation with guilt. Or sometimes the implication is that we can pick and choose which image of salvation we prefer.

Stott's exposition of the cross is written to refute these revisionist tendencies. So, yes, there are a number of images of salvation, since it is a rich and expansive idea. But "they are not alternative explanations of the cross, providing us with a range to choose from, but complementary to one another, each contributing a vital part to the whole."[15] And Stott is emphatic on two key points:

1. Among the models of salvation is propitiation, the turning aside of God's wrath.
2. All the models of salvation are founded on satisfaction through substitution.

Atonement Includes Propitiation

People often see propitiation—the belief that the cross appeases or averts the anger of God—as an offensive doctrine, depicting it as a crude pagan idea in which a god is effectively bribed through a sacrificial offering. Underlying this objection, though, is often an attempt to dilute the reality of divine wrath.

The New Testament noun *hilasmos* (1 John 2:2; 4:10), along with its associated adjectives (Rom. 3:25) and verbs (Luke 18:13; Heb. 2:17), has traditionally been translated "propitiation," with God as its object. It describes the act through which God's wrath toward us is appeased. But Dodd claimed it should be translated "expiation," with humanity as the object. The cross dealt with the human consequences of human sin, Dodd argued, but it did not appease divine wrath. Expiation, as Dodd understood it, produced a change in us—removing from us the stain of sin—but it did not change the way God relates to us. While "propitiation" was how the word was normally understood in the classical world, among Jews, he said, it was understood to mean "expiation."

Drawing on the work of Leon Morris and Roger Nicole, Stott rejects this argument. Dodd's sampling of Judaic usage is too narrow, and in the Old Testament the word is clearly used to describe the appeasement of anger.

[15] Stott, *The Cross of Christ*, 168.

Moreover, the context of its use in the New Testament—especially Romans 3, where it comes as a response to Paul's detailed exposition of human guilt before God in chapters 1–3—suggests that the object of propitiation is God's wrath.[16] In *Basic Christianity*, Stott says Christ "endured instead of us the penalty of separation from God which our sins deserved."[17]

What stops biblical propitiation from descending into pagan notions of bribing or cajoling a deity is that God, not humanity, takes the initiative in our salvation.[18] It is not we who are offering a sacrifice to persuade God but God himself who takes the initiative to offer himself in the person of his Son. We are not acting to make God gracious; *God* is acting because he is *already* gracious.

> It is God himself who in holy wrath needs to be propitiated, God himself who in holy love undertook to do the propitiating, and God himself who in the person of his Son died for the propitiation of our sins. Thus God took his own loving initiative to appease his own righteous anger by bearing it his own self in his own Son when he took our place and died for us. There is no crudity here to evoke our ridicule, only the profundity of holy love to evoke our worship.[19]

Atonement Is Founded on the Self-Substitution of God

"My contention," says Stott, "is that 'substitution' is not a further 'theory' or 'image' to be set alongside the others, but rather the foundation of them all, without which each lacks cogency." Without Jesus dying in our place there could be no propitiation, redemption, justification, or reconciliation.[20] Stott cites a New Testament text for each of these four "images" which links it to the shedding of blood (Rom. 3:25; Eph. 1:7; Rom. 5:9; Eph. 2:13). "All four images plainly teach that God's saving work was achieved through the blood-shedding, that is the substitutionary sacrifice of Christ. . . . Since Christ's death is a symbol of his life laid down in violent death, it is also plain in each of the four images that he died in our place as our substitute."[21]

16 Stott, *The Cross of Christ*, 168–75; Stott, *The Epistles of John: An Introduction and Commentary* (London: Tyndale Press, 1964), 84–88; and Stott, *The Message of Romans: God's Good News for the World* (Leicester: Inter-Varsity Press; Downers Grove, IL: InterVarsity Press, 1994), 113–16.

17 John Stott, *Basic Christianity*, rev. ed. (Leicester: Inter-Varsity Press, 1971), 93.

18 John Stott, "Reconciliation," *Churchman* 68, no. 2 (1954): 80.

19 Stott, *The Cross of Christ*, 175.

20 Stott, *The Cross of Christ*, 168. See Stott, "Reconciliation," 79–83, where Stott speaks of three images: reconciliation, justification, and redemption.

21 Stott, *The Cross of Christ*, 202; see also Stott, *Men with a Message: An Introduction to the New Testament and Its Writers* (London: Longmans, 1954), 91.

Stott makes the same kind of response to Gustaf Aulén's argument in his book *Christus Victor.* Aulén claimed the cross represents victory over Satan and called his approach the "classic" view because of its long pedigree. Stott does not dispute this[22] but says it imposes a false choice on us. The New Testament speaks of the cross as both a defeat of evil and a satisfaction for guilt. Indeed, it speaks of Satan being defeated precisely *because* our guilt is atoned. Commenting on Colossians 2:13–15, Stott says, "Is not this payment of our debts the way in which Christ has overthrown the powers?"[23]

Stott's conclusion, therefore—and this is central to his understanding of the cross—is this: "Substitution is not a 'theory of the atonement.' Nor is it even an additional image to take its place as an option alongside the others. It is rather the essence of each image and the heart of the atonement itself."[24]

To Whom Is Satisfaction Made?

Stott is acutely aware that satisfaction through substitution can be caricatured as a vindictive God being won over by the Son, or an innocent Son sacrificed to fulfill another's purpose. He counters these notions through a careful exposition of substitution.

First, Stott asks to whom satisfaction must be made. He rejects the idea that it was made to the devil, since the devil has no legitimate claims on us. Speaking of redemption, Stott says, "The New Testament never presses the imagery to the point of indicating to whom the ransom was paid, but it leaves us in no doubt about the price: it was Christ himself."[25] Nor does Stott accept that the law, divine honor, or the moral order is what must ultimately be satisfied, as if any of these is an independent entity apart from God to which God must answer. There is some truth in each of these three formulations. But "the limitation they share is that, unless they are very carefully stated, they represent God as being subordinate to something outside and above himself which controls his actions, to which he is accountable, and from which he cannot free himself."[26] Instead, Stott concludes that atonement involves God satisfying *himself*:

---

22 Stott, *Why I Am a Christian*, 60–63.
23 Stott, *The Cross of Christ*, 234.
24 Stott, *The Cross of Christ*, 202–3.
25 Stott, *The Cross of Christ*, 179.
26 Stott, *The Cross of Christ*, 123.

> "Satisfaction" is an appropriate word, providing we realize that it is he himself in his inner being who needs to be satisfied, and not something external to himself. Talk of law, honour, justice and the moral order is true only in so far as these are seen as expressions of God's own character. Atonement is a "necessity" because it "arises from within God himself."[27]

Self-satisfaction in human beings is not an attractive quality, because we are twisted by our selfishness. But God is perfect in his desires. This self-satisfaction therefore means God being true to, or consistent with, the perfections of his character. As the Scriptures say, "he cannot deny himself" (2 Tim. 2:13), for he is "a God of faithfulness and without iniquity" (Deut. 32:4). God is rightly "provoked" to jealous anger by our sins. "Once kindled, his anger 'burns' and is not easily quenched. He 'unleashes' it, 'pours' it out, 'spends' it. This three-fold vocabulary vividly portrays God's judgment as arising from within him, out of his character, as wholly consonant with it, and therefore as inevitable."[28]

This relentless commitment to be true to his holiness and justice creates a "conflict" with his love. Stott cites a number of biblical expressions of this "duality" between love and holiness, righteousness and peace, mercy and wrath, grace and truth. He is aware that such language is anthropomorphic, but he says the Bible is not afraid of such anthropomorphisms. In *Calling Christian Leaders*, Stott comments, "It is not wrong to speak of a divine problem or dilemma solved at the cross."[29]

A discussion of the simplicity of God might have enriched Stott's argument at this stage (though to be fair to him, very few evangelicals were foregrounding the simplicity of God in the twentieth century).[30] The language of "conflict," for example, is appropriate only as an analogical accommodation, for in reality God's attributes are one. He is not composed of his attributes. He is not a mixture of wisdom, love, holiness, and so on, as if these are preexisting building blocks from which God is composed

---

27 Stott, *The Cross of Christ*, 123, citing Ronald S. Wallace, *The Atoning Death of Christ* (Basingstoke: Marshalls, 1981), 113.

28 Stott, *The Cross of Christ*, 126.

29 John Stott, *Calling Christian Leaders: Biblical Models of Church, Gospel and Ministry* (Leicester: Inter-Varsity Press, 2002), 49.

30 See, for example, Matthew Barrett, *None Greater: The Undomesticated Attributes of God* (Grand Rapids, MI: Baker, 2019); James E. Dolezal, *All That Is in God: Evangelical Theology and the Challenge of Classical Christian Theism* (Grand Rapids, MI: Reformation Heritage, 2017); Dolezal, *God without Parts: Divine Simplicity and the Metaphysics of God's Absoluteness* (Eugene, OR: Pickwick, 2011); Katherin A. Rogers, *Perfect Being Theology*, Reason and Religion (Edinburgh: Edinburgh University Press, 2000); Peter Sanlon, *Simply God: Recovering the Classical Trinity* (Nottingham: Inter-Varsity Press, 2014); Thomas G. Weinandy, *Does God Suffer? The Mystery of God's Love* (Notre Dame, IN: Notre Dame University Press, 2000).

or features that could be withdrawn. God's holiness and love are not two separate aspects of his character that must be held together in some kind of balance. His holiness *is* his love, his love is his wisdom, his wisdom is his infinity, and so on. When pure light shines through green glass, it appears green; when it shines through red glass, it appears red. When God's perfect essence interacts with our world, it may appear as holiness; in other circumstances it may appear as love. But all God's attributes are one. So his holiness is always loving, wise, self-sufficient, all-powerful holiness. Stott has some awareness of this, even if it is not as explicit as it might be. "We must never think of this duality within God as being irreconcilable," he says. "For God is not at odds with himself, however much it may appear to us that he is. . . . He must be completely and invariably himself in the fullness of his moral being."[31]

> At the cross in holy love God through Christ paid the full penalty of our disobedience himself. He bore the judgment we deserve in order to bring us the forgiveness we do not deserve. On the cross divine mercy and justice were equally expressed and eternally reconciled. God's holy love was "satisfied."[32]

The point is that forgiveness is not straightforward. It requires satisfaction. This leads to the question "How then could God express simultaneously his holiness in judgment and his love in pardon?" Stott answers, "Only by providing a divine substitute for the sinner, so that the substitute would receive the judgment and the sinner the pardon."[33] "We sinners still of course have to suffer some of the personal, psychological and social consequences of our sins, but the penal consequence, the deserved penalty of alienation from God, has been borne by Another in our place, so that we may be spared it."[34]

This idea of substitution was present in the Old Testament sacrifices, particularly the sacrifice of atonement, when the guilt of the sinner was symbolically placed on the sacrifice through the laying on of hands. The need for the shedding of blood expressed the need for the penalty of death (the significance of the shed blood) to be paid before the sinner could be forgiven. "No forgiveness without blood meant no atonement without

31 Stott, *The Cross of Christ*, 131, 133.
32 Stott, *The Cross of Christ*, 89.
33 Stott, *The Cross of Christ*, 134.
34 Stott, *The Cross of Christ*, 134.

substitution."[35] Yet animal sacrifice could only be a pointer, since the death of an animal could not atone for human guilt. And so the Old Testament looked forward to a greater sacrifice, nowhere more explicitly than in Isaiah 53, which did so much to shape the self-understanding of Jesus and the interpretation of his cross by the apostles.

Who Makes Satisfaction?

Who, then, is the substitute? "The object of the penitent sinner's confidence for acceptance with God is not divine mercy in general but, very specifically, Jesus Christ and him crucified."[36] It is not merely the man Jesus who is our substitute, especially if he is considered an independent third party intervening to pacify an angry God or made the innocent victim of God's initiative. "In both cases God and Christ are sundered from one another: either Christ persuades God or God punishes Christ."[37] This is how penal substitution is often characterized, even vilified, sometimes because its proponents have been sloppy in their language. Stott himself says, "We must never make Christ the object of God's punishment or God the object of Christ's persuasion, for both God and Christ were subjects not objects, taking the initiative together to save sinners."[38] Both the Father and the Son voluntarily accepted the cross, a shared determination born out of a shared holy love. Neither party was reluctant. In *Basic Christianity*, Stott says, "We are not to think of Jesus as a third party wrestling salvation for us from a God unwilling to save. No. The initiative was with God himself."[39]

But neither was it simply God who died in our place. Some biblical language might at first appear to suggest this idea, especially when Paul speaks of "the church of God, which he obtained with his own blood" (Acts 20:28). But immortality belongs to the essence of God. Moreover, "God" in the New Testament often refers specifically to the Father, and the idea that the Father suffered creates a number of Trinitarian problems. Instead, argues Stott, it was "God in Christ" who was our substitute.

> Our substitute, then, who took our place and died our death on the cross, was neither Christ alone (since that would make him a third party thrust

[35] Stott, *The Cross of Christ*, 138.
[36] Stott, *But I Say to You*, 111.
[37] Stott, *The Cross of Christ*, 150.
[38] Stott, *The Cross of Christ*, 151.
[39] Stott, *Basic Christianity*, 94; see also Stott, *Focus on Christ: An Enquiry into the Theology of Prepositions* (Eastbourne: Kingsway, 1979), 31.

> in between God and us), nor God alone (since that would undermine the historical incarnation), but *God in Christ*, who was truly and fully both God and man, and who on that account was uniquely qualified to represent both God and man and to mediate between them.[40]

At the cross the Father was acting in and through the Son to reconcile us to himself (2 Cor. 5:17–18).

> In giving his Son he was giving himself. This being so, it is the Judge himself who in holy love assumed the role of the innocent victim, for in and through the person of his Son he himself bore the penalty which he himself inflicted. . . . In order to save us in such a way as to satisfy himself, God through Christ substituted himself for us. Divine love triumphed over divine wrath by divine self-sacrifice.[41]

In other words, God is not punishing another at the cross. He is punishing himself in the person of his Son. At the cross the Judge and the Judged share one divine being.

One significant observation from this argument is that defective theologies of the atonement arise from defective theologies of the Trinity. Those who find the Bible's teaching on penal substitution offensive do so because they conceive of the Father and the Son as two independent agents, instead of two *hypostases* of one divine, simple being in whom love and holiness are not competing characteristics but coherent features of one divine essence. Stott says, "It is impossible to hold the historic doctrine of the cross without holding the historic doctrine of Jesus Christ as the one and only God-man and Mediator. . . . The person and work of Christ belong together. . . . The incarnation is indispensable to the atonement."[42]

At one point, Stott says, "The righteous, loving *Father* humbled himself to become in and through his only Son flesh, sin and a curse for us, in order to redeem us without compromising his character."[43] I think it would be better to say *God* humbled himself in and through the Son. Stott's statement leaves open the modalism or patripassianism he has worked hard to avoid. But Stott always has in mind the need to refute the opposite error of supposing Christ was a third party. It is this error—against which opponents of

[40] Stott, *The Cross of Christ*, 156.
[41] Stott, *The Cross of Christ*, 159.
[42] Stott, *The Cross of Christ*, 160.
[43] Stott, *The Cross of Christ*, 159; emphasis added.

substitution often react—that he is especially keen to avoid. "What we see, then, in the drama of the cross is not three actors but two, ourselves on the one hand and God on the other. Not God as he is in himself (the Father), but God nevertheless, God-made-man-in-Christ (the Son)."[44]

Atonement Is Necessitated by the Gravity of Sin and the Consistency of God

Why could God not simply forgive our sins? Why the need for blood? After all, we often forgive people without demanding satisfaction. This reasoning, suggests Stott, betrays a failure to grasp the gravity of sin and the majesty of God.

> It overlooks the elementary fact that we are not God. . . . We are private individuals, and other people's misdemeanours are personal injuries. God is not a private individual, however, nor is sin just a personal injury. On the contrary, God is himself the maker of the laws we break, and sin is rebellion against him.[45]

Satisfaction through substitution is necessitated by the gravity of sin and the consistency of God. Behind any inadequate doctrine of the atonement is an inadequate doctrine of God and humanity. "Superficial remedies are always due to a faulty diagnosis."[46] "If we bring God down to our level and raise ourselves to his, then of course we see no need for a radical salvation, let alone for a radical atonement to secure it."[47] Or again, "If we reinterpret sin as a lapse instead of a rebellion, and God as indulgent instead of indignant, then naturally the cross appears superfluous."[48] Only when we see the glory of God's holiness, the depth of our sin, and therefore the reality of judgment does the necessity of substitution "appear so obvious that we are astonished we never saw it before."[49]

Sin is not simply a lapse. It is "godless self-centredness." "Worse still, we have dared to proclaim our self-dependence, our autonomy, which is to claim the position occupied by God alone. Sin is not a regrettable lapse from conventional standards; its essence is hostility to God, issuing in active rebellion against him."[50] And God treats us with dignity as

44 Stott, *The Cross of Christ*, 158.
45 Stott, *The Cross of Christ*, 88; see also Stott, *Why I Am a Christian*, 55.
46 Stott, *The Cross of Christ*, 98–99.
47 Stott, *The Cross of Christ*, 109.
48 Stott, *The Cross of Christ*, 110.
49 Stott, *The Cross of Christ*, 109.
50 Stott, *The Cross of Christ*, 90.

moral agents and therefore holds us accountable for our actions. "To say somebody 'is not responsible for his actions' is to demean him or her as a human being. It is part of the glory of being human that we are held responsible for our actions."[51] There is such a thing as false guilt: humans are not culpable for everything they feel guilty about. But all human beings are guilty before God, whether they "feel" it or not (though Stott does add, "in all evangelism, I find it a constant encouragement to say to myself, 'The other person's conscience is on my side'").[52] We cannot evade that guilt, despite modern claims that a focus on guilt is psychologically unhealthy.[53]

> The concept of substitution may be said, then, to lie at the heart of both sin and salvation. For the essence of sin is man substituting himself for God, while the essence of salvation is God substituting himself for man. Man asserts himself against God and puts himself where only God deserves to be; God sacrifices himself for man and puts himself where only man deserves to be. Man claims prerogatives which belong to God alone; God accepts penalties which belong to man alone.[54]

But the issue is not simply our sin; it is also God's response to our sin. "The obstacle to forgiveness is neither our sin alone, not our guilt alone, but also the divine reaction in love and wrath against guilty sinners."[55] God cannot and will not compromise his holiness. God's wrath is "his holy reaction to evil."[56] Citing the encounters with God experienced by Moses, Job, Isaiah, Ezekiel, Saul on the road to Damascus, and John on Patmos, Stott concludes, "If the curtain which veils the unspeakable majesty of God could be drawn aside but for a moment, we too should not be able to bear the sight."[57] Elsewhere he writes: "God is not interesting. He is deeply upsetting."[58]

Stott cites a number of scholars who have rejected the concept of the wrath of God. Some have argued that Jesus endured the consequences of sin but that these do not include a judicial penalty imposed by God. But,

---

51 Stott, *The Cross of Christ*, 101.
52 Stott, *The Message of Romans*, 89.
53 Stott, *The Cross of Christ*, 96–102; see also Stott, *Confess Your Sins: The Way of Reconciliation* (London: Hodder, 1964), 9, 15–17; and Stott, *The Message of Romans*, 67–68.
54 Stott, *The Cross of Christ*, 160; see also Stott, *Confess Your Sins*, 9, 15–17.
55 Stott, *The Cross of Christ*, 88.
56 Stott, *The Cross of Christ*, 103.
57 Stott, *Basic Christianity*, 73.
58 Stott, *Basic Christianity*, 17.

says Stott, throughout the Bible human death is seen not simply as a natural end to life but as "a penal event,"[59] a penalty for sin.

Part of the problem is that we often conceive of God's anger as like our own, when it is not. "God's wrath is not arbitrary or capricious. It bears no resemblance to the unpredictable passions and personal vengefulness of the pagan deities. Instead, it is his settled, controlled, holy antagonism to all evil."[60]

The Bible explicitly attributes to God anger against sin. These references are reinforced by images of God that highlight the idea that sin cannot exist in his presence (images of height, distance, light, fire, and vomiting). Stott comments, "Unhappily, even in the church we seem to have lost the vision of the majesty of God. There is much shallowness and levity among us. Prophets and psalmists would probably say of us that 'there is no fear of God before their eyes.'"[61]

In *Evangelical Truth*, Stott says, "This sense of our sinfulness, of the blinding holiness of God, and of the absolute incompatibility of the one with the other, is an essential evangelical characteristic, without which our understanding of the necessity and the nature of the cross is bound to be skewed."[62] Stott tackles the moral influence theory of the atonement, which claims that the only condition for salvation is repentance and the purpose of the cross is to evoke this repentance. This, says Stott, does not take the problem of sin seriously. While it is clearly true that Christ's love evokes our love, the cross was not an empty gesture. Someone who dies while saving a drowning person is heroic. But someone who drowns simply to demonstrate love displays folly, not love. "[Christ's] death must be seen to have an objective, before it can have an appeal."[63]

The Humbling of Humanity

Given the logical necessity of satisfaction through substitution and its biblical warrant, why is it so controversial? The answer, argues Stott, is that

59 Stott, *The Cross of Christ*, 65.

60 Stott, *The Epistles of John*, 83. See also Stott, *Christian Mission in the Modern World* (London: Falcon, 1975), 103; Stott, *The Cross of Christ*, 106–7; Stott, *The Message of Ephesians: God's New Society* (Leicester: Inter-Varsity Press, 1979), 75–76; Stott, *The Message of Thessalonians: Preparing for the Coming King* (Leicester: Inter-Varsity Press; Downers Grove, IL: InterVarsity Press, 1991), 42; and Stott, *The Message of Romans*, 71–72, 115.

61 Stott, *The Cross of Christ*, 109.

62 John Stott, *Evangelical Truth: A Personal Plea for Unity, Integrity and Faithfulness*, rev. ed. (Nottingham: Inter-Varsity Press, 2015), 82.

63 Stott, *The Cross of Christ*, 220.

this doctrine humbles us. A failure to appreciate the depth of our sin is perhaps the primary reason why people cannot or will not accept the true meaning of the cross.

> The cross tells us some very unpalatable truths about ourselves. . . . If we could have been forgiven by our own good works . . . we may be quite sure that there would have been no cross. . . . Nothing in history or in the universe cuts us down to size like the cross. All of us have inflated views of ourselves, especially in self-righteousness, until we have visited a place called Calvary. It is there, at the foot of the cross, that we shrink to our true size.
>
> And of course men do not like it. They resent the humiliation of seeing themselves as God sees them and as they really are. They prefer their comfortable illusions. So they steer clear of the cross. They construct a Christianity without the cross, which relies for salvation on their works and not on Jesus Christ's. They do not object to Christianity so long as it is not the faith of Christ crucified. But Christ crucified they detest.[64]

Commenting on Psalm 51, Stott says, "It is when we see ourselves as we are, on the one hand rebels against God and under the judgment of God, and on the other prisoners of a corrupt nature that we come, like David, to despair of ourselves and to cry to God for mercy."[65]

Like Simeon, Stott never accents the label "Calvinist," certainly not in the way his contemporary Martyn Lloyd-Jones did. But his Calvinism is clear from his writings. He defends total depravity,[66] divine election,[67] the necessity of the Spirit to awaken faith and repentance,[68] and the perseverance of the saints (though he is more equivocal in *The Message of 1 Timothy and Titus*, preferring to speak of an "antinomy" of apparently competing affirmations).[69] At the opening of *Basic Christianity* he says, "Before man existed, God acted. Before man stirs himself to seek God, God has sought man."[70] On depravity he says, "Because sin is an inward corruption of human nature we are in bondage. It is not so much certain

---

64 Stott, *The Message of Galatians*, 179; see also Stott, *The Cross of Christ*, 83.
65 John Stott, *Favourite Psalms: Growing Closer to God* (London: Monarch, 2003), 56.
66 Stott, *The Message of Ephesians*, 77–79.
67 John Stott, *The Message of 2 Timothy: Guard the Gospel* (Leicester: Inter-Varsity Press; Downers Grove, IL: InterVarsity Press, 1973), 36; Stott, *The Message of Ephesians*, 36–39, 47–48; Stott, *The Message of Thessalonians*, 31; and Stott, *The Message of Romans*, 248–52, 268.
68 Stott, *But I Say to You*, 129–35; and Stott, *The Message of Ephesians*, 83.
69 John Stott, *The Message of 1 Timothy and Titus* (Leicester: Inter-Varsity Press; Downers Grove, IL: InterVarsity Press, 1996), 64–66, 70–71.
70 Stott, *Basic Christianity*, 11.

acts or habits which enslave us, but rather the evil infection from which these spring."[71]

Stott clarifies what is meant by "total depravity." It does not mean everything a person does is depraved. We still bear the image of God, albeit in a marred way, and so we are still capable of acts of beauty and kindness. The "total" in "total depravity" "refers to extent rather than degree." What it does mean is that we must "firmly deny that we can achieve our own salvation or even contribute to it. This may be humbling but it is a fact."[72] This talk, says Stott, "comes into violent collision with the man-centredness and self-centredness of the world." "Fallen man, imprisoned in his own little ego, has an almost boundless confidence in the power of his own will."[73] But the only way our hearts can be changed is through a miracle accomplished by God in our hearts. This is new birth through the Holy Spirit.

It is true, and Stott will go on to elaborate on this, that the cross motivates us to serve God and provides the pattern for our lives. But Stott is keen to emphasize that this service does not come first. We do not begin with what we do; we begin with what Christ has done. The cross is "the most powerful incentive to a holy life. But this new life follows."[74] First, we have to humble ourselves at the foot of the cross, confess that we have sinned and deserve nothing at his hand but judgment, thank him that he loved us and died for us, and receive from him a full and free forgiveness. "Against this self-humbling our ingrained pride rebels. We resent the idea that we cannot earn—or even contribute to—our own salvation."[75] We want to think there is something we can do to contribute to our salvation, but the cross strips us of all such pretensions. "This is the 'scandal,' the stumbling-block, of the cross. For our proud hearts rebel against it. We cannot bear to acknowledge either the seriousness of sin and guilt or our utter indebtedness to the cross."[76]

So a high view of the cross goes hand in hand with the deep doctrine of sin. Stott's first sermon at All Souls was on the phrase "no difference" in Romans 3:22–23 and 10:12–13 (KJV). There is "no difference" among people with respect to their plight and "no difference" with the

71 Stott, *Basic Christianity*, 76.
72 Stott, *But I Say to You*, 120.
73 Stott, *The Message of Ephesians*, 50.
74 Stott, *The Cross of Christ*, 84.
75 Stott, *The Cross of Christ*, 84.
76 Stott, *The Cross of Christ*, 161.

invitation to salvation. His shorthand notes, written as was his habit on three-by-five-inch cards, contain the line "Important face sin, as then appreciate remedy."[77]

The Cross as Lifestyle

Christ is our Savior before he is our example. Stott is, as we have seen, absolutely clear on this. "The death of Jesus is more than an inspiring example," he says in *Basic Christianity.* "A pattern cannot secure our pardon."[78]

Nevertheless, building on a solid understanding of the cross as the ground of salvation, Stott highlights the New Testament emphasis on the cross as our example. The cross is not only the means by which we are saved; it then imprints itself on the life of the Christian. "The cross is not just a badge to identify us, and the banner under which we march; it is also the compass which gives us our bearings in a disoriented world."[79] It changes the way we view God, ourselves, the church, and the wider world. Even speaking of the cross as our example does not quite capture the radical way it shapes our lives. An example is a model we adopt as the situation demands. But the cross imprints itself on our lives continually. It forms the perpetual pattern of our lives. "Christian discipleship is much more radical than an amalgam of beliefs, good works and religious practices. No imagery can do it justice but death and resurrection."[80] Commenting on the use of the word "daily" in Luke 9:23, Stott says: "The attitude to self which we are to adopt is that of crucifixion. . . . Every day the Christian is to die. Every day he renounces the sovereignty of his own will. Every day he renews his unconditional surrender to Jesus Christ."[81]

Many people have crippling feelings of inferiority, often caused by deprived childhoods, which are reinforced by a competitive marketplace and technological depersonalization. Today we might add the toxic side effects of social media. All this is a reality, but Stott also critiques the counterproductive overreaction that promotes "self-regard, self-awareness and self-actualisation."[82] Again, today we might add the emphasis on self-esteem.[83]

---

[77] Cited in Dudley-Smith, *John Stott*, 1:234.
[78] Stott, *Basic Christianity*, 89; see also Stott, *The Message of Galatians*, 17.
[79] Stott, *The Cross of Christ*, 256.
[80] John Stott, *The Incomparable Christ* (Leicester: Inter-Varsity Press, 2001), 30.
[81] Stott, *Basic Christianity*, 112.
[82] Stott, *The Cross of Christ*, 275.
[83] See, for example, Glynn Harrison, *The Big Ego Trip: Finding True Significance in a Culture of Self-Esteem* (Nottingham: Inter-Varsity Press, 2013).

The cross, suggests Stott, helps us navigate between this self-hatred and self-love. He highlights both the biblical calls to self-denial—especially the call of Jesus to deny ourselves and take up our cross (Mark 8:34)—and the affirmation of our humanity that we see in the teaching and attitude of Jesus.

How do we make sense of this apparent paradox? The answer is to recognize that the human self is complex, neither wholly good nor wholly evil. We are the product of creation, made in the image of God, and we are the product of the fall, so that God's image is now defaced. In the case of Christians, we can add that our self is also the product of re-creation. We are therefore "to put on the new self, created after the likeness of God in true righteousness and holiness" (Eph. 4:24). This double identity helps us discern what self-denial involves: "The self we are to deny, disown and crucify is our fallen self, everything within us that is incompatible with Jesus Christ."[84] This is a helpful clarification. It helps us avoid an unnecessary world-denying attitude in which we reject everything good for fear we are not being self-denying. More significantly, it shows the positive value of self-denial. True self-denial, says Stott, "is not the road to self-destruction but the road to self-discovery." Why? Because it is "the denial of our false fallen self."[85] We can affirm all that we are by virtue of our creation and recreation in God's image, and we must be ruthless in rejecting all that belongs to our fallen nature. We put off the old self so that only the new self remains. Christianity, says Stott in *The Contemporary Christian*, "is freedom from the dark prison of our own self-centredness into a new life of self-fulfilment through self-forgetful service."[86]

But this denial of sin in our lives is not quite the full picture of cross-shaped living. "Sometimes God calls us to deny to ourselves things which, though not wrong in themselves or attributable to the Fall, yet stand in the way of our doing his particular will for us."[87] This is a person-specific denial of self. Our model is still Jesus, who emptied himself of his glory to serve us (Phil. 2:5–9). All Christians have some version of this—things to which they say no in order to fully serve Christ in the context in which God has put them. But what this involves will be specific to each person.

---

[84] Stott, *The Cross of Christ*, 282.
[85] Stott, *The Cross of Christ*, 282; see also Stott, *Men with a Message*, 22.
[86] Stott, *The Contemporary Christian*, 310.
[87] Stott, *The Cross of Christ*, 284.

> Some Christian people are called forgo married life, or a secure job, or professional promotion, or a comfortable home in a salubrious suburb, not because any of these things is wrong in itself, but because they are incompatible with a particular call of God to go overseas or live in the inner city or identify more closely with the world's poor and hungry people.[88]

So we are called to self-sacrificial love and service, patterned on the self-sacrificial love and service exhibited by Christ at the cross. This works itself out not simply in dramatic moments like martyrdom, but in daily life in the home, the church, and the world.

Stott writes with great compassion about suffering. Here his double listening is finely tuned to the reality of pain across history and across the world. His concern is pastoral rather than philosophical, and his focus is on how the cross illuminates suffering. He identifies six ways the cross speaks to our suffering, "which seem to rise gradually from the simplest to the most sublime":[89]

1. The cross of Christ is *a stimulus to patient endurance*. There are times when we must endure suffering as Jesus did at the cross (Heb. 12:1–3; 1 Pet. 2:18–23).
2. The cross of Christ is *the path to mature holiness*. Suffering can be formative (James 1:2–4), as it was for Jesus (Heb. 2:10; 5:8–9).
3. The cross of Christ is *the symbol of suffering service*. "Suffering is indispensable to fruitful or effective service," for, as with a seed falling to the ground, death brings greater fruit (John 12:23–26, 32–33; Eph. 3:1, 13; Col. 1:24; 2 Tim. 2:8–10).[90]
4. The cross of Christ is *the hope of final glory*. Just as we share in Christ's sufferings, so we will share in his glory (Acts 14:22; Rom. 8:17; Rev. 7:9, 14).
5. The cross of Christ is *the ground of a reasonable faith*. It is not that the cross explains the perplexities of suffering, but it does demonstrate God's holy love and justice. "We have to learn to climb the hill of Calvary, and from that vantage-point survey all life's tragedies."[91] In other words, while suffering gives us powerful reasons to doubt the justice and love of God, the cross gives even more powerful reasons to *trust* the justice and love of God. We may not be able to explain the mystery

88 Stott, *The Cross of Christ*, 284–85.
89 Stott, *The Cross of Christ*, 314.
90 Stott, *The Cross of Christ*, 320–21.
91 Stott, *The Cross of Christ*, 329.

of suffering, but we can look to the cross, and there we see the love of God writ large.

6. The cross of Christ is *the proof of God's solidary love*—"his personal, loving solidarity with us in our pain."[92]

The Passibility of God?

In this context, Stott questions the traditional understanding of the impassibility of God. Stott is careful to say that God cannot be influenced against his will. "He is never the unwilling victim either of actions which affect him from without or of emotions which upset him from within."[93] Nevertheless, the cross, says Stott, reveals a God who suffers with us. Stott sympathizes with the church fathers who sought to preserve the perfection and immutability of God. Nevertheless, argues Stott, the testimony of Scripture and the revelation of the Son suggest a God who, while he does not suffer like us, does suffer with us. "If love is self-giving, then it is inevitably vulnerable to pain, since it exposes itself to the possibility of rejection and insult."[94]

This leads to some of the most often quoted words of Stott:

> I could never myself believe in God, if it were not for the cross. The only God I believe in is the One Nietzsche ridiculed as "God on the cross." In the real world of pain, how could one worship a God who was immune to it? I have entered many Buddhist temples in different Asian countries and stood respectfully before the statue of the Buddha, his legs crossed, arms folded, eyes closed, the ghost of a smile playing round his mouth, a remote look on his face, detached from the agonies of the world. But each time after a while I have had to turn away. And in imagination I have turned instead to that lonely, twisted, tortured figure on the cross, nails through hands and feet, back lacerated, limbs wrenched, brow bleeding from thorn-pricks, mouth dry and intolerably thirsty, plunged in God-forsaken darkness. That is the God for me! He laid aside his immunity to pain. He entered our world of flesh and blood, tears and death. He suffered for us. Our sufferings become more manageable in the light of his. There is still a question mark against human suffering, but over it we boldly stamp another mark, the cross that symbolizes divine suffering. "The cross of Christ . . . is God's only self-justification in such a world" as ours.[95]

[92] Stott, *The Cross of Christ*, 329.
[93] Stott, *The Cross of Christ*, 330.
[94] Stott, *The Cross of Christ*, 332.
[95] Stott, *The Cross of Christ*, 335–36, citing P. T. Forsyth, *The Justification of God* (London: Duckworth, 1916), 32.

Stott was writing at a time when both evangelical and non-evangelical theologians were questioning the impassibility and immutability of God. For some, this has reflected a broader departure from classic theism. But many evangelicals maintain the emphasis on the immutability of God's being, will, and revelation within classic theism while, nevertheless, believing that the biblical language used to describe God's response to his world cannot readily be dismissed as mere anthropomorphism—a position variously labeled "biblical personalism" or "theistic mutualism." They argue that God partakes in emotional and relational responses not as a passive victim of external pressures but as he sovereignly determines so to do. This kind of to-and-fro is implied in a covenantal relationship. There is a concern that philosophical categories have historically been privileged over the personal interactions reflected throughout the biblical narrative.[96]

More recently, a strong understanding of divine immutability, and therefore impassibility, has been reasserted,[97] sometimes in polemical terms.[98] Intuitively, we might suppose God responds emotionally to human suffering, but this intuition has been resisted by Christian theology down the centuries because it implies that God changes; and if God changes, then either he used to be perfect and has become less so, or he was less than perfect and has become more so. Either way, his eternal perfection is compromised. This does not make God less caring. God is not "moved" by the plight of specific instances of suffering. He has, as it were, nowhere to go; he is already perfect compassion. God's compassion is not an emotion that comes and goes in accordance with events within history. Instead classic theism describes God as "pure act," existing in a perfect state of unfluctuating compassion.

Clearly, the passibility of God has become an ongoing area for debate within Reformed evangelicalism, a topic that requires the kind of generous dialogue that Stott espoused.

As we have seen, in delineating who made satisfaction for sin on the cross, Stott avoids saying it was the man Jesus, as if he was an independent third party who becomes the victim of divine wrath. But Stott also avoids saying it was God, since God's essence is immortal (and, we might add, im-

---

[96] See, for example, John M. Frame, *Systematic Theology: An Introduction to Christian Belief* (Phillipsburg, NJ: P&R, 2013), 367–77; Frame, *The Doctrine of God* (Phillipsburg, NJ: P&R, 2013), 220–37; and Rob Lister, *God Is Impassible and Impassioned: Toward a Theology of Divine Emotion* (Wheaton, IL: Crossway, 2013).
[97] See, for example, Rogers, *Perfect Being Theology*; Weinandy, *Does God Suffer?*; and Barrett, *None Greater.*
[98] Dolezal, *All That Is in God.*

mutable). Instead, it was God-in-Christ. In Christ, God and man are united in a mysterious way, two natures in one person. In the same way, whatever view one takes of divine passibility, we can and should affirm that God in Christ suffered with humanity. The person of Christ in his human nature suffered with us (Heb. 2:10). In this sense, Stott's oft quoted words above stand with all their power: God in Christ has entered into the human condition to suffer with us and for us.

Cling to the Cross

Stott's contribution to our understanding of the atonement was foundational for a generation of evangelicals. But the cross was never simply a theological puzzle for him. It was the controlling passion of his life.

In 2002, Stott, in his eighties, was in India with his then study assistant, Corey Widmer. During an afternoon break for bird-watching, Stott tripped and lacerated his right leg. The wound became infected, and the leg swollen. Three different doctors could provide no relief. Eventually, the two men contacted Stott's cardiologist in London. He brought little comfort, warning that if things did not improve immediately, they should return to London. "It was as solemn a moment as I ever shared with him," writes Widmer. Both realized the possibility that, if the infection spread, Stott's death could be near. Stott took the opportunity to talk to Widmer about Widmer's desire to be a pastor, speaking of the key elements of pastoral ministry. "Of all that he shared with me in those precious moments, one piece of advice has stayed with me more than any other: 'Above all,' he said, 'cling to the cross.'"[99]

Widmer, now a pastor, comments:

> The cross of Christ, the title of what he considered his most important book and the one in which he invested more of himself than any other, was the paramount theme, the one he returned to again and again. He took quite literally Paul's call in Galatians 6:14, one of his "life verses" as he often called it, to be "obsessed" with the cross. Even when he was not speaking about it directly, the centrality of the cross remained like a deep subterranean undercurrent beneath the body of Uncle John's life and work, affecting and directing so much of his thinking on ethical, theological and pastoral issues. "The Pervasive Influence of the Cross" is

[99] Corey Widmer, in Wright, *John Stott*, 198.

> the title of the epilogue of *The Cross of Christ*. It could just as well serve as an epilogue for his life.[100]

On Stott's gravestone are these words: "Buried here are the ashes of John R. W. Stott . . . who resolved both as the ground of his salvation and as the subject of his ministry to know nothing except JESUS CHRIST and him crucified (1 Corinthians 2:2)."

---

[100] Widmer, in Wright, *John Stott*, 198–99.

CHAPTER 5

REPUDIATION AND SURRENDER

In 1965, John Stott addressed the Keswick Convention. For nearly a century the convention had been strongly associated with a particular view of sanctification; indeed, the view was commonly known as the Keswick holiness tradition. In the early and mid-twentieth century it represented the dominant approach within evangelicalism. Historian David Bebbington says, "It shaped the prevailing pattern of Evangelical piety for much of the twentieth century."[1]

But that was about to change. Although a number of factors contributed to the transformation, Stott's 1965 talks proved the turning point, not least because they were given at the convention itself. According to Charles Price and Ian Randall, "It was probably as significant an address as any ever given at Keswick."[2] It was one of the most crucial ways Stott shaped modern evangelicalism, but it has now become one of his more neglected contributions.

The Keswick Convention and the "Rest of Faith"

The convention had been founded by Canon Thomas Dundas Harford-Battersby, the vicar of St John's, Keswick, in the Lake District. In 1874, aged

1 David W. Bebbington, *Evangelicalism in Modern Britain: A History from the 1730s to the 1980s* (London: Unwin Hyman, 1989), 151.

2 Charles Price and Ian Randall, *Transforming Keswick: The Keswick Convention Past, Present and Future* (Carlisle: OM, 2000), 235.

fifty-one, despite an apparently fruitful ministry, Harford-Battersby was feeling dissatisfied with his inner spiritual life. He wrote in his diary, "How very far I am from enjoying that peace and joy and love habitually which Christ promises."[3]

The year before, Robert Pearsall Smith had arrived in the UK from America with a message emphasizing "holiness by faith." With warm letters of introduction from American church leaders, Pearsall Smith soon found himself invited to address groups of English clergy. His message was welcomed beyond his expectations, so he prolonged his visit. While on holiday in August 1874, Harford-Battersby heard Pearsall Smith at a conference in Oxford. Initially, Harford-Battersby felt Pearsall Smith and the other speakers were one-sided. But then Evan Hopkins, vicar of Holy Trinity, Richmond, challenged his hearers to choose between sanctification by works and sanctification by faith. Afterward, Harford-Battersby wrote in his diary: "Christ was revealed to me so powerfully and sweetly as the present Saviour in His all-sufficiency. I am His, and I do trust him to make good all His promises to my soul."[4] Back in Cumbria, Harford-Battersby began to tell others about his experience. He addressed the Evangelical Union in Kendal under the title "Higher Attainments in Christian Holiness and How to Promote Them." He spoke of holiness as "the fruit of the indwelling of the Lord Jesus Christ in the soul."[5]

After the success of the Oxford conference, a follow-up conference was held in Brighton in May 1875, and it was here that Harford-Battersby conceived the idea of bringing the message of holiness by faith to the north of England. Pearsall Smith agreed to come, but his only free slot was in three weeks' time. So the first Keswick Convention was hastily arranged. Even though Pearsall Smith then had to withdraw at short notice, the convention went ahead with three hundred to four hundred people each night meeting in a tent erected in the churchyard of St John's Church, Keswick. The decision was made to hold a second convention the following year, and ever since the convention has been a mainstay of British evangelicalism, as well as spawning regional meetings and "sister" conventions around the globe.

One of the leading figures in the Keswick movement was Evan Hopkins, whose ministry at the 1874 Oxford conference had so profoundly

[3] Cited in Price and Randall, *Transforming Keswick*, 19.
[4] Cited in Price and Randall, *Transforming Keswick*, 25.
[5] Cited in Price and Randall, *Transforming Keswick*, 27.

impacted Harford-Battersby. Andrew Naselli calls him "Keswick's formative theologian."[6] In his book *The Law of Liberty in the Spiritual Life* (1884), Hopkins identified three views on sanctification within evangelicalism. The first (influenced by the Tractarian movement) believed holiness was achieved through earnest effort. The second was the Wesleyan holiness tradition, which promised the complete eradication of sin in this life. Links are often made between the Wesleyan and Keswick traditions, but those associated with the convention never saw themselves as an extension of the Wesleyan movement. Whereas Wesley thought perfection belonged to a few, the Keswick movement believed all believers could enjoy "a higher life." And the Keswick movement believed not that the sinful nature was eradicated, as Wesley thought, but only that Christ's indwelling presence could counteract it. "The tendency to sin is not eradicated," Hopkins wrote, "but by the power of the Holy Ghost the flesh is kept under as we walk in the Spirit."[7]

The third view, the one Hopkins held (and he believed was compatible with Reformed theology) was that, through an act of consecration and the Spirit's presence, there was the possibility of a "continual counteraction" of sin.[8] Traditional Reformed theology envisions a lifelong battle against temptation through which the believer is gradually transformed into the likeness of Christ. In the old Keswick tradition, the sinful nature remains constant but is now counteracted in the consecrated Christian by the indwelling presence of Christ. Hopkins talked about the "rest of faith"—which became something of a catchphrase for the convention for many years.[9] Hopkins was keen to emphasize that there was always room for progress in sanctification, thus distinguishing the Keswick approach from the Wesleyan emphasis on complete sanctification. "Yet this did not mean a return to human effort," Price and Randall explain. "The call to consecration stressed that holiness was, rather, a gift to be recovered."[10] In 1906, a "manual of Keswick teaching" entitled *Holiness by Faith* was published. In it Bishop Handley Moule described the essence of Keswick teaching as the discovery "of the power of faith, of personal reliance, in the matter of

---

6 Andrew David Naselli, "Keswick Theology: A Survey and Analysis of the Doctrine of Sanctification in the Early Keswick Movement," *Detroit Baptist Seminary Journal* 13, no. 1 (2008): 23.

7 Evan Hopkins, *Christian*, August 12, 1880, 10, cited in David W. Bebbington, *The Dominance of Evangelicalism: The Age of Spurgeon and Moody* (Leicester: Inter-Varsity Press, 2005), 196.

8 Evan Hopkins, *The Law of Liberty in the Spiritual Life* (London: Marshall, 1884), 29.

9 Hopkins, *The Law of Liberty*, 219.

10 Price and Randall, *Transforming Keswick*, 48.

purity and liberty within."[11] Moule said that believers enter the higher life through the twin doors of "surrender and faith."[12]

In practice, convention speakers varied in the degree to which they stressed passivity—letting the presence of Christ counter the pull of sin instead of actively mortifying sin. But there was clearly a strong quietistic note, and this is evident in the hymnody associated with Keswick in its first seventy years. The following hymn lyrics were all popular at the convention and all featured in the convention's first songbook, complied by James Mountain under the title *Hymns of Consecration and Faith*:

Holiness by faith in Jesus,
Not by effort of my own,
Sin's dominion crushed and broken
By the power of grace alone.[13]

I take the promised Holy Ghost,
I take the power of Pentecost,
To fill me to the uttermost.
I take—He undertakes.

I take Thee, blessed Lord,
I give myself to Thee;
And Thou, according to Thy word,
Dost undertake for me.[14]

Jesus I am resting, resting,
In the joy of what Thou art,
I am finding out the greatness,
Of Thy loving heart.[15]

My spirit, soul and body,
Dear Lord, I give to Thee,
A consecrated offering,
Thine evermore to be.

---

[11] H. C. G. Moule et al., *Holiness by Faith* (London: Religious Tract Society, 1906), 24, cited in Price and Randall, *Transforming Keswick*, 47.

[12] Paraphrased in J. C. Pollock, *The Keswick Story: The Authorized History of the Keswick Convention* (Chicago: Moody, 1964), 74.

[13] Frances Ridley Havergal, "Church of God, Beloved and Chosen," in *Hymns of Consecration and Faith*, comp. James Mountain, rev. and ed. Mrs. Evan Hopkins (London: Marshall, 1902).

[14] Albert B. Simpson, "I Clasp the Hand of Love Divine," in Mountain, *Hymns of Consecration and Faith*.

[15] Jean S. Pigott, "Jesus I Am Resting, Resting," in Mountain, *Hymns of Consecration and Faith*.

My all is on the altar;
I'm waiting for the fire;
I'm waiting, waiting, waiting;
I'm waiting for the fire.[16]

Like many convention speakers, Hopkins would often call his hearers to stand and make "a definite transaction"—an act of full surrender to Christ's indwelling presence.[17] Whereas Reformed theology saw sanctification as a gradual process, Keswick theology tended to link progress with crisis moments. "Keswick called for an experience of 'full surrender,' an appropriating of 'holiness by faith,' with consequent victory over sin, as an event usually subsequent to conversion."[18] This tended to create a two-stage view of the Christian life (a merely regenerate state followed by a consecrated state) and therefore also a two-tier hierarchy of Christians. In 1895, Andrew Murray told the convention that there are two types of Christian: the carnal (fleshly) Christian and the spiritual Christian (a distinction Stott himself made early in his ministry);[19] while at the 1929 convention, Stuart Holden gave an address entitled "Only Partially Christian."[20] Some within the holiness tradition described this crisis experience of consecration as "baptism in the Spirit." But after some debate the convention leaders rejected this, believing Spirit baptism referred to conversion, and they preferred the language of "filling with the Spirit." As a result, the language of "baptism in the Spirit" was officially discouraged at the convention.

From the beginning, the word "convention" was chosen because the organizers wanted it to achieve a goal—a crisis experience leading to a new experience of power over sin. It was not a conference considering a *subject*, but a convention pursuing an *object*—the transformation of those attending. To this end, it soon adopted a set pattern for the week designed to lead people to this crisis experience. On day one, speakers sought to raise an awareness of the need as the reality of sin was portrayed. On day two, the focus was on God's provision for that need through the work of the cross and the rest of faith (often focusing on Rom. 6–8). On day three, there was a call to complete consecration or surrender. This was the moment of crisis,

16 Mary Dagworthy James, "My Spirit, Soul and Body," in Mountain, *Hymns of Consecration and Faith*.
17 Cited in Price and Randall, *Transforming Keswick*, 46.
18 Price and Randall, *Transforming Keswick*, 14.
19 John Stott, *Men with a Message: An Introduction to the New Testament and Its Writers* (London: Longmans, 1954), 67–68.
20 *The Keswick Convention*, 1929, 67–74, cited in Steven Barabas, *So Great Salvation: The History and Message of the Keswick Convention* (London: Marshall, Morgan and Scott, 1952), 54–56.

and it was common for people to say, "No crisis before Wednesday." The focus on day four was the promise of a Spirit-filled life. And, finally, on day five, this turned to the resulting need for a life of practical holiness and a call to missionary service. The aim was to create "a spiritual clinic" in which a diagnosis was made and a cure administered. Within each day, too, the evening meetings were oriented toward change. A first speaker would present the biblical foundation for that evening's theme, while a second speaker would make a more existential call to respond.

Nevertheless, differences of emphasis remained with the Keswick movement. Price and Randall comment: "Defining the fine points of Keswick teaching is not a simple exercise, for there has never been in its history an agreed system of the particular truths it has purported to proclaim. A supposed *Keswick view* on something may depend on who is speaking at the time."[21] In 1912, Graham Scroggie, minister of Charlotte Chapel in Edinburgh, spoke at the convention for the first time. He would go on to take the convention's main Bible teaching sessions on twelve occasions and become one of its key thinkers in the mid-twentieth century. He talked about the rest of faith, but also about faith as "a moral and spiritual principle of action."[22] Scroggie believed surrender to Christ's lordship was the distinctive message of Keswick. Price and Randall conclude:

> It was not unusual to have on the same platform at Keswick advocates of a crisis sanctification, who would actively encourage hearers to experience the crisis there and then, and other speakers who were extremely cautious about any such momentary event. The latter group warned against complacency, calling for diligence in spiritual growth. These two issues probably remained in tension for the first seventy years of the Convention's history, and only in its post-war years did the emphasis come down more definitely in favour of the process of growth in holiness.[23]

Stott was the major influence in ensuring that this shift took place.

The Keswick Tradition under Fire

The Keswick holiness movement had already been critiqued from within Reformed circles, and this undoubtedly shaped Stott's response. J. C. Ryle,

21 Price and Randall, *Transforming Keswick*, 34.
22 Price and Randall, *Transforming Keswick*, 75.
23 Price and Randall, *Transforming Keswick*, 15.

the first bishop of Liverpool, wrote his famous book *Holiness* just two years after the convention started. Whereas the Keswick circle spoke of the sinful nature as being counteracted by the indwelling Christ, Ryle spoke of it as being gradually transformed through disciplined effort. The differences between Ryle and Keswick should not be overstated, however, since two years after the publication of *Holiness*, Ryle spoke at the convention on Ezekiel 36:26, a verse that emphasizes the Spirit's presence ("I will remove the heart of stone from your flesh and give you a heart of flesh").

In the 1950s, Martyn Lloyd-Jones voiced his disquiet at what he referred to as the teaching of "a certain town in the Lake District." He was concerned about its subjectivity and passivity. "This type of teaching," he said, "tends to make people dependant upon meetings and the particular atmosphere of certain meetings."[24] They receive a blessing in the highly charged emotional atmosphere of the meeting but then seem to lose it and can regain it only when the emotional atmosphere is recreated. In one sense the convention's numerical success was a sign of the failure of its underlying theology, for, if the crisis people experienced at the convention was so decisive, why did so many return each year for a repeat?

But the foremost assault on Keswick teaching came from a twenty-nine-year-old theologian, J. I. Packer, in an article published in July 1955.[25] While a student at Oxford, Packer had been drawn to the promise of a higher life, but his attempts at self-consecration had left him feeling defeated.[26] Packer accused Keswick theology of being Pelagian. Pelagius was the fifth-century theologian condemned by Augustine for arguing that human beings retained the capacity to keep God's law unaided. At first sight this appears an odd accusation, since the Reformed tradition emphasized disciplined effort and the Keswick tradition taught the need for the indwelling presence of Christ to counterbalance the pull of sin in the soul. But Packer was focusing on the call to an act of consecration, a submission of the will that was itself an act of the will. In the Reformed view, says Packer, "the Holy Spirit uses my faith and obedience (which he himself first works in me) to sanctify me." But in the Keswick view, "I use the Holy Spirit (whom God puts at my disposal) to sanctify myself" so that God does "as much in

24 D. Martyn Lloyd-Jones, *Christ Our Sanctification* (London: Inter-Varsity Press, 1948), 19.

25 J. I. Packer, "'Keswick' and the Reformed Doctrine of Sanctification," *Evangelical Quarterly* 27, no. 3 (1955): 153–67.

26 Alister McGrath, *To Know and Serve God: A Biography of James Packer* (London: Hodder & Stoughton, 1977), 22–24.

[a believer's] life as he is permitted to do."[27] Packer's damning verdict was this: "It is not much of a recommendation when all you can say is that this teaching may help you if you do not take its details too seriously. It is utterly damning to have to say, as in this case I think we must, that if you do take its details seriously, it will tend not to help you but to destroy you."[28]

Others within the Reformed tradition were less confrontational. Eric Alexander, the influential minister of St George's Tron Church in Glasgow, was a regular speaker during the 1960s. And throughout the twentieth century, Reformed thinkers shaped and reshaped the Keswick movement. In 1953, E. F. Kevan, the principal of London Bible College, spoke at the convention, and his treatment of Romans 7 was significant in establishing sanctification as a lifelong process.

But the key reshaper of the Keswick tradition was Stott. According to Price and Randall, "the influence of the teaching of John Stott was to be crucial."[29] And it was his 1965 Bible readings in Romans 5–8, published the following year under the title *Men Made New*,[30] that proved decisive.

E. J. H. Nash, Stott's early mentor, had been favorable toward Keswick and encouraged people to attend. "It was part of my upbringing," said Stott, "to revere the Keswick Convention." But Stott had come to reject the central tenets of its distinctive teaching. Somewhat like Packer, Elisabeth Earnshaw-Smith—the daughter of Stott's predecessor at All Souls—had returned from the convention frustrated at her inability to experience a life-changing state of consecration, and it had fallen to the young curate to counsel her. Indeed, in the preface to *The Message of Romans*, Stott speaks of his own frustration at not experiencing the death to sin he had been taught to expect. "My final deliverance from this chimera," he adds, "was sealed" when he gave his 1965 talks to the Keswick Convention.[31]

So, when he was asked to speak at the 1962 convention, Stott first asked for, and received, an assurance that he would not be required to subscribe to a particular view of holiness. Stott's expositions on 1 Corinthians were well received, and he was invited to return in 1965. Peter Moore, who drove him to the convention, recalls, "I had no idea how important those readings

---

27 Packer, "'Keswick,'" 162, 166.
28 Packer, "'Keswick,'" 159.
29 Price and Randall, *Transforming Keswick*, 71.
30 John Stott, *Men Made New: An Exposition of Romans 5–8* (London: Inter-Varsity Press, 1966). A transcript of the talks was also published in Stott, *John Stott at Keswick: A Lifetime of Preaching* (Milton Keynes: Authentic Media, 2008). See also Stott, *The Message of Romans: God's Good News for the World* (Leicester: Inter-Varsity Press; Downers Grove, IL: InterVarsity Press, 1994), 166–88.
31 Stott, *The Message of Romans*, 10.

would be for the history of Keswick or the evangelical understanding of sanctification; but I do recall John being more than usually nervous on the trip up, and working furiously in the back seat of the small car."[32]

Romans 6 and Our Death to Sin

Romans 6 was a key passage in the understanding of holiness expounded at the Keswick Convention. In 1906, Evan Hopkins said that no other passage had been so prominent at the convention;[33] and, writing in 1952, Steve Barabas suspected that every convention had featured at least one exposition of the chapter.[34]

Verse 6 was a particular focus for the Keswick understanding of holiness: "Knowing this, that our old man is crucified with him, that the body of sin might be destroyed, that henceforth we should not serve sin" (KJV). This, it was claimed, meant the sinful nature had been rendered powerless in a believer. To have died to sin in Christ meant sin no longer exerted any influence on the consecrated believer. Hopkins wrote: "It is [the believer's] privilege to see that because he is identified with Christ in that death, he is also delivered from sin as a ruling principle. Its power is broken. He is in that sense 'free from sin.'"[35] Hopkins called on believers to claim by faith the freedom from sin their death in Christ had secured. This is the rest of faith.

Stott challenged this view head-on. His central idea was that our union with Christ in his death and resurrection does not make sin *impossible*; rather it makes it *incongruous*—what Stott called "the inadmissibility of sin."[36] "It is not the literal impossibility of sin, but the moral incongruity of it, which the apostle is emphasising."[37]

The key question, says Stott, is this: "How, and in what sense, have we died to sin?"[38] At this point he interacts directly with the Keswick tradition, acknowledging that he must first address what death to sin is *not*.

> Frankly, I do not like to be negative, but I fear that it is necessary to be negative here; to demolish before one can construct, because there is abroad

---

[32] Peter Moore, letter to Timothy Dudley-Smith, March 28, 1995, cited in Dudley-Smith, *John Stott*, vol. 2, *A Global Ministry* (Leicester: Inter-Varsity Press, 2001), 36.
[33] *The Keswick Week*, 1906, 94, cited in Price and Randall, *Transforming Keswick*, 228.
[34] Barabas, *So Great Salvation*, 89.
[35] Hopkins, *The Law of Liberty*, 9.
[36] Stott, *John Stott at Keswick*, 18.
[37] Stott, *Men Made New*, 34.
[38] Stott, *Men Made New*, 34.

> in Evangelical circles a popular view of the death unto sin, described in Romans 6, which I submit to you cannot stand up to a careful examination, and leads people rather to disillusion, to deception, or even to despair.[39]

Perhaps he has in mind Packer's experience as a student.

Stott outlines the Keswick view as follows: When you die, your five senses no longer function. You cannot see, hear, touch, taste, or smell. You no longer respond to stimuli. In the same way, so it was claimed, to die to sin is to become insensitive and unresponsive to sin. Its stimuli no longer affect you. "We are told . . . that our old nature in some mystical way was actually crucified. Christ bore not only our guilt, but our 'flesh' . . . and our task (however much evidence we may have to the contrary) is to reckon it dead."[40] Having set it out, Stott responds: "There are serious, indeed fatal, objections to this view."[41]

Stott begins by noting that the phrase "died to sin" occurs three times in Romans 6—twice referring to Christians (vv. 2, 11) and once referring to Christ (v. 10). We therefore need to understand the phrase in a way that applies both to Christians and to Christ. He starts with Christ and verse 10: "For the death he died he died to sin, once for all, but the life he lives he lives to God." Here Christ's death to sin "cannot mean that He became unresponsive to it, because this would imply that He was formerly responsive to it."[42] The idea that Christ had previously been alive to sin is intolerable. What, then, of the Christian? Again, death to sin cannot mean we become unresponsive to it—otherwise Paul would not need to call us to resist sin's stimuli in verses 12 and 13: "Let not sin therefore reign in your mortal body. . . . Do not present your members to sin." "These would be absurd injunctions," Stott comments, "if the flesh were dead and has no desires."[43] Finally, Stott appeals to Christian experience. The fact that we often *do* feel the pull of sin disproves this interpretation. "Far from being dead in the sense of being quiescent, our fallen and corrupt nature is alive and kicking. So much so that we are exhorted not to obey its lust; and so much so that we are given the Holy Spirit for the precise purpose of subduing and controlling it."[44] The result for advocates of this position is a dangerous disjunc-

---

[39] Stott, *John Stott at Keswick*, 23.
[40] Stott, *Men Made New*, 38.
[41] Stott, *Men Made New*, 39.
[42] Stott, *Men Made New*, 39.
[43] Stott, *Men Made New*, 40.
[44] Stott, *Men Made New*, 41.

tion between their theology and their experience. Nor can someone claim this experience of "death to sin" is the experience of a special few—those living a higher life—since Paul explicitly refers to "all of us" in verse 3.

Aware of his audience, Stott adds at this point, "May I say, beloved, that if I have hurt anybody, because this is a cherished view of yours, I am sorry; but I believe that if you will absorb this, it will lead you into a new dimension of Christian living, a new liberty."[45] There is a pastoral sensitivity here. But he is also turning the rhetoric of the higher life teaching on itself with its promise as a new dimension of Christian living and liberty.

What, then, are we to make of the phrase "dead to sin"? Instead of likening this death to a human corpse, Stott reasons, we should consider biblical understandings of death. The Keswick view, he says, illustrates the dangers of arguing from a false analogy.[46] Our death to sin is not like becoming a corpse. Death in the Scriptures is not just a physical reality; it is also a moral and legal reality. Death is "the grim but just penalty for sin."[47] "Whenever sin and death are spoken of together in the Scripture, the essential relationship between them is that death is sin's penalty. . . . Sin and death are linked in Scripture as an offence and its just reward."[48] Stott cites Romans 1:32 and 6:23. "This, then, is how dying and death are to be understood: not as a state of insensibility, but as the just reward of sin."[49] Romans 6:10 can only mean that Christ died to sin "in the sense that He bore's sin's penalty."[50] And this therefore is also the sense in which Christians have died to sin. "We have died to sin in the sense that in Christ we have borne its penalty. Consequently, our old life is finished; a new life has begun."[51]

Freed from the Dominion of Sin but Not Its Influence

Stott then analyzes the key verse, Romans 6:6, in detail, dividing it into three parts:

1. We know that our old self *was* crucified with Him
2. in order that the sinful body might be destroyed,
3. in order that we might no longer be enslaved to sin.

[45] Stott, *John Stott at Keswick*, 27.
[46] Stott, *Men Made New*, 42.
[47] Stott, *Men Made New*, 42.
[48] Stott, *Men Made New*, 42.
[49] Stott, *John Stott at Keswick*, 28.
[50] Stott, *Men Made New*, 43.
[51] Stott, *Men Made New*, 43.

Stott employs his own translation here to draw attention to the way "something happened, in order that something else might happen, in order that something else might happen."[52] The ultimate goal is freedom from bondage to sin. How does this happen? Through the destruction of the body of sin. This is not the human body, which is not in itself sinful. "It means rather the sinful nature which belongs to the body."[53]

"Now, careful!" says Stott at this point.[54] Though he does not say so explicitly, there is a danger of slipping back into the old Keswick holiness mind-set, thinking the danger of sin has been eradicated because the sinful body is described as being destroyed. But the word "destroyed" is used of Satan in Hebrews 2:14. "It means not to become extinct, but to be defeated; not to be annihilated, but to be deprived of power. Our old nature is no more extinct than the devil; but God's will is that the dominion of both should be broken."[55] This is an important distinction. We have been freed from both the penalty and the dominion of sin. But this does not mean sin's influence evaporates. It no longer necessarily controls us (as it does the unregenerate person), but it still exerts a pull on us. *De jure*, its power is broken, but, *de facto*, its power continues to be felt. It is no longer a master we *must* obey, but we may still feel its call.

This defeat of the sinful nature took place when our old self was crucified with Christ. The "old self" here cannot mean the "sinful nature," since Stott has already identified "the body of sin" as the sinful nature. "No. The 'old man' denotes, not our old unregenerate nature, but our old unregenerate life . . . not a part of me called my old nature, but the whole of me as I was before I was converted. My 'old self' is my pre-conversion life, my unregenerate self."[56]

How does dying to sin—in the sense of having its penalty borne—lead to overcoming the sinful nature and deliverance from bondage to sin? Romans 6:7, says Stott, gives the answer: "Because he who has died has been justified from his sin." Stott criticizes the KJV and RSV for translating this "has been freed from his sin," when the word is translated "justified" every other time it is used in Romans. "The only way to be justified from sin is to receive the wages of sin. There is no other escape from sin but to bear its penalty."[57] In

[52] Stott, *Men Made New*, 44.
[53] Stott, *Men Made New*, 44.
[54] Stott, *John Stott at Keswick*, 29.
[55] Stott, *Men Made New*, 44.
[56] Stott, *Men Made New*, 45.
[57] Stott, *Men Made New*, 46.

our human judicial system, the only way to escape your crime is to pay the penalty the law demands. In a similar way, the penalty for sin is death, and so the only way to escape the claims of sin is to die. In *The Cross of Christ*, Stott says, "There is only one sense in which it may be said that Jesus 'died to sin,' and that is that he bore its penalty, since 'the wages of sin is death' (v. 23)."[58] A death sentence, of course, is not normally an escape! But our death to sin in Christ is followed by resurrection. In summary:

> We deserve to die for our sin. By union with Jesus Christ we did die—not in our own person (that would have meant eternal death) but in the Person of Christ our Substitute, with whom we have been made one in faith and baptism. And, by union with the same Christ, we have risen again to live the life of a justified sinner, a life that is altogether new.[59]

Five Steps to Holiness

This detailed examination of the phrase "dead to sin" comes in the middle of a five-step exposition of what, positively, it means to die to sin.

Step 1. "Christian baptism is baptism into Christ."[60] "A Christian is not merely a justified believer. He is someone who has entered into a vital, personal union with Jesus Christ. . . . And baptism signifies this union with Christ."[61] This is why the New Testament often describes baptism as baptism "into" Christ. "This union with Christ, invisibly effected by faith, is visibly signified and sealed by baptism."[62]

Step 2. "Baptism into Christ is baptism into His death and resurrection."[63] Our union with Christ is not something vague or general. We share in his death and resurrection.

Step 3. "Christ's death was a death unto sin, and His resurrection was a resurrection to God."[64] This is where Stott's explanation of "died to sin" fits. In summary he says that, through our union with Christ by faith-baptism, we have died to the *penalty* of sin. As a result, our former life, which was heading inexorably toward death, is now behind us, and we have risen to live a new life for God.

---

58 John Stott, *The Cross of Christ*, 2nd ed. (Leicester: Inter-Varsity Press, 1989), 277.
59 Stott, *Men Made New*, 47.
60 Stott, *Men Made New*, 34.
61 Stott, *Men Made New*, 34–35.
62 Stott, *Men Made New*, 35.
63 Stott, *Men Made New*, 36.
64 Stott, *Men Made New*, 37.

Step 4. "Since we have died to sin and live to God, we must reckon it so," as Romans 6:11 says.[65] Stott is keen to emphasize that this is not an act of make-believe. We are not conjuring up faith in something that is not the case. "We are not to pretend that our old nature has died when we know perfectly well that it has not."[66] Our old man or our former self really did die in Christ, and so the penalty of sin really has been paid. Stott likens it to a biography in two parts. Volume 1 is the story of our old self, and that part of the biography is now over. It ended with our judicial death in Christ. Now we are living in volume 2, the story of our new self. It is *not impossible* to live as though we still belong in volume 1, but it should be *inconceivable* to go backward in this way.

> Can a married woman still live as though she were a single girl? Well, yes, I suppose she can. It is not impossible. But let her feel that ring on the fourth finger of her left hand, the symbol of her new life, the symbol of her identification with her husband, let her remember who she is, and let her live accordingly. Can a born-again Christian live as though he were still in his sins? Well, yes, I suppose he can. It is not impossible. But let him remember his baptism, the symbol of his identification with Christ in His death and resurrection, and let him live accordingly.[67]

In *Focus on Christ*, Stott points out that we sometimes speak of the death of a wish, a hope, a dream, a friendship, or even a marriage. What we mean is that it has come to an end. We speak of finality. "So when Paul wants to emphasize that our old pre-Christian life has come to an end, he says that he 'died' to it. . . . We are set free from the bondage of the old life."[68]

Step 5. "As those who are alive from the dead, we must not let sin reign within us, but yield ourselves to God."[69] In other words, we must live with God as our King rather than sin as our king.

Stott then deals with the second half of Romans 6 more briefly. Paul contrasts two slaveries: slavery to sin, which begins at birth, develops through moral deterioration and leads to death; and slavery to God, which begins at conversion, develops through sanctification and leads to eternal life.

---

65 Stott, *Men Made New*, 48.
66 Stott, *Men Made New*, 49.
67 Stott, *Men Made New*, 50–51.
68 John Stott, *Focus on Christ: An Enquiry into the Theology of Prepositions* (Eastbourne: Kingsway, 1979), 94.
69 Stott, *Men Made New*, 51.

Stott concludes by identifying the whisper of Satan in our ear: "Why not continue to sin? . . . God will forgive you." Our first response should be "God forbid!" But we can go further and give a reason. We need to tell ourselves: "Don't you know that you are one with Christ? That you have died to sin and risen to God? Don't you know that you are a slave of God and therefore committed to obedience?"[70]

Characteristically, Stott makes the mind the focus: "The secret of holy living is in the mind."[71] He draws attention to the use of the word "know" in verses 3 and 6, and "reckoning" or, as Stott puts it, "intellectually realising" in verse 11. "Our minds are so to grasp the fact and the significance of our death and resurrection with Christ, that a return to the old life is unthinkable."[72] Whereas the old Keswick holiness teaching appealed to the will, Stott appeals to the mind. The mind drives the will. As the mind recognizes our new identity in Christ, so the will chooses to live out the reality of that identity.

Stott's talks in 1965 created a stir during and after the convention. The editor of *The Keswick Week*, Herbert Stevenson, wrote, "The standard of Scriptural teaching was very high . . . although direct appeal for immediate response . . . was not so forceful as is sometimes the case"—a coded way of saying there was not a call to a crisis experience of consecration.[73] Alan Redpath, a regular Keswick speaker, was present during Stott's talks and unhappy with their content. "This is not Keswick," he is reported to have said. Two years later he gave an alternative reading of Romans 6:6 at the convention: "Freedom from sin's dominion is a blessing we may claim by faith, just as we claim pardon. . . . That is basically why the Keswick Convention was founded." Redpath exhorted his hearers not to settle for "half-salvation."[74]

Stott's and Redpath's contrasting approaches generated lengthy debate at meetings of the convention council in 1968. The council decided that the convention should allow both points of view. But Packer and Stott had decisively shifted the approach to sanctification taken by the convention and the wider British evangelical world. The convention dropped the format of "the spiritual clinic" and instead built its evening meetings around an annual theme. Today the call to Christlike transformation, practical holiness, and

70 Stott, *Men Made New*, 56–57.
71 Stott, *Men Made New*, 50.
72 Stott, *Men Made New*, 50–51.
73 *The Keswick Week*, 1965, 118, cited in Price and Randall, *Transforming Keswick*, 240.
74 *The Keswick Week*, 1967, as cited in Price and Randall, *Transforming Keswick*, 241.

missionary service continues at the convention. But the call to consecration is associated no longer with a one-off crisis experience leading to a higher life but with an ongoing submission to God in the battle with sin.

Repudiation and Surrender

Stott's position was essentially a restatement of a classic Reformed understanding of sanctification. In *The Contemporary Christian* he describes sanctification as a process involving "ruthless repudiation" and "unconditional surrender."[75]

Though Stott does not state this explicitly, these correspond to the process of mortification and vivification that were so central to John Calvin's view of our union with Christ and have been the mainstay of Reformed spirituality ever since.[76] Mortification is the "ruthless" repudiation of sin and the influence of the sinful nature. There must be a renunciation of sin and self.[77] Elsewhere Stott says, "A Christian's rejection of his old nature is to be pitiless . . . painful . . . decisive. . . . We must renew every day this attitude towards sin of ruthless and uncompromising rejection."[78] But we can undertake this repudiation only by surrendering to the influence of the Spirit. In *Christian Basics* he correlates repudiation and surrender to the battle between the flesh and the Spirit. We take sides in the battle, repudiating the flesh and surrendering to the Spirit.[79]

In his exposition of Romans 6, Stott does not focus on the role of the Spirit, since the passage does not address this. But elsewhere Stott says, "The Christian faith and life depend entirely upon the Holy Spirit."[80] It is the Spirit who implants in us new desires for holiness. Using the imagery of Galatians 5, Stott often speaks of the flesh and Spirit as combatants, battling for control of our hearts.

> This [presence of the Spirit] does not mean that from now on we are exempt from the possibility of sinning. On the contrary, in some ways the

---

75 John Stott, *The Contemporary Christian: An Urgent Plea for Double Listening* (Leicester: Inter-Varsity Press, 1992), 154–55; see also Stott, *Men with a Message*, 67.

76 See Stott, *Men Made New*, 91–92, where Stott speaks of "mortification" ("putting to death by the power of the Spirit the deeds of the body") and "aspiration" ("setting our minds on the things of the Spirit"). See also Stott, *The Message of Romans*, 228–30.

77 John Stott, *Balanced Christianity: A Call to Avoid Unnecessary Polarisation*, 2nd ed. (Nottingham: Inter-Varsity Press, 2014), 109–12.

78 John Stott, *The Message of Galatians: Only One Way* (Leicester: Inter-Varsity Press; Downers Grove, IL: InterVarsity Press, 1968), 150–51.

79 John Stott, *Christian Basics: An Invitation to Discipleship* (London: Hodder, 1991), 88.

80 Stott, *Balanced Christianity*, 97; see also Stott, *Men Made New*, 84.

> conflict is intensified. . . . We continue to be conscious of sinful desires which are tugging us down; but we are now also aware of a counteracting force pulling us upwards to holiness. . . . Towards "the flesh" we must take up such an attitude of fierce resistance and ruthless rejection that only the word "crucifixion" can describe it; but to the indwelling Spirit must trustfully surrender the undisputed dominion over our lives.[81]

But what is striking is the language Stott uses to describe his position. Again we see a dialectic approach, where two apparent opposites are combined to produce not a halfway house but a powerful synthesis.

It is important to recognize the context in which the Keswick movement emerged. The dominant religious movement in England in the second half of the nineteenth century was the Oxford movement or Tractarianism, what became Anglo-Catholicism. Even in evangelical Anglican parishes, it was reshaping the architecture of Christian worship. And this influence extended to Harford-Battersby, the founder of the Keswick Convention. While he had grown up in an evangelical home, at Oxford he had been influenced by the pursuit of deeper holiness within the Tractarian movement. It was only when he realized that the Tractarian emphasis on duty did not match what he found in Scripture or satisfy the longings of his heart that he returned to evangelical spirituality. At the same time, the Victorian era in England was marked by an emphasis on outward respectability. "It was easier to conform than to change."[82] In the late nineteenth century, evangelicals felt that the advances they had made in the first half of the century (following on the Great Awakening at the end of the eighteenth century) were being reversed by the rationalism of the Enlightenment. So the holiness movement, says David Bebbington, emerged when "vital religion seemed threatened at the same time by the twin foes of rationalism and ritualism."[83] This arid environment explains why people were drawn to an emphasis on supernatural power and personal consecration. Reacting against the self-reliance of the era, many found at the Keswick Convention a profound and liberating experience.

Stott combines this longing for spiritual reality with the Reformed emphasis on disciplined effort. In doing so, he takes the language of the Keswick movement and repurposes it to emphasize that our activity takes

81 Stott, *Basic Christianity*, 101; see also Stott, *The Incomparable Christ* (Leicester: Inter-Varsity Press, 2001), 46–47.
82 Price and Randall, *Transforming Keswick*, 191.
83 Bebbington, *Evangelicalism in Modern Britain*, 152.

place in and through the power of the Holy Spirit. So he speaks of "unconditional surrender" and "a counteracting force." But these no longer imply a single act of consecration leading to a state in which the indwelling Christ constantly prevails against the flesh. Instead, they refer to a battle raging in our souls that can be won only by fighting the flesh and surrendering to the Spirit. Meanwhile, the language of "ruthless repudiation" reflects the traditional emphasis on disciplined mortification expressed in Puritan thinkers like John Owen, the main influence on Packer. So Stott is combining both traditions or, better still, drawing the Keswick tradition back into balance.

> To "sow to the flesh" is to pander to it, to cosset, cuddle and stroke it, instead of crucifying it. . . . Every time we allow our mind to harbour a grudge, nurse a grievance, entertain an impure fantasy, or wallow in self-pity, we are sowing to the flesh. Every time we linger in bad company whose insidious influence we know we cannot resist, every time we lie in bed when we ought to be up and praying, every time we read pornographic literature, every time we take a risk which strains our self-control, we are sowing, sowing, sowing to the flesh. Some Christians sow to the flesh every day and wonder why they do not reap holiness.[84]

In *The Contemporary Christian*, Stott says, "Both our repudiation of the flesh and our surrender to the Spirit need to be repeated daily, however decisive our original repudiation and surrender may have been."[85] He does not invalidate a past act of consecration, but the key word is "daily." Consecration is not completed through a crisis experience but is a daily reality. The cross and resurrection shape not (or not just) a onetime or occasional crisis experience but a continuous, repeated pattern of Christian spirituality.

Again, this is characteristic of the Reformed tradition. In his book *The Practice of Piety*, historian Charles Hambrick-Stowe studied the day-to-day piety of the Puritans as it was actually practiced. One striking conclusion of Hambrick-Stowe's work is the way the cross and resurrection shaped the rhythms of Puritan piety. For the Puritans, conversion involved coming to an end of yourself—a recognition of your sin and your inability to put things right. This then leads you to embrace Christ in faith and receive new life from him through the Spirit. So each conversion is a kind of death and

---

[84] Stott, *The Message of Galatians*, 170.
[85] Stott, *The Contemporary Christian*, 155; see also Stott, *The Cross of Christ*, 348–49; and Stott, *Focus on Christ*, 67.

resurrection. But what Hambrick-Stowe highlights is that for the Puritans this pattern continued throughout their lives:

> The pattern of spiritual stages first established in conversion continued to mark the journey to heaven. The devotional life of the saints, the means by which they progressed on the pilgrimage, was a system of ritual self-emptying in preparation for the renewed experience of being filled by God with his grace. The redemptive cycle of Christ's death and resurrection was translated into a set of spiritual exercises, devotional acts that became the path of renewed repentance and fulfilment.[86]

Disciplined Habits of Life

Stott says, "Both our repudiation and our surrender are also to be worked out in disciplined habits of life."[87] The Christian life requires effort. "Holiness," says Stott, "is not a condition into which we drift."[88] So, for Stott, *discipline* is always a key component of the Christian life. He cites Martyn Lloyd-Jones: "I am more and more convinced that most people get into trouble in the living of the Christian life because of their molly-coddling of themselves spiritually."[89]

In the introduction of *The Radical Disciple*, the last book Stott wrote, he explains why he has used the word "disciple" rather than "Christian." After pointing out that "Christian" is used only three times in the New Testament, he says, "One wishes in some ways the word 'disciple' had continued into the following centuries, so that Christians were self-consciously disciples of Jesus, and took seriously their responsibility to be 'under discipline.'"[90] "Jesus never concealed the fact that his religion included a demand as well as an offer."[91]

This commitment to discipline and to the disciplines was a feature of Stott's own personal piety. "Fundamental to all Christian leadership and ministry," he said, "is a humble, personal relationship to the Lord Jesus Christ, devotion to him expressed in daily prayer, and love for him expressed in daily obedience."[92] Stott himself had a number of disciplines

---

86 Charles E. Hambrick-Stowe, *The Practice of Piety: Puritan Devotional Principles in Puritan New England* (Chapel Hill: University of North Carolina Press, 1982), 89–90.
87 Stott, *The Contemporary Christian*, 155.
88 John Stott, *The Message of Ephesians: God's New Society* (Leicester: Inter-Varsity Press, 1979), 193.
89 Cited in John Stott, *The Radical Disciple: Wholehearted Christian Living* (Leicester: Inter-Varsity Press, 2010), 121, quoting D. M. Lloyd-Jones, *Romans 6: The New Man* (Edinburgh: Banner of Truth, 1992), 93.
90 Stott, *The Radical Disciple*, 16.
91 Stott, *Basic Christianity*, 107.
92 John Stott, *Calling Christian Leaders: Biblical Models of Church, Gospel and Ministry* (Leicester: Inter-Varsity Press, 2002), 116.

he adhered to resolutely. He did not impose them on others in a legalistic way, but they were the framework for his own walk with Christ. His normal pattern was to rise at 5:00 a.m.—a pattern of early rising he learned from Simeon.[93] Stott would greet each member of the Trinity in turn before offering a petition for the day ahead.[94] It was also common for him to recite the ninefold fruit of the Spirit or, mindful of the call of Romans 12:1 to present our bodies as a living sacrifice, to offer each limb of his body in service to God. Then he would listen to the news on the radio while washing, before spending an hour reading his Bible and in prayer. All his adult life Stott followed the Bible reading plan developed by Robert Murray M'Cheyne, which involved reading four chapters each day—three each morning, one of which he studied in more depth, and one at night.

Bible reading was followed by intercession,[95] conducted with the aid of a leather notebook containing names and issues for prayer, and stuffed with letters and pamphlets. Not that prayer was straightforward for Stott—he often spoke of the need to win "the battle of the prayer threshold." He would imagine God waiting within a walled garden. But in front of the door into the garden stands the devil with a drawn sword, who must be defeated in the name of Christ. "Many of us give up praying," comments Stott, "before we have tried to fight this battle. The best way to win, in my experience, is to claim the promises of Scripture, which the devil cannot undo."[96]

Stott became rector of All Souls at the young age of twenty-nine "to everybody's astonishment (especially mine)," he says, and he describes how the responsibilities soon got on top of him.[97] "I guess that at the time I was not far from a nervous breakdown."[98] At this point he heard L. F. E. Wilkinson, the principal of Oak Hill Theological College, commending to a group of church leaders the practice of spending one day a month as a quiet day away from the parish. Stott immediately planned a "Q" day into his diary, a practice he continued throughout his ministry. "All I can say is that this little prudential arrangement saved my life and my ministry. . . . Although I was still challenged by the job, I was not overwhelmed by

---

[93] John Stott, "Charles Simeon: A Personal Appreciation," in *Evangelical Preaching: An Anthology of Sermons by Charles Simeon* (Portland, OR: Multnomah, 1986), xxxvi.

[94] Roger Steer, *Inside Story: The Life of John Stott* (Nottingham: Inter-Varsity Press, 2009), 246–47.

[95] See Stott, *Christian Basics*, 121–35; and Stott, *Understanding the Bible* (London: Scripture Union, 1972), 244–45, where Stott commends daily Bible reading and prayer.

[96] John Stott, *Authentic Christianity: From the Writings of John Stott*, ed. Timothy Dudley-Smith (Downers Grove, IL: InterVarsity Press, 1995), 226.

[97] John Stott, *The Living Church: Convictions of a Lifelong Pastor* (Leicester: Inter-Varsity Press, 2007), 165.

[98] Stott, *The Living Church*, 183.

it."[99] In fact, as the busyness of ministry increased, so did the frequency of his Q days, from monthly to biweekly, and from biweekly to weekly. Every Thursday he would drive to a house in north London in which two elderly spinsters hosted him.

Stott would give up chocolate (one of the abiding passions of his life) and other treats during Lent.[100] His friend John Wyatt recalls how Stott once told him that he was in the habit, when walking alone, "of remembering that every fresh breath, every heartbeat, was a gift from God which could be taken away at any time"—a good example of what John Calvin calls "the meditation on the future life."[101]

Stott was once asked whether he had ever felt like giving up his ministry. He acknowledged that pastors are often subject to discouragements and that these can easily lead to burnout. But then he added:

> I have never really been tempted to this because I have taken precautions. I have recognised that human beings are psychosomatic creatures, so that our bodily condition has a powerful influence on our spiritual life. I have tried to maintain a disciplined life, ensuring adequate sleep, food and exercise.

He characteristically commends bird-watching, citing the physical recreation and mental relaxation it provides, along with the exposure to wilderness. "I don't think birdwatchers get nervous breakdowns," he adds, somewhat tongue in cheek. Finally, he concludes, "I found, however, that most important of all is a disciplined devotional life, with a determination to meet Christ every day."[102]

There is no doubt Stott was by temperament a disciplined person, a natural bent further reinforced by his social background and upbringing. But, although he commended discipline as part of the Christian life, he was slow to impose his own routines on other people.

Recent years have seen a welcome emphasis on being gospel-centered and an approach to the Christian life that is energized by grace rather than driven by legalism. But there is a danger in this of viewing any emphasis on discipline with suspicion. This is where Stott helps us. His dialectic of

---

99 Stott, *The Living Church*, 184; see also Stott, *Between Two Worlds: The Art of Preaching in the Twentieth Century* (Grand Rapids, MI: Eerdmans, 1982), 202–3.

100 Matthew Smith, in *John Stott: A Portrait by His Friends*, ed. Chris Wright (Nottingham: Inter-Varsity Press, 2011), 202.

101 John Calvin, *Institutes of the Christian Religion*, ed. John T. McNeill, trans. Ford Lewis Battles (Philadelphia: Westminster, 1960), 3.9.

102 Cited in Steer, *Inside Story*, 251–52.

"ruthless repudiation" and "unconditional surrender" averts a false choice between discipline and grace. Instead, we pursue Spirit-empowered discipline. We are sanctified by faith. But it is a faith that gladly crucifies whatever belongs to the flesh and actively sows to the Spirit. It avails itself of the means of grace not as a synonym for human achievements but as gifts God gives us that we might enjoy life-changing communion with him.

Romans 8:12–13 captures this combination well: "So then, brothers, we are debtors, not to the flesh, to live according to the flesh. For if you live according to the flesh you will die, but if by the Spirit you put to death the deeds of the body, you will live." What must we do? We must put to death the deeds of the body. We must be active, proactive, violent, resolute. There is no room for passivity or quietism. It is kill or be killed. Either we put to death the deeds of the body or we die. And yet this is not a call to self-reliance. Instead, Paul is calling us to reliance on the Spirit. We put to death the deeds of the body "by the Spirit." We may not see or feel the Spirit (John 3:8). All we do is fight against sin with all our might. But we know that we are enabled in this fight by the Spirit. We enter the fray confident that he will stand with us and strengthen our arms. And we fight confident that the Spirit will give us the ultimate victory. For in the previous verse Paul says: "If the Spirit of him who raised Jesus from the dead dwells in you, he who raised Christ Jesus from the dead will also give life to your mortal bodies through his Spirit who dwells in you" (Rom. 8:11).

CHAPTER 6

LIFE IN THE SPIRIT

"What is the wrong with the Church to-day? Why is it so ineffective?"[1] These are the opening words of an extended, five-page editorial by the respected scholar Philip E. Hughes in the September 1962 edition of the Anglican journal *Churchman*. The editorial was subsequently printed in pamphlet form and sold thirty-nine thousand copies. Hughes pulled no punches.

> We need desperately to break free from the impersonal hand of institutionalism, from the puppetry of formalism, and from the smugness of respectability—not, however, by conforming to the world and its crazes (which is only to publicize our powerlessness) but by returning to genuine Christianity; and that means the Christianity of the New Testament. When we consider the gloriously triumphant power of the Holy Spirit in the lives of ordinary Christians as described in the Acts of the Apostles, the Church today almost seems to be a stranger to vibrant Christian dynamics.[2]

Hughes lamented a preoccupation with committee reports and pastoral platitudes. Instead, he called on his readers to seek God's grace: "If in humility and sorrow we seek His face, He will, in accordance with Christ's promise, pour upon us the transforming blessing of His Holy Spirit yet again. Indeed, there are already indications of a new movement of the Holy Spirit within the Church at the present time."[3]

1 Philip E. Hughes, "Editorial," *Churchman* 76, no. 3 (1962): 131.
2 Hughes, "Editorial," 131.
3 Hughes, "Editorial," 131.

Hughes had recently returned from the United States, where, he told his readers, he had witnessed that "the Breath of the Living God is stirring among the dry bones of the major, respectable, old-established denominations."[4] He particularly cited the "strange" and "incongruous" phenomenon of Episcopalians speaking in tongues. He then quoted a letter from a disillusioned Anglo-Catholic whose rule keeping had failed to satisfy, but who had then been baptized in the Spirit and spoken in tongues. As a result, the man's "whole life had begun to be transformed," and he had "gained an entirely new conception of Christianity."[5] Finally, Hughes added his own endorsement:

> This experience, your Editor found, has been enjoyed by large numbers of other church-people. It is transforming lives. It is revitalizing congregations. It is not confined to one church or to one district. Nor is it induced from without, but has every appearance of being a spontaneous movement of the Holy Spirit. . . . Much more impressive than the glossolalia were the love, the joy, the devotion, which flowed out from their lips and their lives—and their consciousness of spiritual power: power to witness to their faith freely and daily in the world, and power to pray for the miraculous healing of the sick and to see the victorious answer to these prayers. Is not all this reminiscent of the situation with which we are confronted in the book of the Acts?[6]

For many readers, this was their first exposure to what became known as the "charismatic movement." With its emphases on a post-conversion experience of the Holy Spirit that many identified as "the baptism of the Spirit," on the gifts of tongues and prophecy, and on freedom in worship, it brought with it not only renewed life for many but also a good deal of controversy. Nor was (or is) it in any way monolithic. Not all charismatics shared the classic Pentecostal understanding of the baptism of the Spirit as a second experience subsequent to conversion. Some emphasized the importance of miraculous signs and wonders; for others the primary change was in the style of worship they adopted.

In the early 1960s these divisions emerged within the staff team at All Souls. Michael Harper, then one of Stott's curates, had an experience of "renewal." Although the nascent charismatic movement provided a context

[4] Hughes, "Editorial," 131.
[5] Hughes, "Editorial," 132.
[6] Hughes, "Editorial," 133.

for what happened, Harper's experience took place not in a meeting but in private as he was meditating on the fullness of God in Ephesians 3. "It was earth-shaking," he said later, "baptized in the Spirit, everything leapt off the page."[7] On a staff away day, Stott invited Harper to tell his story. At the end, the senior curate John Lefroy declared, "Michael, I believe you've been baptized in the Spirit."[8] It was an expression Harper himself had not met before. Fearful of divisions forming within the church, Stott allowed Harper to speak of his experience but not to preach on the subject.

Martyn Lloyd-Jones was supportive of the movement, influenced as he was by a strain of Puritan thinking, particularly associated with Thomas Goodwin, that spoke of assurance as an experience of the Spirit subsequent to conversion. It was also a position taken by Charles Simeon.[9] This was different from classic Pentecostalism: the focus was on assurance rather than empowerment, and it was not tied to the gift of tongues. But it made Lloyd-Jones open to what was happening. He famously told a delegation of pastors who were embracing the new movement, "Gentlemen, I believe that you have been baptized with the Holy Spirit."[10]

Stott was always going to be driven by what he was convinced the Bible taught, but, given his emphasis on the mind, he was also instinctively inclined to view non-rational speech with suspicion. "John Stott was very interested," says Harper, "he was very intrigued, very gripped by it, but the turn-off was when I spoke in tongues."[11] Tongues divided the staff team. A number of people urged Stott to dismiss Harper, but Stott was loyal. Harper stayed two more years before eventually leaving in 1964 to found Fountain Trust to promote charismatic renewal.

Around this time Roopsingh Carr, a member of All Souls, asked Stott whether there was such an experience of the baptism of the Spirit, to which Stott replied, "I do not know, Roopy."[12] Stott himself had first encountered the charismatic movement in the 1950s during visits to California. His longing for revival meant he was initially and instinctively open to what he

---

7 Robbie Low, "An Interview with Michael Harper," *New Directions*, October 1996, cited in Timothy Dudley-Smith, *John Stott*, vol. 2, *A Global Ministry* (Leicester: Inter-Varsity Press, 2001), 21.

8 John Stott, interview by Timothy Dudley-Smith, July 27, 1994, in Dudley-Smith, *John Stott*, 2:22.

9 Charles Simeon, sermon on Rom. 8:15, *Horae Homileticae*, vol. 15, cited in Derek Prime, *Charles Simeon: An Ordinary Pastor of Extraordinary Influence* (Leominster: Day One, 2011), 32.

10 David Watson, *You Are My God* (London: Hodder & Stoughton, 1983), 57; see also John Stott, *The Cross of Christ*, 2nd ed. (Leicester: Inter-Varsity Press, 1989), 143–44, 235–36, for Stott's assessment of this perspective.

11 Raymond Luker, *All Souls: A History* (London: All Souls Church, 1979), 18, cited in Dudley-Smith, *John Stott*, 2:23.

12 Roopsingh Carr, letter to Timothy Dudley-Smith, August 4, 1995, cited in Dudley-Smith, *John Stott*, 2:37.

saw. But, as always, the Bible would be his touchstone. Years later he wrote to a correspondent:

> When the movement began some years ago in this country I personally searched the Scriptures deliberately in order to discover the truth about the subject. I opened my mind afresh to all that was being said, written and claimed, and spent two years reading, thinking, praying and discussing. It was as a result of this prolonged period of study that I came to my conclusions.[13]

In 1964, Stott shared those conclusions at the Islington Clerical Conference. In 1827, Daniel Wilson, the vicar of Islington, had invited a group of twelve clergy friends to discuss the subject of prayer together. Ever since, the vicar of Islington had convened an annual conference, primarily for evangelical Anglican clergy. In 1964 the theme was "The Holy Spirit in the Life of the Church," and Stott's paper was entitled "The Individual Christian and the Fullness of the Holy Spirit." That year the conference attracted its largest attendance in living memory. Most came looking for guidance on how they should respond to the charismatic movement, and it was Stott to whom they looked. "This was a period of much heart searching, diligent study and many meetings," says David Watson, a prominent charismatic Anglican.[14] One way or another it was going to be a decisive moment for evangelicalism in Britain and beyond. Stott's lecture was published as a booklet. In the years that followed, a number of people wrote to Stott because they had heard rumors that he had changed his mind and "become charismatic." So in 1975 he reprinted and revised *Baptism and Fullness*, partly to squash these rumors.[15] But the second edition also allowed him to modify his initial antagonism. In the new preface he confesses his own "immaturity both in having been too negative towards the charismatic movement and in having been too reluctant to meet its leaders and talk with them."[16] Speaking of the revised edition of *Baptism and Fullness*, Stott said in 1995: "I practically rewrote the book, principally because I felt I had been less than generous in my

---

[13] John Stott, letter to Edward Doring, October 29, 1995, Church of England Record Centre, STOTT/5/22, cited in Dudley-Smith, *John Stott*, 2:38.
[14] Watson, *You Are My God*, 58.
[15] John Stott, *Baptism and Fullness: The Work of the Holy Spirit Today*, 2nd ed. (Leicester: Inter-Varsity Press, 1975), 9.
[16] Stott, *Baptism and Fullness*; see also Stott, *The Message of Ephesians: God's New Society* (Leicester: Inter-Varsity Press, 1979), 156.

evaluation of the movement. So, I wanted to put on record that I had no doubt that God had blessed the charismatic movement to both individuals and local churches."[17]

Stott's instinct was always to be irenic, and he became more irenic on this issue as time went on. *Baptism and Fullness* warns those who took the same position as he did against looking on other people's experience with cynicism.[18] "There is a need for all of us, whatever our precise stance on this issue may be, to remain in fruitful fellowship and dialogue with one another."[19] Stott himself was involved in a series of meetings between Fountain Trust and the Church of England Evangelical Council,[20] though Harper described Stott's attitude at the time as "icy."[21]

In *Baptism and Fullness*, Stott is keenly aware of the church's failure to reach Western society and our own personal need for renewal. "We hunger and thirst for more. . . . We also long for true revival."[22] Speaking of our constant need to seek the fullness of the Spirit, Stott appeals to all Christians: "Can we not gladly occupy this common ground together, so that there is no division among us?"[23]

The Baptism of the Spirit

Nevertheless, Stott cannot accept that baptism of the Spirit is a second experience subsequent to conversion. "The Christian life is life in the Spirit. . . . So every Christian believer has an experience of the Holy Spirit from the very first moments of his Christian life."[24] He points to a number of texts to demonstrate that to be a Christian is to have the Spirit. All the key elements of the Spirit's work—regenerating us as God's children, mediating Christ's presence, sanctifying believers, creating community, motivating mission, guaranteeing our inheritance—all show that "from the very beginning to the very end of our Christian life, we are dependent on the work of the Holy Spirit."[25]

---

17 John Stott, *Balanced Christianity: A Call to Avoid Unnecessary Polarisation*, 2nd ed. (Nottingham: Inter-Varsity Press, 2014), 96.
18 Stott, *Baptism and Fullness*, 73–74.
19 Stott, *Baptism and Fullness*, 9.
20 *Gospel and Spirit: A Joint Statement* (Esher: Fountain Trust; London: The Church of England Evangelical Council, 1977).
21 Michael Harper, "Divided Opinions," *Renewal* no. 187 (December 1991): 20, cited in Andrew Atherstone, David Ceri Jones, and William K. Kay, "Lloyd-Jones and the Charismatic Controversy," in *Engaging with Martyn Lloyd-Jones*, ed. Andrew Atherstone and David Ceri Jones (Nottingham: Apollos, 2011), 120.
22 Stott, *Baptism and Fullness*, 14.
23 Stott, *Baptism and Fullness*, 74.
24 Stott, *Baptism and Fullness*, 19.
25 Stott, *Baptism and Fullness*, 21.

Stott sets the seven New Testament uses of the phrase "baptism of the Spirit" in the context of Old Testament promises of an outpouring of the Spirit, an outpouring that would be one of the main distinctives of the new age (2 Cor. 3:8). Although the Spirit has always been at work in God's world, the prophets promised that the Spirit would be poured out in a new way in the new age (Isa. 32:15; 44:3; Ezek. 39:28–29; Joel 2:28). John the Baptist, the last prophet of the old age, likewise promised that the coming Messiah would "baptize you with the Holy Spirit" (Mark 1:8). In the Synoptics, John the Baptist says Jesus will baptize with the Holy Spirit, suggesting a once-for-all future activity (which was fulfilled at Pentecost). But in John's Gospel, he uses a present participle: "He on whom you see the Spirit descend and remain, this is he who baptizes with the Holy Spirit" (John 1:33). "It describes not the single event of Pentecost, but the distinctive ministry of Jesus."[26] In John 1:29 the same grammatical construction is used to describe Jesus as the one "who takes away the sin of the world." "If we put verses 29 and 33 together," says Stott, "we discover that the characteristic work of Jesus is twofold. It involves a removal and a bestowal, a taking away of sin and a baptizing with the Holy Spirit. These are the two great gifts of Jesus Christ our Saviour."[27] These are also the two promises of the new covenant prophesied in Jeremiah 31:31–34 (see also Ezek. 36:25–27). And these are, therefore, the two gifts that Peter promised on the day of Pentecost to all who would repent (Acts 2:38). "We could sum it up by saying that these penitent believers received the *gift* of the Spirit which God had *promised* before the Day of Pentecost, and were thus *baptized* with the Spirit whom God *poured out* on the Day of Pentecost."[28] When Cornelius received the Spirit at his conversion, Peter referred to it as both the "baptism" and the "gift" of the Spirit (Acts 11:16–17).

Putting all this together, Stott says it seems clear "that the 'baptism' of the Spirit is the same as the promise or gift of the Spirit and is as much an integral part of the gospel of salvation as the remission of sins."[29] "When sinners repent and believe, Jesus not only takes away their sins but also baptizes them with his Spirit."[30]

"The outpouring or baptism of the Spirit is not only a *distinctive* blessing of the new age (in that it was not available previously) but also a *univer-*

[26] Stott, *Baptism and Fullness*, 23.
[27] Stott, *Baptism and Fullness*, 24.
[28] Stott, *Baptism and Fullness*, 25.
[29] Stott, *Baptism and Fullness*, 25.
[30] Stott, *Baptism and Fullness*, 26.

sal blessing (in that it is now the birthright of all God's children)."[31] Peter's quotation from Joel on the day of Pentecost speaks of the Spirit being poured out on "all flesh"—that is, on every believer without distinctions of age, sex, ethnicity, or rank (Acts 2:17). Whereas empowerment for service was the experience of a few in the Old Testament, now all believers are indwelt by the Spirit. The experience of the 120 on the day of Pentecost was unique because they were believers who then received the Holy Spirit as an indwelling power in a way no previous generation of old covenant believers had done. Our experience today as new covenant believers is more like the three thousand on the day of Pentecost who received the Spirit at conversion along with the forgiveness of sins (Acts 2:33, 39). In one sense, Pentecost was an unrepeatable event—the moment in the story of salvation when the Spirit was poured out as part of the inauguration of the new age. But, because the Spirit has now been poured out, he has become the glorious possession of every believer. "In itself it is unrepeatable, as unrepeatable as the Saviour's death, resurrection and ascension which preceded it. But its blessings are for all who belong to Christ."[32] We must derive our understanding of the Spirit not from a description of what happened to the 120 on the day of Pentecost but from the interpretation of the event that Peter provides in his sermon. "What was normative . . . was the experience specifically promised in Peter's conclusion to all whom God calls and who respond in penitent faith, namely that they would receive both forgiveness and the Holy Spirit."[33] This is what Paul also taught. Paul says Christians received the Holy Spirit "by hearing with faith" the gospel (Gal. 3:2, 14).

Stott then addresses two incidents in the book of Acts that might appear to confirm that believers receive the Holy Spirit subsequent to their conversion—the Samaritan believers in Acts 8:5–17 and the Ephesian disciples in Acts 19:1–7. In both cases, Stott claims there is "something unusual, something irregular."[34]

In the case of the Samaritan believers, the apostles sent a delegation on hearing the news—something they had not had cause to do before (Acts 8:13). This is not because the reception of the gospel by the Samaritans was defective, for Luke describes how they "had received the word of God" (Acts 8:14). Instead, it was because they were the first believers outside Judea.

---

31 Stott, *Baptism and Fullness*, 26; see also Stott, *The Message of Acts: To the Ends of the Earth* (Leicester: Inter-Varsity Press; Downers Grove, IL: InterVarsity Press, 1990), 78.

32 Stott, *Baptism and Fullness*, 29; see also Stott, *The Message of Acts*, 60.

33 Stott, *Baptism and Fullness*, 30.

34 Stott, *Baptism and Fullness*, 31.

Moreover, they were Samaritans, who had for centuries been in theological dispute with the Jews (John 4:9). For Luke—shaping his narrative as he does around Christ's promise that the disciples will be his witnesses in Jerusalem, Judea, and Samaria, and the ends of the earth (Acts 1:8)—this is of huge significance. Were these true believers? Would they be accepted by Jewish believers? Would two separate churches, one Jewish and another Samaritan, develop?

> Is it not reasonable to suppose that it was precisely in order to avoid the development of such a situation that God deliberately withheld the gift of his Spirit from the Samaritan believers (or at least outward evidence of the gift) until two of the leading apostles came down to investigate and, by the laying on of their hands, acknowledged and confirmed the genuineness of the Samaritans' conversion?[35]

The Samaritan experience, argues Stott, can no more be used to justify a normative post-conversion receipt of the Spirit than it can be used to justify the imparting of the Holy Spirit by the episcopal successors of the apostles (as Roman Catholics believe).

As for the Ephesian disciples of John the Baptist, Stott argues that they were not true Christians when Paul first met them. The very fact that Paul asked if they had received the Spirit suggests he had reason to doubt the credibility of their profession (since he consistently taught that the Spirit was given at conversion). It turns out that the Ephesians had not heard of the Spirit, nor had they been baptized in the triune name (perhaps because they had heard the incomplete teaching of Apollos as suggested in Acts 18:24–26). Even more significant was Paul's response their situation. He did not call them to some higher teaching or deeper experience. Instead, "he went right back to the beginning, to the very essence of the gospel," and proclaimed Christ.[36] These were not believers who now, at a date after their conversion, received the Spirit. These were unbelievers who were converted and, as a result, received the Spirit.

Stott concludes, "The gift of the Holy Spirit is a *universal* Christian experience because it is an *initial* Christian experience."[37] Stott reinforces this by highlighting the link between Spirit baptism and water baptism. The lan-

[35] Stott, *Baptism and Fullness*, 33; see also Stott, *The Message of Acts*, 151–59.
[36] Stott, *Baptism and Fullness*, 35; see also Stott, *The Message of Acts*, 303–5.
[37] Stott, *Baptism and Fullness*, 36.

guage of Spirit baptism is intended to evoke water baptism; or, rather, water baptism is the symbolic confirmation of the Spirit baptism that has taken place in conversion. Therefore, since water baptism is initiatory, Spirit baptism must be as well. Cornelius's Spirit baptism, for example, is a sign that he has been saved, and it therefore becomes the basis for his water baptism (Acts 10:47; 11:16). "The New Testament authors take it for granted that God has 'given' their readers his Holy Spirit (e.g. Rom. 5:5; 1 Thess. 4:8; 1 John 3:24; 4:13); there is no single occasion on which they exhort them to receive him."[38]

This view is confirmed by the one remaining New Testament reference to baptism by the Spirit: "For in one Spirit we were all baptized into one body—Jews or Greeks, slaves or free—and all were made to drink of one Spirit" (1 Cor. 12:13). What is striking about this verse is that, far from identifying two classes of Christian (those who have been baptized by the Spirit and those who have not) or calling on Paul's readers to pursue the baptism of the Spirit, it actually emphasizes the opposite. It affirms that all believers have received Spirit baptism, irrespective of gender or race. Believers have different gifts from the Spirit, but underlying this is a common, unifying experience of the Spirit. Throughout the chapter, Paul speaks of "the one Spirit" or "the same Spirit" (1 Cor. 12:4, 8, 9, 11, 13).

Finally, Stott points to the broad exhortation of the New Testament. He notes that advocates of baptism of the Spirit as a second experience either point recipients back to their Spirit baptism or point non-recipients forward to it as the key to holiness. But this is never the outlook of the New Testament writers.

> When they are looking back, they are recalling that great act which God performed when he put us in Christ, justified, redeemed, regenerated and recreated us. To that they constantly appeal. And when they are looking forward, it is to their readers' growth into maturity and, beyond that, to the perfection which awaits the glorious appearing of the Saviour. . . . But never, not once, do they exhort and instruct us to "be baptized with the Spirit." There can be only one explanation of this, namely that they were writing to Christians, and Christians have already been baptized with the Holy Spirit.[39]

As is so often the case, in the end Stott's argument is Christocentric. "This is not a mere argument about words," he says. "The fundamental

[38] Stott, *Baptism and Fullness*, 38.
[39] Stott, *Baptism and Fullness*, 44–45.

truth which is involved is that, by uniting us to Christ, God has given us everything."[40] We have already been blessed "in Christ with every spiritual blessing" (Eph. 1:3). There is no deficit in Christ's work. "You have been filled in him" (Col. 2:10). "If God has given us the Lord Jesus Christ in his fullness, and if Christ already dwells within us by his Spirit, what more can God possibly add? Is not the very suggestion that there is some additional gift still to come derogatory to the fullness and the satisfactoriness of Jesus?"[41] The tentative way in which Stott answered Roopsingh Carr's question has been replaced with a defiant jealously for Christ's honor.

The Fullness of the Spirit

Stott then moves on to speak more positively of what life in the Spirit involves. "When we speak of the baptism of the Spirit we are referring to a once-for-all gift; when we speak of the fullness of the Spirit we are acknowledging that this gift needs to be *continuously and increasingly appropriated*."[42]

A survey of the use of the term, suggests Stott, shows "filling" could be used of the normal experience of dedicated Christians, as well as an endowment for a particular role or specific task. Jesus himself is said to be "full of the Spirit" to equip him for his ministry (Luke 3:22; 4:1, 14, 18). In addition to these descriptive statements, Ephesians 5:18 commands us to be filled with the Spirit or, more precisely, to go on being filled with the Spirit. At the same time, Paul can rebuke the Corinthians for being *un*-spiritual or fleshly rather than spiritual or Spirit-filled (1 Cor. 3:1–4), even though they have been baptized with the Spirit (1 Cor. 12:13). The reason for this rebuke is their jealousy and rivalry. What this adds up to is this: "As an initiatory event the baptism is not repeatable and cannot be lost, but the filling can be repeated and in any case needs to be maintained. If it is not maintained, it is lost. If it is lost, it can be recovered."[43]

Stott rejects the notion that the sign of being filled with the Spirit is speaking in tongues. Only three groups speak in tongues as a sign that they have received the Spirit (Acts 2:14; 10:44–46; 19:1–6). With other groups no mention is made of tongues. Moreover, in 1 Corinthians 12 and 14, Paul specifically talks of tongues as one gift among many without affording it any special status.

---

[40] Stott, *Baptism and Fullness*, 45.
[41] Stott, *Baptism and Fullness*, 45–46.
[42] Stott, *Baptism and Fullness*, 47.
[43] Stott, *Baptism and Fullness*, 47.

What, then, is the sign of being filled with the Spirit? And how may his fullness be enjoyed? According to John 7:37–39 we receive the thirst-quenching fullness of the Spirit by thirsting, coming, drinking, and believing in Jesus. The grammar, says Stott, suggests a continual coming. We constantly come to Jesus in faith to receive thirst-quenching life from him through the Spirit. Moreover, as we do so, blessing flows out from us to others. "Notice the disparity between the water we drink and the water that flows out. We can drink only small gulps, but as we keep coming, drinking, believing so by the mighty operation of the Holy Spirit within us, our little sips are multiplied to a mighty confluence of flowing streams."[44] And notice again the Christocentric approach that Stott adopts. He concludes his look at John 7 by saying: "There is no way to ensure a constant inflow and a constant outflow, except to keep coming to Jesus and to keep drinking. For the fullness of the Spirit is to be continuously appropriated by faith."[45]

Turning to Ephesians 5:18–21, Stott notes that the marks of the Spirit's fullness are "moral not miraculous."[46] Spirit-fullness here is contrasted with drunkenness. This is not, says Stott—his focus always on the right functioning of the mind—because Spirit-fullness is a kind of spiritual intoxication. Quite the opposite. We are filled with the Spirit so that we might exercise self-control, not lose it (Gal. 5:23). "The fullness of the Spirit leads to restrained and rational moral behaviour."[47] Indeed, Paul's signs of Spirit-fullness are fellowship, worship, gratitude, and mutual submission (Eph. 5:18–21). "It is in these spiritual qualities and activities, not in supernatural phenomena, that we should look for primary evidence of the Holy Spirit's fullness."[48]

As for the command to be filled, Stott notes[49] that it is in

- the imperative mood (it is a command rather than a recommendation);
- the plural form (it is addressed to all believers rather than a privileged few);
- the passive voice (we yield to the Spirit rather than manipulating him);
- the present tense (it is a continual appropriation rather than a one-off crisis experience).

---

44 Stott, *Baptism and Fullness*, 54.
45 Stott, *Baptism and Fullness*, 54.
46 Stott, *Baptism and Fullness*, 54.
47 Stott, *Baptism and Fullness*, 57.
48 Stott, *Baptism and Fullness*, 54.
49 Stott, *Baptism and Fullness*, 60–61; see also Stott, *The Message of Ephesians*, 208–9.

There is no doubt that Stott fully appreciates the importance of the work of the Spirit in the life of the believer and the ministry of the church.

> Without the Holy Spirit, Christian discipleship would be inconceivable, even impossible. There can be no life without the life-giver, no understanding without the Spirit of truth, no fellowship without the unity of the Spirit, no Christlikeness of character apart from his fruit, and no effective witness without his power. As a body without breath is a corpse, so the church without the Spirit is dead.[50]

Interpreting Our Experience

Stott attempts to correlate the biblical data with experience. First, he considers the many Christians who do not appear to possess the Spirit. This, he suggests, assumes a certain image of what Spirit baptism involves. People assume it looks like the wind and fire of Pentecost. But these should no more shape our expectations than Paul's story should lead us to expect a bright light and audible voice to feature in every conversion. Indeed, regeneration is not normally a conscious process. As Jesus himself says in John 3:8, just as we cannot see the wind but can feel its effects, so we cannot see the work of the Spirit but can see the effects of his work in repentance and faith. The reason Christians live sub-Christian lives is not that they have failed to receive the baptism of the Spirit but that "we continue to live on a level lower than our Spirit baptism has made possible, because we do not remain filled with the Spirit."[51] More pointedly, Stott adds that Christlikeness is evident among both charismatic and non-charismatic Christians, while un-Christlike Christians are also evident in both groups.

Second, Stott considers what we are to make of those experiences of the Spirit which people interpret as post-conversion baptisms of the Spirit. He first offers three explanations that he thinks do not represent the majority of cases but are true in some instances: the experiences can be demonic, merely psychological, or actual conversions. Apart from these explanations, though, many encounters "are authentic, deeper experiences of God" in believers.[52] While the norm presented in the Bible is one of "steady growth in holiness," "within this process of growth there

[50] Stott, *The Message of Acts*, 60.
[51] Stott, *Baptism and Fullness*, 66.
[52] Stott, *Baptism and Fullness*, 67.

may be many deeper experiences."[53] "What the New Testament teaches . . . is not a stereotype of two stages, but rather the initial blessing of regeneration by the Spirit, followed by a process of growth into maturity, during which we may indeed be granted many deeper and richer experiences of God."[54] Some subsequent experiences may, for example, precede fresh responsibility, while others may follow periods of spiritual decline. Also, such experiences can vary according to our natural temperament, since the Spirit respects our distinctive human personalities. In *Balanced Christianity*, Stott wrote, "Our temperament has more influence on our theology than we often realize or concede!"[55] So Stott issues this warning to those who have experienced the Spirit in a fresh way: "Let your exhortation to others be grounded not upon your experiences but upon Scripture."[56]

However dramatic our experiences may be, they are all secondary to "God's first work of grace" in our lives. Sometimes Christians talk as if they have been subsequently set free from bondage, but, says Stott, "they must be mistaking subjective feelings for objective reality."[57] Regeneration involves a new creation: those who were slaves are now children of God; those who were condemned are now justified. People may come to experience a greater *sense* of these realities, but the realities themselves occurred at their conversion.

Stott also invites us to recognize that all these subsequent experiences are incomplete. Not only do some people talk as if nothing much happened before their new experience; they also assume nothing much can happen afterward. But the New Testament expects us to hunger and thirst for righteousness, and to groan for the new creation (Matt. 5:6; Rom. 8:23). "So let neither those who have had unusual experiences, nor those who have not, imagine that they have 'attained,' and that God cannot fill them any fuller with himself!"[58]

The practical application of this approach can be seen in a 1965 letter Stott wrote to the president of CICCU, who had sought his advice on how the charismatic phenomena should be handled within the Christian Union:

---

[53] Stott, *Baptism and Fullness*, 68.
[54] John Stott, *Christian Basics: An Invitation to Discipleship* (London: Hodder, 1991), 89.
[55] Stott, *Balanced Christianity*, 15.
[56] Stott, *Baptism and Fullness*, 54.
[57] Stott, *Baptism and Fullness*, 74.
[58] Stott, *Baptism and Fullness*, 75.

> There is little doubt that some have had a genuine spiritual experience, perhaps a new infilling of the Holy Spirit like Acts 4:31. It is not necessary or right for us to try to invalidate these experiences; our quarrel is that so many Pentecostals try to make their experience the norm for everybody. . . . There is no need to paint the question about their experiences in such a way as to insist that they are either divine or devilish in origin. I tend to think that much of it is psychological. . . . If it is psychological, it is not surprising that it is accompanied by a sense of great release or freedom.[59]

Stott bases his contention that these experiences are psychological on his observation that they seem to need to be "induced" through various techniques. He also notes the parallels with experiences outside Christianity. "The results which are claimed," he adds, "are subjective." The lack of objective fruit, such as an increase of Christlike character and evangelistic effectiveness, "makes me suspicious that the experience itself is not what it is cracked up to be." Nevertheless, Stott advises against a "public showdown" and urges his correspondent to be "patient and prayerful."[60]

The Fruit of the Spirit

In *Baptism and Fulness*, Stott next expounds the fruit of the Spirit in Galatians 5:22–23. Much of what he says touches on themes that were characteristic of his whole ministry, but certain elements are accentuated in the context of the charismatic debate. He highlights three things.

The first is the *supernatural origin* of the fruit. "This fruit . . . is the best available evidence—because it is solidly objective—of the indwelling fullness of the Holy Spirit."[61] Though Stott does not say so, there is a polemic edge to this statement. His point is that godly character rather than extraordinary experiences or tongues speaking is the true sign of the Spirit's work.

Second, Stott highlights the *natural growth* of spiritual fruit. Again, his focus has a polemic edge. He emphasizes the need to create the right growing conditions, an emphasis Paul himself makes in Galatians 6:7–8. If we want the Spirit to grow fruit in our lives, we must "sow to the Spirit." This brings Stott back to one of his common themes: the need for discipline. "By the 'sowing' the apostle appears to be referring to the whole pattern of

---

[59] John Stott, letter to R. Stephen Baldock, then President of CICCU, May 13, 1965, Church of England Record Centre, STOTT/5/22.
[60] John Stott, letter to R. Stephen Baldock.
[61] Stott, *Baptism and Fullness*, 79.

our thoughts and habits, our life-style, life-direction and life-discipleship." Stott cites the company we keep and what we watch as examples.

Finally, Stott emphasizes the *gradual maturity* of the fruit. Fruit does not appear overnight. Once again there is unspoken polemic. "This emphasis on the gradualness of sanctification is not meant to condone our continued sinfulness, or to encourage our laziness, or to lower our expectations, but rather to warn us against quack gardeners who offer us ripe fruit on the spot."[62] He clearly has in mind those who promise a higher level of Christian living through a onetime experience. If the natural growth of the fruit calls for *discipline*, then its gradual maturity calls for *patience*.

Spiritual Gifts

Turning to the issue of spiritual gifts, Stott begins by saying, "The church owes its unity to *charis* (grace) and its diversity to *charismata* (gifts of grace)."[63] He defines spiritual gifts as "certain capacities, bestowed by God's grace and power, which fit people for specific and corresponding service."[64] He considers the New Testament lists of gifts to be representative rather than exhaustive (Rom. 12:3–8; 1 Cor. 12; Eph. 4:7–12; 1 Pet. 4:10–11). In some cases gifts are clearly supernatural, but in others, more mundane (though equally important in the life of the church). Stott also highlights the way each list emphasizes that gifts are given to all within the church. Indeed, he goes further, describing the "charismatic movement" as "a protest against clericalism (the clerical suppression of the laity) and a plea for the liberation of the laity."[65] This was an aspect of the movement with which, as we shall see, he had considerable sympathy, having been a pioneer of lay involvement from the early 1950s.

What about the miraculous gifts—the gifts of miracles, apostleship, prophecy, and tongues?

Miracles

Stott refuses to rule out miracles, for "the God we believe in is the free and sovereign Creator of the universe. . . . Who are we to circumscribe his power and tell him what he may or may not do?"[66] Nevertheless, a miracle

[62] Stott, *Baptism and Fullness*, 83.
[63] Stott, *Baptism and Fullness*, 86.
[64] Stott, *Baptism and Fullness*, 87.
[65] Stott, *Baptism and Fullness*, 105.
[66] Stott, *Baptism and Fullness*, 96.

by definition is an extraordinary event. Even within the biblical narrative miracles cluster around key moments of revelation to provide confirmation for that revelation. Moreover, God is at work through both the extraordinary and the ordinary. "Once we begin to see the living God ceaselessly at work through the process of history and nature, we shall begin (for example) to recognise that all healing is divine healing, whether without the use of means or through the use of physical, psychological or surgical means."[67] What, then, should our attitude be? "It should be neither a stubborn incredulity . . . nor an uncritical gullibility, but rather a spirit of open-minded enquiry."[68]

As rector of All Souls, Stott introduced monthly healing services in the early 1950s, long before the charismatic movement took shape. They were not showy affairs and did not cater to large numbers. No one was asked the nature of his or her complaint, nor were results ever investigated, let alone publicized. Stott knew that some people had been healed while others had felt their pain alleviated. "Others do not seem to have had any physical result, but all say that it has been a real spiritual blessing."[69]

Apostles

In *The Message of Romans*, Stott recognizes that the word "apostle" is used in the New Testament of what we would call today "missionaries"—people sent by the churches as emissaries (Phil. 2:25) or pioneer missionaries (Acts 14:14; 2 Cor. 8:23).[70] "Missionary" is the Latin form of the Greek word "apostle," which literally means "sent one." To this we could add that in 1 Corinthians 9:1–2, Paul ties his apostleship both to the fact that he witnessed the risen Christ and to the fact that he planted the church in Corinth. "Am I not free? Am I not an apostle? Have I not seen Jesus our Lord? Are not you my workmanship in the Lord? If to others I am not an apostle, at least I am to you, for you are the seal of my apostleship in the Lord."

But more often in the New Testament the term is used of the foundational twelve plus Paul—those personally appointed and equipped by Jesus to provide an authoritative record of his work. It is their testimony that we have in the New Testament. Stott believes there is good biblical evidence to

[67] Stott, *Baptism and Fullness*, 97.
[68] Stott, *Baptism and Fullness*, 98; see also Stott, *The Message of Acts*, 100–104.
[69] John Stott, letter to Dr. A. P. Waterson, August 25, 1955, in Mrs. E. M. Waterson's papers, cited in Timothy Dudley-Smith, *John Stott*, vol. 1, *The Making of a Leader* (Leicester: Inter-Varsity Press, 1999), 268.
[70] John Stott, *The Message of Romans: God's Good News for the World* (Leicester: Inter-Varsity Press; Downers Grove, IL: InterVarsity Press, 1994), 396.

suggest apostles no longer exist today in this sense of the word. In the list of gifts, he argues, it refers to the twelve plus Paul who were witnesses to the resurrection in a unique way.[71] They head up each list because they are foundational, and now that foundation has been laid. He therefore argues against the use of the term today for fear of creating confusion or conflict between the authority of the foundational apostles in the New Testament and the authority of contemporary apostles.

Prophecy

Stott treats prophecy in a similar way. Prophecy, he says, has always been seen as an organ of divine revelation. But now God's revelation has come to a close in Christ, the apostolic testimony, and the finalization of the canon of Scripture. Stott recognizes that some people want to define prophecy in other ways—as a prediction of the future or as an interpretation of political events or as preaching. But in each case, he feels these understandings fall short of a biblical definition.

It could be argued that Stott has failed to pay due attention to the way the apostles function as the New Testament equivalent of Old Testament prophets. It is prophets and apostles, as bringers of revelation in the Old and New Testaments, who are foundational (Eph. 2:20). So the apostolic testimony corresponds to Old Testament prophets. This means that New Testament prophecy is not the same as Old Testament prophecy. Prophecy in the New Testament must be weighed (1 Cor. 14:29; 1 Thess. 5:19–22), whereas Old Testament prophecy must be obeyed. It was the prophet, not the prophecy, who was tested in the Old Testament, with death being the sanction for a false prophet (Deut. 18:19–22). Thus, we should share Stott's concern to safeguard the finality of divine Scripture—something that was threatened in the context in which he was writing (as it often continues to be today), where the immediacy of prophetic claims tended to eclipse the centrality of the Bible. Speaking at the Keswick Convention in 1975, Stott told of a gift of prophecy in preaching in which the preaching becomes especially and specifically encouraging or consoling. But he ruled out a contemporary ministry of prophets like that described in the New Testament.[72]

[71] Stott, *Baptism and Fullness*, 99–100; Stott, *The Message of Ephesians*; and Stott, *The Message of Acts*, 34–37.

[72] *The Keswick Week*, 1975, 94, cited in Charles Price and Ian Randall, *Transforming Keswick: The Keswick Convention Past, Present and Future* (Carlisle: OM, 2000), 185; see also Stott, *The Message of Ephesians*, 161–63.

Tongues

An even bigger question mark hangs over contemporary tongues, in Stott's mind. It is clear, he says, that tongues on the day of Pentecost were foreign languages, intelligible to the different ethnic groups in the crowd (Acts 2:4–11), and there are strong reasons to think they should be understood in this way in 1 Corinthians 12, rather than as an ecstatic language. The same word is used in both passages, and outside the New Testament the noun *glōssa* is used only of a spoken language. Moreover, the whole thrust of Paul's argument in 1 Corinthians 12–14 is toward intelligibility, with unintelligibility regarded as childish (1 Cor. 14:20).

Stott recognizes that some have found private tongues speaking to offer a new degree of fluency before God or to bring "psychic release." But Paul's prohibition of speaking in tongues without interpretation suggests it should not be used where the speaker cannot understand what has been said. Paul does say, "The one who speaks in a tongue builds up himself, but the one who prophesies builds up the church" (1 Cor. 14:4). But, given his central concern for mutual edification and the use of gifts to serve others, Stott concludes that this must be ironic, even sarcastic. This is not a commendation of uninterpreted tongues but a condemnation, since they serve no real purpose. Key for Stott are Paul's words in 1 Corinthians 14:13–15:

> Therefore, one who speaks in a tongue should pray that he may interpret. For if I pray in a tongue, my spirit prays but my mind is unfruitful. What am I to do? I will pray with my spirit, but I will pray with my mind also; I will sing praise with my spirit, but I will sing with my mind also.

We should not pray unless our minds are engaged; otherwise our praying is "unfruitful." "It is clear that he simply cannot contemplate Christian prayer and praise in which the mind is not actively engaged."[73] Stott is speaking of the apostle Paul here, but Stott's comment also functions as a self-portrait. He constantly emphasized the importance of the mind, and this emphasis shaped his approach to tongues.

If these arguments seem familiar to you, then it is almost certainly because the people who influenced you were influenced by people who, in turn, were influenced by Stott. I read *Baptism and Fullness* as a teenager in 1986 before I left home for the university, and it was formative in my

[73] Stott, *Baptism and Fullness*, 114; see also Stott, *The Message of Acts*, 65–68.

understanding and in anchoring me to God's word. Though Stott's was by no means the only voice, it was one of the most significant.

What emerges from Stott's treatment of spiritual gifts is an overriding concern for the centrality of the word. Having stressed that all gifts are given through grace for the common good so that there is no scope for personal superiority or inferiority, he nevertheless argues that some gifts are more valuable, not least because Paul himself speaks of "the higher gifts" (1 Cor. 12:31). And, since they are given to edify the church, "the teaching gifts have the highest value, for nothing builds up Christians like God's truth."[74] This is why teaching-related gifts top the New Testament lists. "The apostles' insistence on the priority of teaching has considerable relevance to the contemporary church. All over the world the churches are spiritually undernourished owing to the shortage of biblical expositors."[75] From any other preacher, this might sound like self-interested special pleading to bolster one's own status. But Stott's behavior betrayed no self-aggrandizement. More to the point, he was writing in a context where a focus on extraordinary phenomena was in danger of eclipsing the central importance of the "ordinary" preaching of God's word. But Stott was not pleading for the word instead of the Spirit; rather, he was recognizing that the Spirit works *through* the word. Stott was once asked what he thought as he walked to the pulpit to preach. "As I make that journey to the pulpit," he replied, "I just say over and over again, 'I believe in the Holy Spirit.'"[76]

For Stott, belief in the Spirit was always tied to belief in Christ and his finished work. Stott shared the charismatic movement's longing for a greater experience of God, but for Stott such experiences take us not beyond the gospel of Jesus Christ but deeper into Christ: "Of course we have much more to learn, but God has no more to say than he has said in Jesus Christ. Again, we have much more to receive, but God has no more to give than he has given in Jesus Christ. In Jesus Christ God's word and work are complete, and we ourselves come to completion in him."[77]

[74] Stott, *Baptism and Fullness*, 112; see also Stott, *Christian Basics*, 94; and Stott, *The Message of Ephesians*, 164.
[75] Stott, *Baptism and Fullness*, 112.
[76] Cited in Roger Steer, *Inside Story: The Life of John Stott* (Nottingham: Inter-Varsity Press, 2009), 123.
[77] John Stott, "Address given by JRWS on Receiving an Honorary DD from Brunel University on 14 October 1997," Church of England Record Centre, STOTT/2/4.

CHAPTER 7

EMBEDDED IN THE CHURCH

John Stott was an international figure, global speaker, best-selling author, and evangelical statesman, and it was in one or more of these capacities that most people knew him. But we must not forget that throughout much of his ministry he was the pastor of a local church. Only when he "retired" did local church responsibilities stop while the wider ministry continued. Even then he remained an active member of the local church. For Stott commitment to the church of Christ meant commitment to All Souls, the church of which he was a member throughout his life. He writes movingly of his lifelong involvement with All Souls in "an autobiographical sketch" at the end of *The Living Church*,[1] and he begins the book with these words:

> The church lies at the very centre of the eternal purpose of God. It is not a divine afterthought. It is not an accident of history. On the contrary, the church is God's new community. For his purpose, conceived in a past eternity, being worked out in history, and to be perfected in a future eternity, is not just to save isolated individuals and so perpetuate our loneliness, but rather to build his church.[2]

The argument is clear: the church is central to the purposes of God revealed in the Scriptures, and therefore it must be central to our lives as Christians.[3] Stott articulates this communal approach most forcefully in

[1] John Stott, *The Living Church: Convictions of a Lifelong Pastor* (Leicester: Inter-Varsity Press, 2007), 163–65.
[2] Stott, *The Living Church*, 19–20.
[3] John Stott, *The Message of Ephesians: God's New Society* (Leicester: Inter-Varsity Press, 1979), 129.

his commentary on Ephesians. Warning against "a privatised gospel," he says: "One of our chief evangelical blind spots has been to overlook the central importance of the church. We tend to proclaim individual salvation without moving on to the saved community."[4] Stott uses similar language in *The Cross of Christ*, where he is keen to stress that salvation is not simply an individual affair. "The very purpose of [Christ's] self-giving on the cross was not just to save isolated individuals, and so perpetuate their loneliness, but to create a new community whose members would belong to him, love one another and eagerly serve the world."[5]

The centrality of church in the Bible's exposition of salvation inevitably and radically shifts the focus of our lives as Christians. "Conversion to Christ means also conversion to the community of Christ, as people turn from themselves to him, and from 'this corrupt generation' to the alternative society which he is gathering round himself."[6] God is building "a new society in the midst of the old."[7] This leads to a compelling vision of the Christian community:

> I wonder if there is anything more urgent today, for the honour of Christ and for the spread of the gospel, than that the church should be, and should be seen to be, what by God's purpose and Christ's achievement it already is—a single new humanity, a model of human community, a family of reconciled brothers and sisters who love their Father and love each other, the evident dwelling place of God by his Spirit. Only then will the world believe in Christ as Peacemaker. Only then will God receive the glory due to his name.[8]

We are intended to live life in community, and for Christians that means living in the Christian community, the church. Stott relates, "I sometimes hear old people, including Christian people who should know better, say 'I don't want to be a burden to anyone else . . .' But this is wrong. We are all designed to be a burden to others."[9] What makes these words all the more striking is that at this point Stott was an old person and he was a burden to

---

[4] Stott, *The Message of Ephesians*, 9; see also 111–12, 126–30.
[5] John Stott, *The Cross of Christ*, 2nd ed. (Leicester: Inter-Varsity Press, 1989), 255; see also Stott, *Christian Basics: An Invitation to Discipleship* (London: Hodder, 1991), 138, where Stott uses similar language.
[6] Stott, *The Cross of Christ*, 244.
[7] Stott, *The Message of Ephesians*, 24.
[8] Stott, *The Message of Ephesians*, 111–12.
[9] John Stott, *The Radical Disciple: Wholehearted Christian Living* (Leicester: Inter-Varsity Press, 2010), 112; see also Stott, *The Message of Thessalonians: Preparing for the Coming King* (Leicester: Inter-Varsity Press; Downers Grove, IL: InterVarsity Press, 1991), 178–79.

others (although one, no doubt, they were happy to bear). In the introduction to *The Radical Disciple*, the book in which these words come, he writes of his appreciation to the staff of the College of St Barnabas, the residential home where he spent his final years, and the leaders of the nearby St John's Church, Felbridge, who transported him to its service when he was able to attend. Having borne the burdens of many throughout his ministry, Stott himself was now a burden. He is writing these words from personal experience. They come at the end of a moving chapter, again born of his own experience, on dependence—dependence on both God and others—as a key characteristic of Christian discipleship. Stott continues: "You are designed to be a burden to me and I am designed to be a burden to you. And the life of the family, including the life of the local church family, should be one of 'mutual burdensomeness.'"[10]

Mobilizing the Laity

In the 1950 issue of the All Souls Church newsletter that announced his appointment as the new rector, Stott wrote two articles. One was "Call to Prayer," which exhorted the congregation to attend the weekly prayer meeting. The second was "A Five-Point Manifesto," a summary of his first sermon as rector-designate. His starting point was the description of the church in Acts 2:42: "And they devoted themselves to the apostles' teaching and the fellowship, to the breaking of bread and the prayers." Study, fellowship, worship, and prayer would all be priorities "together with evangelism." Then, speaking of evangelism, he wrote, "The task is beyond the power of the clergy. . . . There are only two alternatives. Either the task will not be done, or we must do it together, a task force of Ministers and people thoroughly trained and harnessed as a team for evangelism."[11]

The centerpiece of the strategy was the "Guest Service," held monthly on a Sunday evening and quarterly on a Sunday morning (Simeon had done something similar in Cambridge with a Sunday evening evangelistic "lecture"). Those who responded at the guest service were invited to an "At Home" to meet the staff team and hear a talk on growing as a Christian. They were then put into "Nursery Classes" led by lay leaders for follow-up. The guest service resembled the evangelistic lectures of his university

[10] Stott, *The Radical Disciple*, 113.
[11] *All Souls*, September 1950, cited in Timothy Dudley-Smith, *John Stott*, vol. 1, *The Making of a Leader* (Leicester: Inter-Varsity Press, 1999), 251.

Christian Union, while the follow-up drew from Stott's experience with the Scripture Union camps.

Stott also organized a six-month "Training School" for lay people in the theology and practice of evangelism, with twelve lectures on alternate Monday evenings followed by a written exam and interview. These culminated in a commissioning service to create what were known as "Commissioned Workers." The commissioned workers were involved in parish visitation, care for the sick, children's and youth work, welcoming internationals, and leading fellowship groups. The program could readily be replicated year after year with a summary of the lectures for successive curates to use. All Souls was not the only parish to equip the laity; Maurice Wood was doing something similar at St Ebbe's in Oxford, but it was a pioneering approach. "Today such a 'Training School' is part of the life of many churches—but in 1950 it was radically new," wrote Timothy Dudley-Smith, and was "more than any other single factor, to establish the unique position of All Souls as trail-blazer in parochial evangelism."[12]

Soon Stott had an opportunity to commend this strategy of lay mobilization for mission to others. In June 1952 he was asked to speak at the London Diocesan Conference on "Parochial Evangelism by the Laity." Our congregations must realize, he told his hearers, that we, the clergy, "believe in evangelism" and "that we believe they must evangelize in their parish."[13] This talk became an eight-page booklet that went through several editions. Six months later he addressed the Islington Clerical Conference along similar lines. His address was reported by *The Times* newspaper: "Mr Stott said that until every Christian became as enthusiastic for his church work as every Communist was for his party's propaganda they would not see this country evangelised. . . . The man-power was there—'slumbering drowsily in the pews.'"[14] The focus of Stott's early speaking was university missions, but whenever he was asked to address church leaders as he toured the world, he would speak on mobilizing laypeople for evangelism, often showing a filmstrip of the All Souls evangelistic program.

Stott further elaborated on the theme when he was invited to give the 1968 pastoral lectures at the Divinity Faculty of Durham University, lec-

12 Dudley-Smith, *John Stott*, 1:281, 253.

13 John Stott, *Parochial Evangelism by the Laity* (Westminster: Church Information Board/London Diocese, 1952), 4.

14 Raymond Luker, *All Souls: A History* (London: All Souls Church, 1979), 57, cited in Dudley-Smith, *John Stott*, 1:283–84.

tures published under the title *One People: Clergy and Laity in God's Church.*[15] Although he describes the practice of All Souls to illustrate how lay involvement might be implemented, he is keen to emphasize that, while the principles are of "permanent validity," they can be applied in "a multitude of different ways."[16]

Stott highlights the growing interest in lay ministry, driven, he suggests, by the need for more manpower, the fear of losing underutilized people, and the increasingly egalitarian mood of the times. Stott's concern, though, is to provide a biblical rationale for lay mobilization. "The real reason for expecting the laity to be responsible, active and constructive church members is biblical not pragmatic, grounded in theological principle not expediency."[17]

Stott begins his argument for lay ministry by exploring the nature of the church. "The church," he says, "is a people, a community of people, who owe their existence, their solidarity and their corporate distinctiveness from other communities to one thing only—the call of God."[18] In other words, it is the gospel that creates and defines the church, not the clergy. Moreover, since the gospel breaks down the divisions of race and class, we should not create other divisions in the form of clericalism. "It is only against the background of the equality and unity of the people of God that the real scandal of clericalism may be seen."[19] Concentrating power in the hands of a few annuls the essential oneness of God's people. "I do not hesitate to say that to interpret the church in terms of a privileged clerical caste or hierarchical structure is to destroy the New Testament doctrine of the church."[20] The New Testament's key metaphors and images ("bride," "vine," "flock," "kingdom," "household," "building," "body") all define the church in terms of God's gracious initiative or his people as a united community. None of them define the church in terms of its clergy. The church *as a whole* is a priestly and missionary people. "The evangelistic agency God employs then is His people the Church."[21]

This emphasis of the church as a whole does not deny the importance of different ministries within the church. Stott rejects not only clericalism

---

15 John Stott, *One People: Clergy and Laity in God's Church* (London: Falcon, 1969); see also Stott, *Our Guilty Silence: The Church, the Gospel and the World* (London: Hodder & Stoughton, 1967), 73–92.
16 Stott, *One People*, 92.
17 Stott, *One People*, 18.
18 Stott, *One People*, 15.
19 Stott, *One People*, 19; see also Stott, *The Message of Ephesians*, 166–68.
20 Stott, *One People*, 19–20.
21 Stott, *Our Guilty Silence*, 58.

but also anticlericalism. He also rejects what he calls "dualism"—the idea that the clergy and laity have their own distinctive spheres that must be carefully delineated.[22] There are not two classes, priest and people, for in the new covenant all God's people are priests; we have become a priestly people. Indeed, Stott says there is no function a minister may perform which a layman may not perform. Where we impose such restrictions, he says, it is "a question of *order* not of *doctrine*." The Thirty-Nine Articles, he argues, restrict the administration of communion to the clergy (art. 23) not because the clergy are a distinct class apart from the laity but to ensure that the sacraments are conducted in an orderly fashion. Instead, Stott defines the relationship between clergy and laity in terms of "service." Citing Ephesians 4:11–12, he says that the clergy are "to seek to equip [the laity] to be what God intends them to be."[23]

Stott laments the way the laity are often defined in negative terms as those who are not the clergy. "Instead," he says, "we must start defining the clergy in relation to the laity. The laity are the whole people of God, purchased by His precious blood, and some of us are given the great privilege of their oversight, shepherding and serving them for Christ's sake."[24] It is not the laity who belong to the clergy but the clergy who belong to the laity. This requires "a complete mental somersault" from everyone.[25] Stott nevertheless stops short of saying that the clergy are first and foremost members of the laity, a subset of the people, distinguished only by their role—a pastor is a sheep before he is a shepherd.

If the role of the clergy is to prepare God's people for service, what is that service? Here, in addition to identifying the roles the laity can play in the local church, Stott highlights a theme that would become increasingly prominent in his ministry—the importance of Christian vocation in the home, workplace, and neighborhood.

In 1965, All Souls replaced the weekly prayer meeting with "Fellowship Groups" in different homes. In a policy statement, Stott wrote, "We are convinced from Scripture and history of the importance and value of small Fellowship Groups."[26] All Souls was a large congregation, and so these groups were intended to be the context in which people could find

---

22 Stott, *One People*, 38.
23 Stott, *One People*, 42.
24 Stott, *One People*, 47.
25 Stott, *One People*, 51.
26 John Stott, "Fellowship Groups: A Policy Statement," March 1965, Church of England Record Centre, STOTT/1/4.

a meaningful sense of community and pastoral care. In *One People*, Stott elaborates on the *koinōnia*, the New Testament word for "fellowship" or "community." We have a common gospel, a common witness, and a common life, he argues. The All Souls fellowship groups aimed to reflect these three dimensions through the study of God's word, working together in service, and the provision of mutual care.[27] Again, Stott may have taken his cue from Simeon, who organized his congregation into "societies" modeled on those of Methodism.[28]

Forty years later, Stott reiterated the case for small groups in *The Living Church*.[29] Fellowship, he says, "bears witness to three things we hold in common. First, it expresses what we share in together (our common inheritance); secondly, what we share out together (our common service); and thirdly, what we share with each other (our mutual responsibility)."[30]

There is a sense in which his thinking on the local church never really moved on once he had stepped aside from local church leadership. He never placed much emphasis, for example, on the need for church planting.

The Local Church as the Locus for Evangelism

When he writes about evangelism in *The Contemporary Christian*, Stott acknowledges the validity of personal and mass evangelism. After all, Stott himself rose to prominence through university missions. But his heart remained in the local church. Despite the success of other means, he concludes, "*local church evangelism* can claim to be the most normal, natural and productive method of spreading the gospel today."[31] He maintains this on the basis of both Scripture and strategy. Mission is written into the DNA of New Testament churches. "Every Christian congregation is called by God to be a worshipping, witnessing community."[32] And "each local church is situated in a particular neighbourhood. . . . The congregation is strategically placed to reach the locality."[33]

For the church to realize this potential, it must understand itself aright. Stott uses a phrase from Alec Vidler to describe this right understanding:

[27] Stott, *One People*, 75–81.
[28] Derek Prime, *Charles Simeon: An Ordinary Pastor of Extraordinary Influence* (Leominster: Day One, 2011), 57–60.
[29] Stott, *The Living Church*, 92–95.
[30] Stott, *The Living Church*, 96.
[31] John Stott, *The Contemporary Christian: An Urgent Plea for Double Listening* (Leicester: Inter-Varsity Press, 1992), 241; see also Stott, *The Living Church*, chap. 3.
[32] Stott, *The Contemporary Christian*, 241.
[33] Stott, *The Contemporary Christian*, 241.

"holy worldliness." We are called from the world for the world. We come out of the world to worship and then are sent back into the world in mission. We must be distinct from the world yet, at the same time, embedded in it. If we lose our holiness, we will have nothing to say—we will just echo the world. If we lose what Stott calls our worldliness, we will have no one to say it to—the church will become an enclosed echo chamber.

So churches must organize themselves for mission. Once again Stott commends a form a double listening: he suggests that churches do community and church surveys.[34] Only with a good understanding of their context can churches develop a strategy for mission. Given this emphasis on context-specific solutions, it would be inappropriate for Stott to outline missional structures, but he does allow himself to wonder if many churches have too many meetings.

It is not just that the local church owns the task of evangelism. The church itself through its common life commends the message.

> The church is supposed to be God's new society, the living embodiment of the gospel, a sign of the kingdom of God, a demonstration of what human community looks like when it comes under his gracious rule. In other words, God's purpose is that the good news of Jesus Christ is set forth visually as well as verbally . . . that it be made known "by word and deed."[35]

Stott expounds this by comparing John 1:18 and 1 John 4:12. The apostle John begins both verses in the same way: "No one has ever seen God." "The invisibility of God," says Stott, "is a great problem for faith."[36] The same problem of an unseen God challenges us today. People brought up on the scientific method have been taught to examine everything with their five senses. Like people of old, they want to see so that they might believe. How has God solved the problem of his own invisibility? First and foremost, by sending his Son into the world, the Word made flesh. This is the answer given in John 1:18: "No one has ever seen God; the only God, who is at the Father's side, he has made him known." But, of course, Jesus can no longer be seen. This is where 1 John 4:12 comes in: "No one has ever seen God; if we love one another, God abides in us and his love is perfected in us." Stott comments:

---

[34] Stott, *The Contemporary Christian*, 247–51.
[35] Stott, *The Contemporary Christian*, 253–54.
[36] Stott, *The Contemporary Christian*, 254.

> The invisible God, who once made himself visible in Christ, now makes himself visible in Christians, *if we love one another.* God is love in his essential being, and has revealed his love in the gift of his Son to live and die for us. Now he calls us to be a community of love, loving each other in the intimacy of his family—especially across the barriers of age and sex, race and rank—and loving the world he loves in its alienation, hunger, poverty and pain. It is through the quality of our loving that God makes himself visible today. We cannot proclaim the gospel of God's love with any degree of integrity if we do not exhibit it in our love for others.[37]

Evangelical Divisions

In the wake of Billy Graham's 1954 Harringay Crusade, Stott and Martyn Lloyd-Jones joined a group set up by the British Council of Churches, the main ecumenical body in Britain. The council wanted to explore the differences between its members and the evangelical churches who had supported the crusade. It soon emerged that on a range of key doctrines—atonement, the nature of regeneration, the person of Christ, the nature of sin—there was no agreement. Stott withdrew early on. Again and again Stott insisted in his writings that there can be no true or lasting unity at the expense of the truth of the gospel.[38] Somewhat ironically, given what later transpired, it was Lloyd-Jones who persisted until 1961, when the British Council of Churches brought the process to a close.

The 1960s were the high-water mark of ecumenical optimism. In the UK the Presbyterians and Congregationalists were in a process of coming together that led to formation of the United Reformed Church in 1972. Anglicans and Methodists were considering a similar proposal to unite. In 1964 the British Council of Churches resolved to form one united church in Britain by Easter 1980. These moves, though, were viewed with suspicion by evangelicals, because unity was privileged above truth. Evangelical Congregationalists refused to join the new United Reformed Church, and evangelicals were in the forefront of defeating the Anglican-Methodist merger.

In 1963, John Robinson published *Honest to God*, which questioned the existence of an objective divine Being "up there," and although Robinson was the Anglican bishop of Woolwich, he received no censure from the

[37] Stott, *The Contemporary Christian*, 255–56.

[38] See, for example, John Stott, *The Epistles of John: An Introduction and Commentary* (London: Tyndale Press, 1964), 203; Stott, *The Message of Romans: God's Good News for the World* (Leicester: Inter-Varsity Press; Downers Grove, IL: InterVarsity Press, 1994), 25; Stott, *The Contemporary Christian*, 265–69; and Stott, *But I Say to You: Christ the Controversialist* (Nottingham: Inter-Varsity Press, 2013), 15–25, 78–79.

Church of England. The following year Mass vestments were legalized for use in the Anglican Church, and two years later prayers for the dead were permitted. In 1966, Michael Ramsey, the archbishop of Canterbury, visited the pope, and together they declared their meeting to be "a new stage in the development of fraternal relations."

As a result of these events a number of evangelical clergy left the Church of England. Herbert Carson, the vicar of St Paul's, Cambridge, left in response to a challenge from Lloyd-Jones at the annual lecture of the Evangelical Library in 1962 to put truth before denominational allegiance. In 1966, Iain Murray, Lloyd-Jones's former assistant, published *The Forgotten Spurgeon*, which explored the reasons why Spurgeon had left the Baptist Union in the nineteenth century. Spurgeon's position, he said, was that "to be linked in association with ministers who do not preach the gospel of Christ is to incur moral guilt," and to remain in mixed denominations breaks the unity of the true church.[39] Both H. J. W. Legerton, general secretary of the Lord's Day Observance Society, and Geoffrey Carr, rector of Aborfield near Reading, called for a concerted act of secession. Historian Andrew Atherstone speaks of "the Anglican secession crisis."[40]

The Islington Clerical Conference in 1965 in fact marked a concerted effort to quell thoughts of secession. Peter Johnston (the conference president), Maurice Wood (principal of Oak Hill Theological College), Roger Beckwith (librarian of Latimer House, Oxford), and John Pearce (rector of St Paul's, Homerton) all lined up to call on evangelicals to remain in the Church of England and pursue its reform. Stott echoed these sentiments in an address to the annual meeting of the Church Society in June 1965:

> Some Evangelicals of the Free Churches are talking of seceding from their different Churches in order to form a United Evangelical Church. I, for one, ardently hope they will not do so. I believe that history as well as Scripture is against them, and I am quite sure that they would not carry more than a small handful of Anglican Evangelicals with them.[41]

This is the background to one of the most dramatic moments in twentieth--century evangelical history. On October 18, 1966, with John Stott in the

---

[39] Iain H. Murray, *The Forgotten Spurgeon* (Edinburgh: Banner of Truth, 1966), 164–64.
[40] Andrew Atherstone, "Lloyd-Jones and the Anglican Succession Crisis," in *Engaging with Martyn Lloyd-Jones: The Life and Legacy of "the Doctor,"* ed. Andrew Atherstone and David Ceri Jones (Nottingham: Apollos, 2011), 261–92.
[41] Cited in Atherstone, "Lloyd-Jones and the Anglican Succession Crisis," 267.

chair, Dr. Martyn-Lloyd Jones stood up to give the opening address of the Second National Assembly of Evangelicals, under the auspices of the Evangelical Alliance. The year before, the first assembly, intended to be a kind of evangelical synod, had created a commission to produce a report on evangelical unity, and this was the focus on the 1966 gathering. A few weeks before the meeting, Lloyd-Jones had asked if Stott would consider being his successor at Westminster Chapel. Stott, somewhat taken aback by the suggestion, said he felt no call to leave All Souls, nor the Church of England.[42]

At the beginning of the meeting Stott was given ten minutes for "chairman's remarks," which he used to say that spiritual unity should be founded on biblical truth with room for divergence on secondary issues, and that this unity should be expressed visibly in some way with a recognition of ministries and sacraments (by which he meant shared communion).

What happened next was the source of considerable controversy and even today remains the subject of heated debate.[43]

Evangelicals faced a new situation, Lloyd-Jones began. The ecumenical movement was pushing toward church unions, though not union built around truth. In contrast, evangelicals showed little interest in unity. Indeed, typically evangelicals were fighting rearguard actions against proposed new configurations. "The most pathetic thing of all, to me, is that our attitude towards the question of church union is always a negative one."[44] Citing Jesus's prayer that "they may all be one . . . that the world may know" (John 17:21–23), Lloyd-Jones said church unity must be visible as well as spiritual, since it is to be seen by the world.[45] "Are we content, as evangelicals," he asked, "to go on being nothing but an evangelical wing of the church?" He spoke of a "paper church," united around ambiguous statements that all can interpret as they choose.[46] It is not enough to point to a statement of faith, however orthodox, if that statement is being routinely denied by a denomination. He pointed to the incongruity of evangelicals coming together for occasional conferences but expressing ongoing, visible

---

42 Roger Steer, *Inside Story: The Life of John Stott* (Nottingham: Inter-Varsity Press, 2009), 131.

43 See, for example, Iain H. Murray, *David Martyn Lloyd-Jones: The Fight of Faith 1939–1981* (Edinburgh: London, 1990), 522–28; Murray, *Evangelicalism Divided: A Record of the Crucial Change in the Years 1950 to 2000* (Edinburgh: London, 2000); Timothy Dudley-Smith, *John Stott*, vol. 2, *A Global Ministry* (Leicester: Inter-Varsity Press, 2001), 65–71; John Brencher, *Martyn Lloyd-Jones (1899–1981) and Twentieth Century Evangelicalism* (Milton Keynes: Paternoster, 2002), 92–106; Andrew Atherstone and David Ceri Jones, "Lloyd-Jones and His Biographers," in Atherstone and Jones, *Engaging with Martyn Lloyd-Jones* (Nottingham: Apollos, 2011), 11–37; Atherstone, "Lloyd-Jones and the Anglican Secession Crisis," 261–92.

44 Martyn Lloyd-Jones, "Evangelical Unity: An Appeal," in *Knowing the Times: Addresses Delivered on Various Occasions 1942–1977* (Edinburgh: Banner of Truth, 1989), 249.

45 Lloyd-Jones, "Evangelical Unity," 247.

46 Lloyd-Jones, "Evangelical Unity," 251.

unity within their denominations with those who deny the truth. True schism, he said, was for evangelicals to be divided from one another "in the main tenor of our lives and for the bulk of our time."[47]

As he came toward the end of his address, Lloyd-Jones moved to his central purpose: "Let me therefore make an appeal to you evangelical people here present this evening. What reasons have we for not coming together?"[48] He did not call for a unified evangelical denomination as such, but instead spoke of "a fellowship, or an association, of evangelical churches."[49] He did not define what this might involve, but, given that he was speaking at an Evangelical Alliance event, he must have meant something more than the kind of parachurch alliance represented by the EA. Lloyd-Jones recognized the problems involved in such a venture but reminded his hearers of those who had stood sacrificially for truth in the past. "We are living in tremendous times," he concluded. "It is a glorious day of opportunity."[50]

The general thrust of this address was known in advance by the council of the Evangelical Alliance and Stott as chair of the meeting. But some believe that, in turning his address into an appeal, Lloyd-Jones exceeded his brief to set out his position and he thereby preempted the rest of the assembly. The primary theme of his talk was a call for evangelical unity in some kind of association, but the call to secede from mixed denominations was clear. Others thought the Evangelical Alliance was at fault in failing to manage expectations (it had changed general secretaries between the planning of the assembly and the assembly itself).

At the end of the address, instead of simply giving a few words of thanks as was normal for the chair of such a meeting, Stott added to the drama by using his role as chair to offer an impromptu response. History was against Lloyd-Jones, he said, because previous attempts at evangelical denominations had failed, and Scripture was against him because it consistently speaks of a faithful remnant within the visible church. "From the platform," Stott said later, "I could see younger men with flushed faces, sitting on the edge of their seat, hanging on every word, and probably ready to go home and write their letter of resignation that very night. I hoped at least to restrain some hotheads from doing this."[51]

47 Lloyd-Jones, "Evangelical Unity," 254.
48 Lloyd-Jones, "Evangelical Unity," 254.
49 Lloyd-Jones, "Evangelical Unity," 257.
50 Lloyd-Jones, "Evangelical Unity," 256.
51 John Stott, memorandum to Timothy Dudley-Smith, September 1996, cited in Dudley-Smith, *John Stott*, 2:67.

Some people thought Lloyd-Jones exceeded his brief; others thought Stott abused his role as chair. But, of course, the real heat was generated by the issue itself. The dispute created a breach between Anglican and Free Church evangelicals in the UK that has taken a generation to heal.

Stott called Lloyd-Jones a few days later to apologize, not for the substance of what he had said, but for turning the occasion into a debate. In 1978, Stott visited Lloyd-Jones with a view to reconciliation. The relationship between the two men was warm, though they continued to air their differences.

The year after the Evangelical Alliance assembly, British evangelical Anglicans met together at Keele University for the first National Evangelical Anglican Congress. It had not been Stott's idea, but he was enthusiastic about the proposal and chaired the organizing committee. Keele was a "watershed" for evangelical Anglicans.[52] For two generations, evangelicals had felt like an embattled minority trying to keep the flame of orthodoxy alive through dark times. But at Keele there was a radically different, almost euphoric spirit. Evangelicals were now growing in numbers and in confidence.[53] "This was largely due to the status and influence of one man," claims Canon Paul Welsby, "John Stott."[54]

Keele had been two years in the making, so it was not created as a response to Lloyd-Jones's address, but it served to cement a determination to stay and reform the Church of England. The Keele Congress took evangelical Anglicans in a direction opposite to the one advocated by Lloyd-Jones. The final declaration explicitly said, "We do not believe secession to be a live issue in our present situation."[55] Ironically, the need to include this statement is a good indication of just how much secession was in fact a live issue! Instead, the congress agreed to invest in the structures of the Church of England with a view to bringing change. They burrowed into the Anglican Church rather than coming out of it or existing on the fringe. The final statement said: "We are deeply committed to the present and future of the Church of England. We believe that God has led us to this commitment,

---

52 Kenneth Hylson-Smith, *Evangelicals in the Church of England 1734–1984* (Edinburgh: T&T Clark, 1989), 291; see also Andrew Atherstone, "The Keele Congress of 1967: A Paradigm Shift in Anglican Evangelical Attitudes," *Journal of Anglican Studies* 9 (2011): 175–97.

53 See Tim Chester, *Awakening to a World of Need: The Recovery of Evangelical Social Concern* (Leicester: Inter-Varsity Press, 1993), 22–24.

54 Paul A. Welsby, *A History of the Church of England 1945–1980* (Oxford: Oxford University Press, 1984), 213.

55 Philip Crowe, ed., *Keele '67: The National Evangelical Anglican Congress Statement* (London: Falcon, 1967), §87.

and we dare to hope and pray that through it God will bring His word to bear with new power upon this Church."[56] Stott himself said:

> God is evidently raising up in our generation evangelical churchmen of intellectual and spiritual power. . . . We are increasingly anxious to play our part actively and constructively in the Church of England. . . . We do not want to remain for ever on the defensive, but to take the initiative to speak positively and evangelically to what is going on around us.[57]

In 1969, Stott and Lloyd-Jones were both present when delegations from the British Evangelical Council (now Affinity) and the Church of England Evangelical Council met to foster greater respect. But the situation worsened the following year when J. I. Packer and Colin Buchanan, together with two Anglo-Catholics, published *Growing into Union*. Its primary intent was to oppose plans for Anglican-Methodist union, but to the Free Church leaders it reinforced the idea that Anglican evangelicals were more interested in Anglican unity than evangelical unity.

Archbishop Donald Coggan, in a lecture on Charles Simeon, stated: "He loved the Church of England. He loved its liturgy and he was content to live and die a son of the Church of England, even though within that Church he suffered so much and saw so much that was weak and unworthy in its priests and people."[58] Paul Carr comments, "It is widely accepted that Simeon, by his loyalty to the Church of England, was instrumental in keeping evangelical Anglicans within the fold rather than following the Dissenters into Nonconformity."[59] The same could have been said of Stott. Andrew Atherstone summarizes Stott and his Anglican-evangelical colleagues as follows:

1. *Historically*, they argued that the constitutional basis of the Church of England was Protestant and Reformed, seen in the Reformation formularies like the Thirty-Nine Articles of Religion and the Book of Common Prayer. So evangelicals held the legal "title deeds" to the Church of England, and the liberals and catholics should get out, not them.
2. *Biblically*, they argued that many New Testament churches were doctrinally confused or morally compromised, like the church in Corinth

---

[56] Crowe, *Keele '67*, §87.
[57] John Stott, "Statement to Be Made at the 133rd Islington Clerical Conference," January 10, 1967, cited in Dudley-Smith, *John Stott*, 2:78.
[58] F. D. Coggan, *These Were His Gifts* (Exeter: University of Exeter Press, 1974), 16, cited in Paul A. Carr, "Are the Priorities and Concerns of Charles Simeon Relevant for Today?," *Churchman* 114, no. 2 (2000): 160.
[59] Carr, "Priorities and Concerns of Charles Simeon," 160.

that was muddled about the resurrection, or the church in Sardis that numbered only "a few" godly people (Rev. 3:4). But believers in those churches are told to hold fast to the gospel, and to fight against false teachers, not to leave the church and set up a new one.

3. *Pragmatically*, Stott and his friends argued that the Church of England provided many gospel opportunities for evangelicals, and that it would be a dereliction of duty to hand over their pulpits to unbelieving clergy. What then would become of their congregations?[60]

I am not so rash as to think I can adjudicate on this division. The debate is still raw after more than half a century. But here are some reflections.

First, this is in many ways the latest iteration of a long-running debate. After the persecutions of Emperor Diocletian in the fourth century, the church faced the issue of what to do with the *traditores*—those who "handed over" their Christian books to be burned (the source of the English word "traitor"). When a former *traditor* was consecrated as bishop of Carthage in 311, a breakaway movement known as the Donatists (after their African leader, Donatus) called for a pure church. Augustine, however, while acknowledging that *traditio* was a serious sin, believed schism to be more serious. Appealing to the parable of the wheat and the tares in Matthew 13:24–30, he argued that in history the church is a "mixed body" (*corpus permixtum*) containing both saints and sinners. We must wait for the end of history for a pure church, since only God can make these judgments. The holiness of the church is the holiness not of its members but of its head, Jesus Christ.

Lloyd-Jones explicitly looked to Luther as his model: a man who had left the church to remain true to the gospel. Referring to the precedent set at the Reformation, Lloyd-Jones said in his 1966 address that to leave an apostate church is not schism but a Christian's duty.[61] But, in fact, Luther and the other magisterial Reformers followed Augustine in arguing for a mixed church. Luther wanted to reform the church, and only when Rome excommunicated him for preaching justification by faith did he separate from the Catholic Church. Calvin made a distinction between the visible church (the people making up the congregation together with the structures of

---

60 Justin Taylor, "50 Years Ago Today: The Split between John Stott and Martyn Lloyd-Jones," an interview with Andrew Atherstone, *The Gospel Coalition*, October 18, 2016, https://www.thegospelcoalition.org/blogs/evangelical-history/50-years-ago-today-the-split-between-john-stott-and-martyn-lloyd-jones; emphasis added.

61 Lloyd-Jones, "Evangelical Unity," 254.

the church) and the invisible church (the company of true believers under Christ). It was the Anabaptists who believed the church should pursue purity by welcoming only those baptized on the basis of a credible profession of faith and disciplining those who did not live accordingly.

Second, temperament and background undoubtedly played its part in the division. Lloyd-Jones was Welsh, while Stott was English. John Brencher says Lloyd-Jones's "anti-Anglicanism . . . was essentially a Welsh view of the English."[62] The word "essentially" overstates the case—theological issues were central. But both men were profoundly influenced by the differing cultures of their home nations. It is often said that after 1970, Lloyd-Jones stopped cooperating with Anglicans. But, while this was largely true in England, it was not true in Wales,[63] perhaps because evangelicals in the church in Wales were too few in number to adopt a patrician attitude.

Lloyd-Jones had been shaped by his early ministry in the working-class town of Aberavon, while Stott was shaped by his establishment upbringing. One reason for Stott's ongoing allegiance to Anglicanism was an aversion to joining the Free Churches. This was perhaps due in part to social class—the Free Churches were generally lower class, a culture alien to Stott—and a perceived ghetto mentality among Free Churches at the time. Free Churches have always tended to have an outsider mentality, to see themselves as on the margins—not least because they have historically been marginalized. It was, for example, not until 1828 that non-conformists in Britain were allowed to be government officials.

Why was Stott so loyal to the Anglican Church? In part, the answer must be that it was all he had known. Alister Chapman comments: "John Stott was a cradle Anglican. The Church of England was the church of his birth, the church of his school, the church of his college, and the church of his ordination."[64] All Souls was his church, and he was loyal to his church. Plus, he could not see the Free Churches as a force for the evangelization of the nation. The Free Churches were not part of mainstream culture, and that was what Stott wanted to reach. He did not want to enter what Chapman calls "the cultural wilderness."[65] Yet, a generation on, the Anglican

62 Brencher, *Martyn Lloyd-Jones*, 172.

63 David Ceri Jones, "Evangelical Resurgence in the Church in Wales in the Mid-Twentieth Century," in *Evangelicalism and the Church of England in the Twentieth Century: Reform, Resistance and Renewal*, ed. Andrew Atherstone and John Maiden (Woodbridge: Boydell, 2014), 236.

64 Alister Chapman, *Godly Ambition: John Stott and the Evangelical Movement* (New York: Oxford University Press, 2012), 79.

65 Chapman, *Godly Ambition*, 94.

Church itself is no longer mainstream of secular Britain; it, too, is entering the wilderness.

The success of the National Evangelical Anglican Congress in 1967 and its follow-up ten years later seemed to promise a new era of evangelical ascendancy within the Church of England. But after the second congress (1977), Stott himself admitted privately that he saw "disturbing signs . . . a new 'liberal evangelicalism'" that made him fear a new "battle for the Bible."[66] Anglican evangelicalism was broadening, and in the coming years its common voice was weakened. The charismatic debate overshadowed the second congress. A controversial article on biblical authority in *Churchman*, the traditional journal of evangelical Anglicanism, by the New Testament scholar James Dunn led to the launch of a second journal, *Anvil* (Stott declared he would subscribe to both). Writes Oliver Barclay, "Stott's now frequent trips abroad had weakened his influence at home, and less conservative views began to be heard."[67] Evangelicals have not "won" the Anglican Church, as debates over the ordination of women and the status of same-sex relationships reveal.

Many of those evangelicals who invested in the Anglican system perhaps inevitably become more Anglican than evangelical. Stott himself remained staunchly evangelical. Indeed, as he traveled outside the UK, he recognized that elsewhere in the world the life of the church lay outside the Anglican communion. His position was that the Church of England was orthodox in its formularies. "At least until it becomes apostate and ceases to be a church, we believe it is our duty to remain in it and bear witness to the truth as we have been given to understand it."[68] Addressing the Guildford Diocesan Evangelical Fellowship in the 1980s, Stott called himself a Christian first, an evangelical second, and an Anglican evangelical third.

> I am not an Anglican first, since denominationalism is hard to defend. It seems to me correct to call oneself an Anglican evangelical (in which evangelical is the noun and Anglican the descriptive adjective) rather than an evangelical Anglican (in which Anglican is the noun and evangelical the adjective).[69]

---

[66] John Stott, letter to Archbishop Sir Marcus Loane, August 5, 1977, JRWS Papers, cited in Dudley-Smith, *John Stott*, 2:164.

[67] Oliver Barclay, *Evangelicalism in Britain 1935–1995: A Personal Sketch* (Leicester: Inter-Varsity Press, 1997), 101. For a full account of this controversy, see Andrew Atherstone, *An Anglican Evangelical Identity Crisis: The Churchman—Anvil Affair of 1981–1984* (London: Latimer Trust, 2008).

[68] John Stott, *Essentials for Tomorrow's Christians* (London: Scripture Union, 1978), 7, cited in Dudley-Smith, *John Stott*, 2:70.

[69] Cited in Steer, *Inside Story*, 191.

Stott's support for the Anglican Church was not unqualified. Asked in 1995 under what circumstances he would leave the Church of England, he identified two. The first was a major doctrinal departure concerning the person of Christ, such as a denial of his divine-human identity, or concerning the work of Christ, such as a denial of justification by grace alone. Back in 1958 he had said: "We cannot have Christian fellowship with those who deny the divinity of Christ's person or the satisfactoriness of His work on the cross for our salvation. . . . There is no room for negotiation or appeasement here."[70]

In 1977, *The Myth of God Incarnate*, written by a collection of British academics, some of whom were ordained Anglican clergymen, rejected Chalcedonian Christology. In the wake of the public debate this provoked, Stott called for them to be disciplined. "Is it too much to hope and pray," he wrote, "that some bishop sometime will have the courage to withdraw his licence from a presbyter who denies the incarnation?"[71] Individuals may say what they will as scholars and citizens, he said, not advocating any denial of academic or civil liberty. But they could not continue as teachers of a church whose standards they promised to uphold at their ordinations. At Stott's instigation, the Church of England Evangelical Council pursued this idea in a booklet entitled *Truth, Error and Discipline in the Church*.[72] But no action was taken.

The second line that Stott drew in the sand would be any departure from biblical norms on a major ethical issue. "I would say that if the church were officially to approve of homosexual partnerships as a legitimate alternative to heterosexual marriage, this so far diverges from the sexual ethic of the Bible that I would find it exceedingly difficult to stay."[73]

In 1993, Stott publicly debated the ethics of homosexuality with the liberal American bishop John Spong. In his handwritten notes, Stott says, "We can no more defend homosexual conduct on the ground that it is 'created' and therefore 'natural,' than we can defend any other deviation of temperament or behaviour, or indeed the basic selfishness with which we are all born." Responding to the claim that it is unrealistic to expect

---

70 John Stott, *What Christ Thinks of the Church: Expository Addresses on the First Three Chapters of the Book of Revelation* (London: Lutterworth, 1958), 56.

71 John Stott, *Authentic Christianity: From the Writings of John Stott*, ed. Timothy Dudley-Smith (Downers Grove, IL: InterVarsity Press, 1995), 121.

72 Church of England Evangelical Council, *Truth, Error and Discipline in the Church* (London: Vine, 1978). See also John Stott, *Confess Your Sins: The Way of Reconciliation* (London: Hodder, 1964), 43–50, where Stott makes the case for church discipline. Stott also wrote his own response in *The Authentic Jesus: A Response to Current Scepticism in the Church* (Basingstoke: Marshall, Morgan and Scott, 1985).

73 Reproduced in John Stott, *Balanced Christianity: A Call to Avoid Unnecessary Polarisation*, 2nd ed. (Nottingham: Inter-Varsity Press, 2014), 75–76.

people to restrain their sexual urges, Stott argues that ethics are defined not by whatever we deem "realistic" but by what God reveals to be right. He also adds, "Bishop Spong himself is not advocating promiscuity, which indicates that he does believe in the possibility of self-control." Anything less, suggests Stott, reduces our humanness, since we become like animals driven simply by instincts. Stott then anticipates the argument that since God's love is universal, he must approve of same-sex relationships. He responds that "God's love, like the love of parents, seeks our highest welfare, which is our holiness."[74]

Evangelical Unity

Stott's father had hoped John would enter the British diplomatic service, little realizing the diplomatic role Stott would play within worldwide evangelicalism.[75] Despite the confrontation with Lloyd-Jones, Stott repeatedly played the role of conciliator on the world stage. It is a reflection of his commitment to balanced Christianity that he constantly tried to hold together positions that might otherwise have torn apart. Indeed, this desire to hold together divergent views is one reason Stott was reluctant to leave the Anglican Church to create what he feared would become a polarized body. Again Simeon's influence is significant. Simeon, writing of himself in the third person, once noted, "He bitterly regrets that men will range themselves under human banners and leaders, and employ themselves in converting the Inspired Writers into friends and partisans of their peculiar principles."[76] Stott says: "Some of the right wing have already dismissed me as a quasi-liberal . . . while others to the left of me regard me as much too conservative for their liking. I often find myself caught in the cross-fire between these groupings."[77]

As their subtitles reveal, Stott's books *Balanced Christianity* and *Evangelical Truth* are essentially "a call to avoid unnecessary polarisation" and "a personal plea for unity" (along with integrity and faithfulness).[78] In *The*

[74] John Stott, "Christian Sexual Ethics: Presuppositions," July 7, 1993, Church of England Record Centre, STOTT/2/4.

[75] In John Stott, *The Message of Acts: To the Ends of the Earth* (Leicester: Inter-Varsity Press; Downers Grove, IL: InterVarsity Press, 1990), 25–29, Stott writes appreciatively of Luke's role as a diplomat in the book of Acts.

[76] Charles Simeon, *Horae Homileticae* (London: Richard Watts, 1819), 1:6.

[77] John Stott, in David L. Edwards with John Stott, *Essentials: A Liberal-Evangelical Dialogue* (London: Hodder & Stoughton, 1988), 34.

[78] Stott, *Balanced Christianity: A Call to Avoid Unnecessary Polarisation*; and Stott, *Evangelical Truth: A Personal Plea for Unity, Integrity and Faithfulness*, rev. ed. (Nottingham: Inter-Varsity Press, 2015).

Message of Ephesians he says, "The fact of the church's indestructible unity is no excuse for acquiescing in the tragedy of its actual disunity."[79] Stott says of domestic evangelical debates:

> When we stay apart, and our only contact is to lob hand grenades at one another across a demilitarized zone, a caricature of one's "opponent" develops in one's mind, complete with horns, hooves and tail! But when we meet, and sit together, and begin to listen, not only does it become evident that our opponents are not after all demons, but actually normal human beings, and even sisters and brothers in Christ, the possibility of mutual understanding and respect grows.[80]

If God has revealed himself in Scripture and the Spirit illuminates Scripture, why do Christians disagree? Stott replies: "My general answer is this, that we actually agree with one another a great deal more than we disagree, and that we would agree more still if we fulfilled the following five conditions":[81]

1. We must accept the supreme authority of Scripture.
2. We must remember that the chief purpose of Scripture is to bear witness to Jesus Christ as the Saviour of sinners.
3. We must develop sound principles of biblical interpretation.
4. We must study Scripture together.
5. We must come to the biblical text with a humble, open, receptive spirit.[82]

"I'm a great believer," he says, "in small, private, international, representative consultations in which we're prepared to listen to one another." It had been his own experience on a number of occasions to see polarized positions resolved into mutual understanding through personal contact and a willingness to understand other people's underlying concerns. "Why did they feel this so strongly? What is it that they want to safeguard? The extraordinary thing was that in many cases you find that you want to safeguard it too. And then you reach the point of creative development

---

[79] Stott, *The Message of Ephesians*, 153. See also Stott, *The Message of the Sermon on the Mount: Christian Counter-Culture* (Leicester: Inter-Varsity Press; Downers Grove, IL: InterVarsity Press, 1978), 50–51; Stott, *The Message of Acts*, 197, 268–70; Stott, *The Message of Romans*, 355–75; and Stott, "Blessed Are the Peacemakers: The Cost of Reconciliation," Jamaica, May 4, 2002, Church of England Record Centre, STOTT/2/3.
[80] Stott, *The Contemporary Christian*, 108–9.
[81] John Stott, *Calling Christian Leaders: Biblical Models of Church, Gospel and Ministry* (Leicester: Inter-Varsity Press, 2002), 80–81.
[82] Stott, *Calling Christian Leaders*, 80–81; see also Stott, *Focus on Christ: An Enquiry into the Theology of Prepositions* (Eastbourne: Kingsway, 1979), 102–8.

or creative solutions."[83] Stott's dialectical approach of bringing together the truths in apparently competing ideas enabled him to mediate between divergent positions.

Stott spent much of his ministry battling for the church. Sometimes he fought for its integrity by combatting error; sometimes he fought for its unity by working to reconcile divisions. But always his concern was to strengthen the people for whom Christ had died.

[83] John Stott, "Rehabilitating Discipleship: An Interview with John Stott," *Prism*, July–August 1995, cited in Dudley-Smith, *John Stott*, 2:327.

CHAPTER 8

REACHING A LOST WORLD

In 1961 the International Missionary Council (IMC) was integrated into the World Council of Churches (WCC), the global body for ecumenical cooperation.[1] The IMC had been formed in 1921 from the continuation committee of the first great global missionary conference in Edinburgh in 1910 to coordinate churches and mission societies in the task of world evangelization. With the formation of the WCC in 1948, however, it came under pressure to become the WCC's missionary arm. The move was controversial but almost inevitable. Many expressed strong reservations about the effect of this integration upon the IMC and the missionary movement as a whole. Others, however, hoped its presence would place the task of evangelization once again at the heart of the ecumenical movement. The IMC became the Commission on World Mission and Evangelism (CWME) of the WCC with the following stated aim: "To further proclamation to the whole world of the gospel of Jesus Christ, to the end that all men may believe and be saved."

The Ecumenical Drift in Missiology

In the years following its formation the CWME lost many of its key staff, and a number of posts were vacant for some time. Without this leadership

[1] For a detailed examination of developments in the WCC's understanding of mission from an evangelical perspective, see Harvey T. Hoekstra, *Evangelism in Eclipse: World Mission and the World Council of Churches* (Exeter: Paternoster, 1979). For Stott's summary, see John Stott, *The Incomparable Christ* (Leicester: Inter-Varsity Press, 2001), 115–19. See also Orlando Costas, *The Church and Its Mission: A Shattering Critique from the Third World* (Wheaton, IL: Tyndale, 1974), 153–301; David Bosch, *Witness to the World: The Christian Mission in Theological Perspective* (London: Marshall, Morgan and Stott, 1980), 159–95; and Arthur Johnston, *The Battle for World Evangelism* (Wheaton, IL: Tyndale, 1970).

the CWME failed to make an impact on the WCC. Instead, it was the WCC that influenced the CWME. A number of factors were involved. Many evangelical mission societies that had been part of the IMC left, either because they were non-denominational (and the WCC could receive only churches as members) or because they felt unable to participate in the broader ecumenical movement. With the decline of colonialism many ecumenical leaders felt that a new, less imperialist missionary model was needed. Indeed, the WCC was at times highly, and somewhat indiscriminately, critical of its missionary forebears. Finally, all too often ecumenical cooperation in mission meant missionary no-go areas. The Eastern Orthodox churches, for example, which joined the WCC in 1961, feared Western Protestant churches would seek to evangelize their many nominal members.

The first meeting of the CWME was held in Mexico City in 1963. With churches now determining delegates, those delegates tended to be denominational representatives who were not necessarily directly involved in mission. They met under the slogan "Mission to Six Continents." It was chosen to underline the fact that the church is always in a missionary situation—mission is needed in the West as well as the Global South. Emphasizing the church's responsibility to its own locality, however, had the effect of turning attention away from the many unevangelized people outside the sphere of any church. Instead, the central issues at Mexico City revolved round the relationship between God's activity in the church and in the world.

In 1968 the fourth assembly of the WCC met at Uppsala, Sweden. Here the talk was of "new mission." Whereas leading people to Christ had been the traditional goal of mission (Christianization), now the concern was enabling people to be truly human (humanization). Also challenged was the belief that God related to the world through the church. The pattern God-church-world became God-world-church. In other words, the emphasis shifted from God speaking to the world through his people toward God speaking to the church through what he was doing in the world. Mission was still understood as a participation in the *missio Dei*, the mission of God, but now this was understood as "entering into partnership with God in history." The *missio Dei* was linked to secular movements, and the task of the church was to discern God's purposes in such movements and back them. As a result, the supposed activity of the Spirit in the secular world claimed authoritative status along with the Bible in determining the mission of the church.

John Stott attended the Uppsala Assembly as an official advisor, authorized to speak but not to vote. His friend Oliver Barclay had written a strong letter to Stott warning about the message his attendance would send.[2] And before leaving, Stott had told the congregation at All Souls that he had made it clear to the WCC that he did not share the emerging ecumenical view of mission. Nevertheless (or perhaps as a result), he felt it was his duty to attend and put forth an evangelical perspective. Although Stott would become well known in evangelical circles for his advocacy of social involvement, in ecumenical circles he was courageous in his call to keep evangelism at the center.

Stott found he shared much of the concern for social justice. "I do not regret this emphasis at all," he wrote on his return, "*except* that there appeared to be no comparable compassion for the spiritual hunger of the unevangelized millions, no comparable call to go to them with the Bread of Life."[3] At the assembly itself he felt compelled to speak in the plenary session on world mission.

> The church's first priority . . . remains the millions and millions . . . who (as Christ and his apostles tell us again and again) being without Christ are perishing. . . . The World Council of Churches professes to acknowledge Jesus Christ as Lord. Well, the Lord Jesus Christ sent his church to preach the good news and make disciples; I do not see this Assembly as a whole eager to obey his command. The Lord Jesus Christ wept over the impenitent city which had rejected him; I do not see this Assembly weeping any similar tears.[4]

Historian David Edwards described it as a "brave protest."[5] In the light of the input by Stott and other evangelicals, the final report was somewhat modified, but the original thrust remained.

Most evangelicals reacted strongly against the assembly's changes in the understanding of mission. Even before the Uppsala Assembly, Donald McGavran had written an article asking, "Will Uppsala Betray the Two Billion?" in which he expressed his fear that the assembly would not give

---

[2] Oliver Barclay, letters to John Stott, March 1, 1968, and March 25, 1968; and John Stott, letters to Oliver Barclay, March 22, 1968, and April 8, 1968, Church of England Record Centre, STOTT/4/1.

[3] John Stott, *All Souls Newsletter*, September 1968, cited in Timothy Dudley-Smith, *John Stott*, vol. 2, *A Global Ministry* (Leicester: Inter-Varsity Press, 2001), 125.

[4] John Stott, *Christian Mission in the Modern World* (London: Falcon, 1975), 19. Stott's handwritten notes for his Uppsala intervention can be seen at the Church of England Record Centre, STOTT/4/1.

[5] David L. Edwards with John Stott, *Essentials: A Liberal-Evangelical Dialogue* (London: Hodder & Stoughton, 1988), 5.

attention to the need to reach the unreached.[6] In Germany, Peter Beyerhaus, a former missionary in South Africa, issued a challenge to the ecumenical view of mission in a book entitled *Humanisierung—Einzige Hoffnung der Welt? (Humanization—The Only Hope of the World?)*.[7] When this received no response from the German Missionary Council, a group of German theologians led by Beyerhaus adopted a declaration in March 1970 entitled "The Frankfurt Declaration on the Fundamental Crisis in Christian Missions." The Frankfurt Declaration, as it became known, was modeled on the Barmen Declaration, the statement made in response to Nazism by the "Confessing Church" in Germany. It spoke of an "inner decay" in contemporary ecumenical mission and "the displacement of their primary tasks by means of an insidious falsification of their motives and goals."[8] Of the various programs set up to implement this new understanding of mission by the WCC, the most notorious was the Programme to Combat Racism, which attracted considerable press attention when it made grants to guerrilla groups in Rhodesia (Zimbabwe).[9]

This new ecumenical conception of mission was further consolidated at the next CWME conference in Bangkok, which met under the title "Salvation Today." It was evident from the preparatory material that salvation was to be determined by what God was perceived to be doing in the world today, whether within the church or outside. Although evangelism was included in the final statements, it received little attention, and no mention was made of the unreached. Instead, the goal of mission was seen as bringing a just socioeconomic order. Stott did not attend the Bangkok conference, but he "followed it with deep interest and concern."[10]

The Bangkok affirmation of Uppsala's emphases on new mission and humanization served only to polarize further ecumenicals and evangelicals. The Berlin Declaration on Ecumenism, drawn up between Bangkok 1973 and the evangelical Lausanne Congress in 1974, attacked the WCC for its acceptance of "an ungodly humanism." Like the Frankfurt Declaration, the Berlin Declaration emanated from the Theological Convention of Confessing Fellowships, a conservative movement within the Lutheran

6 Donald A. McGavran, "Will Uppsala Betray the Two Billion?," *Church Growth Bulletin* 4, no. 5 (1968): 149–53.
7 Published in English as Peter Beyerhaus, *Missions: Which Way? Humanization and Redemption* (Grand Rapids, MI: Zondervan, 1971).
8 Cited by Costas, *The Church and Its Mission*, 190.
9 See Hoekstra, *Evangelism in Eclipse*, 237–42.
10 Stott, *Christian Mission in the Modern World*, 9.

church, with Peter Beyerhaus again involved. The Berlin Declaration was a response to Bangkok just as the Frankfurt Declaration had been a response to Uppsala. It spoke of an "unavoidable division," an "antithesis," between "the biblical profession of Jesus Christ and a secularist ecumenical movement," and it accused the WCC of forsaking the gospel for "an anti-Christian ideology."

All of this is background to John Stott's plenary address to the Lausanne Congress in 1974.

Recovering the Priorities of Missions

Since the WCC could receive only denominations into membership, interdenominational or unaffiliated missionary societies were effectively excluded. In 1957, for example, only 42 percent of all American missionaries were related to member churches of the American National Council of Churches, and thus to the WCC. By 1969 this had dropped still further to 28 percent, and in 1975 it was only 14 percent.[11] This exclusion, along with concerns about the drift in WCC missiology, created an opportunity for missionary fellowship among evangelicals on an international scale. David Bosch says, "A new movement would be launched: the 'evangelical ecumene.'"[12] This movement took shape at the Lausanne Congress in July 1974. Officially entitled the International Congress on World Evangelization, it brought together 2,473 participants from 150 countries—together with 570 observers and 410 reporters.[13] It was the largest and perhaps most significant gathering of evangelical leaders ever held, a conscious attempt to take up the mantle of the early ecumenical commitment to evangelization that evangelicals believed had been forsaken by the WCC.

At Lausanne, Stott was given the task of bringing clarity to the ecumenical-evangelical discussion and chose to do so by providing biblical definitions of the words "mission," "evangelism," "dialogue," "salvation," and "conversion."[14] He acknowledged that, "during the last few years, especially between Uppsala and Bangkok, ecumenical-evangelical relations hardened into something like a confrontation."[15] Characteristically, he

---

[11] Bosch, *Witness to the World*, 181.
[12] Bosch, *Witness to the World*, 181.
[13] The congress papers were published in *Let the Earth Hear His Voice*, ed. J. D. Douglas (Minneapolis: World Wide Publications, 1975).
[14] John Stott, "The Biblical Basis of Evangelism," in Douglas, *Let the Earth Hear His Voice*, 65–78.
[15] Stott, "The Biblical Basis of Evangelism," 65.

sought to show the common ground between the two groups, confessing that evangelicals could learn from ecumenicals. Ultimately, however, he remained highly critical of the missiology and soteriology reflected at Uppsala and Bangkok.[16] The year after the Lausanne Congress, Stott was invited to give the Chavasse Lectures at Wycliffe Hall in Oxford and took the opportunity to expand his contribution to Lausanne in lectures that were subsequently published as *Christian Mission in the Modern World*. The lectures steer a path between an evangelicalism that was suspicious of social action (a theme to which we will return in the following chapter) and an ecumenism that was abandoning the task of proclaiming Christ to the lost. Despite these immediate concerns, or perhaps because of them, the result is a rounded, balanced (of course), biblical understanding of mission. As Christopher Wright comments, again and again Stott's analyses have proved "farsighted."[17]

Much of the focus of the opening section of his Lausanne plenary address and first Chavasse lecture is on an evangelical audience, as Stott makes the case for the inclusion of social action within a biblical definition of mission. Nevertheless, he begins by critiquing ecumenical redefinitions of mission. Stott contrasts two "extreme" views of mission. The first is "the older or traditional view" that sees mission as just evangelism. But at the opposite extreme is the ecumenical perspective that sees God at work in historical processes, especially the development of social harmony and justice. Stott is quite explicit in his criticisms of the Uppsala Assembly, especially its misuse of Scripture. God's eschatological cry, "Behold, I am making all things new" (Rev. 21:5) was repeatedly used at Uppsala to endorse social change within history. But, as Stott says, "the God who is the Lord of history is also the Judge of history."[18] We cannot identify historical change with the kingdom of God.

Stott accepts that "the primal mission is God's" rather than the church's—a common claim made by the ecumenical movement. For ecumenicals this claim was used to redefine mission as cooperating in whatever God was thought to be doing in history to bring social justice. Stott, in contrast, characteristically defines it Christocentrically: the Son was

16 Stott, "The Biblical Basis of Evangelism," 74.

17 John Stott with Christopher J. H. Wright, *Christian Mission in the Modern World*, 2nd ed. (London: Inter-Varsity Press, 2015), 13.

18 Stott, *Christian Mission* (1975), 18; see also Stott, "Jesus Christ, the Life of the World," *Churchman* 97, no. 1 (1983): 6. Stott includes an eight-point "manifesto of evangelism" in *The Message of Romans: God's Good News for the World* (Leicester: Inter-Varsity Press; Downers Grove, IL: InterVarsity Press, 1994), 313–15.

sent by the Father as the culmination of God's purposes in history to redeem a people, and now the Son sends us to continue his mission. This brings Stott to the Great Commission in its various forms. Citing Matthew 28:19–20, Mark 16:15, Luke 24:47, and Acts 1:8, he says: "The cumulative emphasis seems clear. It is placed on preaching, witnessing and making disciples."[19]

Stott returns to this theme in his lecture on evangelism. He endorses the Lausanne Covenant's declaration, which he himself drafted, that "in the church's mission of sacrificial service evangelism is primary."[20] "How can we seriously maintain that political and economic liberation is just as important as eternal salvation?" he asks.[21] Paul was in anguish for his fellows Jews not because they were under the colonial heel of Rome but because they were alienated from God (Rom. 9:1–3; 10:1–4).

Evangelism, says Stott, cannot be defined in terms of its results or methods—an implicit critique of the technological and managerial approaches to world evangelization that some in the Lausanne movement were keen to apply. Instead, it must be defined by its message. Stott acknowledges that the gospel is expressed in the New Testament in a diversity of ways, but he claims that there is, nevertheless, a common and coherent unity (1 Cor. 15:11). "There is only one gospel, and in its essence it never changes."[22] Stott defines this in terms of *the gospel events* of the cross and resurrection, affirmed by *the gospel witnesses*, with *the gospel affirmations* of the ongoing lordship of Christ, proclaimed with *the gospel promises* of forgiveness and the Spirit, together with *the gospel demands* of faith and repentance.[23]

> Evangelism, therefore, is sharing the good news with others. The good news is Jesus. And the good news about Jesus which we announce is that he died for our sins and was raised from death, and that in consequence he reigns as Lord and Saviour at God's right hand, and has authority both to command repentance and faith, and to bestow forgiveness of sins and the gift of the Spirit on all those who repent, believe and are baptised. And

[19] Stott, *Christian Mission* (1975), 22.
[20] Stott, *Christian Mission* (1975), 35.
[21] Stott, *Christian Mission* (1975), 35.
[22] Stott, *Christian Mission* (1975), 42.
[23] Stott, *Christian Mission* (1975), 35–54. See also Stott, *Our Guilty Silence: The Church, the Gospel and the World* (London: Hodder & Stoughton, 1967), 32–55; Stott, *The Incomparable Christ*, 32–33; Stott, *The Message of Acts: To the Ends of the Earth* (Leicester: Inter-Varsity Press; Downers Grove, IL: InterVarsity Press, 1990), 79–81; and Stott, *The Message of Thessalonians: Preparing for the Coming King* (Leicester: Inter-Varsity Press; Downers Grove, IL: InterVarsity Press, 1991), 187.

> all this is according to the Scriptures of the Old and New Testament. It is more than that. It is precisely what is meant by "proclaiming the Kingdom of God." For in fulfilment of Scripture God's reign has broken into this life of men through the death and resurrection of Jesus. This reign or rule of God is exercised from the throne by Jesus, who bestows salvation and requires obedience.[24]

The reference to the kingdom of God is significant. The ecumenicals were using the kingdom motif to justify involvement in secular movements as mission. Stott, in contrast, defines the kingdom in terms of Christ and the gospel.

Stott then examines *dialogue*. The background was an ecumenical call to engage in dialogue with other religions with a view to mutual understanding and enlightenment. This was born out of a postcolonial concern not to impose ideas on others, and a growing belief that salvation could be found in other religions (led by Karl Rahner's claim that sincere adherents of other religions could be thought of as "anonymous Christians"), along with the general switch of focus from evangelism to social justice. If the movement was no longer God-church-world, but now God-world-church, then why not include other religions in the "world" that speaks to the church? Christ, it was argued, is already present in other faiths, and so we should not arrogantly attempt to bring him where he is already to be found.

Characteristically, Stott is both conciliatory and clear. He cites examples of dialogue in the Scriptures and calls on evangelicals to listen attentively to the world (anticipating his subsequent emphasis on double listening). Dialogue is an act of love because it seeks to overcome prejudices, see the world through others' eyes, and sympathize with their fears.[25] While Stott was always opposed to religious or philosophical pluralism (the belief that all worldviews are equally valid), he recognized pluralism as a social phenomenon. We now live with a diversity of cultures, ethnicities, and worldviews. As such, social cohesion requires that we communicate well with one another.

Nevertheless, after citing examples of Paul's use of dialogue, Stott makes clear that this was very different from the kind of dialogue being

---

24 Stott, *Christian Mission* (1975), 54.

25 Stott, *Christian Mission* (1975), 80; see also Stott, *The Authentic Jesus: A Response to Current Scepticism in the Church* (Basingstoke: Marshall, Morgan and Scott, 1985), 81–82.

proposed in ecumenical circles. "Paul's dialogue was clearly a part of his proclamation and subordinate to his proclamation."[26] In other words, Paul listened so he could present the gospel more appropriately. In contrast, "modern dialogue of Christians with non-Christians seems to savour rather of unbelief than of faith, of compromise than of proclamation."[27] It is true that the pre-converted Cornelius is described as "a devout man who feared God" (Acts 10:2), but God's response to his prayers is to send a preacher through whose message he is saved. There is a universal knowledge of God throughout the world, as Paul affirms in Romans 1, but people suppress that truth by their unrighteousness. All that is good and true owes its origins to God, even if people do not acknowledge this, but this universal light is not saving light. Hence the Bible's consistent denouncement of all forms of what it calls "idolatry." Stott concludes:

> Although there is an important place for "dialogue" with men of other faiths, there is also a need for "encounter" with them, and even for "confrontation," in which we seek both to disclose the inadequacies and falsities of non-Christian religion and to demonstrate the adequacy and truth, absoluteness and finality of the Lord Jesus Christ.[28]

When it comes to the word "salvation," Stott is clearly concerned that the title of the CWME's 1973 Bangkok conference, "Salvation Today," implies a departure from the understanding of salvation "yesterday" in the apostolic witness. "Salvation," he says, "is not socio-political liberation."[29] The main biblical justification for Bangkok's focus on social justice was the precedent set by the liberation of Israel from Egyptian oppression. But Stott points to Israel's special covenantal relationship with the Lord. "Hence in the New Testament the exodus becomes a picture of our redemption from sin by Christ, not a promise of liberation for all politically oppressed minorities."[30]

Stott defines salvation as freedom from judgment for sonship, from self for service, and from decay for glory.[31] He is keen to emphasize that liberation from oppression is a desirable goal, pleasing to God the Creator.

---

[26] Stott, *Christian Mission* (1975), 63.
[27] Stott, *Christian Mission* (1975), 63.
[28] Stott, *Christian Mission* (1975), 69; see also Stott, *The Message of Acts*, 198–99.
[29] Stott, *Christian Mission* (1975), 82, 87.
[30] Stott with Wright, *Christian Mission* (2015), 151–52. The original 1975 edition of *Christian Mission in the Modern World* contains an unfortunate typo which omits the crucial middle portion of this sentence.
[31] Stott, *Christian Mission* (1975), 100–107.

> But to call socio-political liberation "salvation" and to call social activism "evangelism"—this is to be guilty of a gross theological confusion. It is to mix what Scripture keeps distinct—God the Creator and God the Redeemer, the God of the cosmos and the God of the covenant, the world and the church, common grace and saving grace, justice and justification, the reformation of society and the regeneration of men. For the salvation offered in the gospel of Christ concerns persons rather than structures.[32]

Stott later qualifies this by adding an eschatological perspective: "One day both body and society will be redeemed."[33] His position might have been clearer if he had expanded on this eschatological perspective. Social justice is part of the gospel promises, but this aspect of salvation is eschatological. Only with the second coming of Christ will justice reign on the earth. The same distinction could be made of physical health: we are promised healing in the gospel (as the prosperity gospel rightly emphasizes), but this is guaranteed only with the redemption of our bodies in the new creation (which the prosperity gospel refuses to recognize, with disastrous pastoral consequences). Commenting on Stott's presentation, Wright suggests that we should divide up salvation not in terms of its content, which is consistently broad and rich, but in terms of its *timing*, recognizing that some aspects of salvation are not promised to us now,[34] something Stott does elsewhere.[35]

Stott ends with a defense of personal conversion to Christ. He warns evangelicals against trying to win converts by muting the call to repentance or making that call so vague that it requires no specific changes of behavior. Here Stott finds common cause with the Bangkok Report's claim that "personal conversion leads to social action."[36] "Conversion," comments Stott, "must not take the convert out of the world but rather send him back into it, the same person in the same world, and yet a new person with new convictions and new standards."[37]

Here again, though, Stott finds ecumenical missiology deficient. The call for conversion has been muted (1) by syncretism, which believes no one need switch religion, since no religion can claim ultimate finality, and (2) by universalism, which claims no one need switch religion, since ev-

[32] Stott, *Christian Mission* (1975), 94.
[33] Stott, *Christian Mission* (1975), 94.
[34] Wright, in Stott with Wright, *Christian Mission* (2015), 168.
[35] John Stott, *Understanding the Bible* (London: Scripture Union, 1972), 15–17.
[36] Stott, *Christian Mission* (1975), 119–20.
[37] Stott, *Christian Mission* (1975), 120.

eryone will be saved.[38] Elsewhere Stott expands on the need to call people from other religions, or none, to follow Christ.

> If it is God's desire that everybody acknowledge Jesus, it must be our desire as well. Hindus speak of "the Lord Krishna" and Buddhists of "the Lord Buddha," but we cannot accept these claims. Only Jesus is Lord. He has no rivals. There is no greater incentive to world mission than the lordship of Jesus Christ. Mission is neither an impertinent interference in other people's private lives, nor a dispensable option which may be rejected, but an unavoidable deduction from the universal lordship of Jesus Christ.[39]

In *The Contemporary Christian*, Stott argues that, as the title of chapter 19 puts it, "our God is a missionary God." Stott traces the missionary import of five key sections of the Bible: the Old Testament, the Gospels, the book of Acts, the Letters, and the book of Revelation. His section on the Old Testament is notably brief. It would take Christopher Wright, director of the Langham Partnership, one of the key organizations that Stott established, to fill out our appreciation of the missiological importance of the Old Testament.[40] Nevertheless, the key themes are present. Stott concludes:

> So the religion of the Bible is a missionary religion. The evidence is overwhelming, irrefutable. Mission cannot be regarded as a regrettable deviation from religious toleration, or as the hobby of a few eccentric enthusiasts. On the contrary, it arises from the heart of God himself, and is communicated from his heart to ours. Mission is the global outreach of the global people of a global God.[41]

Stott never lost his passion for proclaiming Christ. Wright describes visiting him in the care home where, increasingly infirm, he spent the final four years of his life. "His face lit up," says Wright, "as he told me how he had shared the way of salvation with one of the staff in response to a

---

[38] Stott expressed similar concerns before the sixth assembly of the WCC in 1983, in John Stott, "Jesus Christ, the Life of the World," *Churchman* 97, no. 1 (1983): 6–15.

[39] John Stott, *The Contemporary Christian: An Urgent Plea for Double Listening* (Leicester: Inter-Varsity Press, 1992), 98.

[40] Wright, in Stott with Wright, *Christian Mission* (2015), 35–41; Wright, *The Mission of God: Unlocking the Bible's Grand Narrative* (Nottingham: Inter-Varsity Press, 2006); and Wright, *The Mission of God's People: A Biblical Theology of the Church's Mission* (Grand Rapids, MI: Zondervan, 2010).

[41] Stott, *The Contemporary Christian*, 335; see also Stott, "The Bible in World Evangelization" and "The Living God Is a Missionary God," in *Perspectives on the World Christian Movement: A Reader*, ed. Ralph D. Winter and Steven C. Hawthorne (Pasadena, CA: William Carey Library, 1981), 3–9, 10–18.

question, as she wheeled him back from the dining room to his own small apartment."[42] Having surveyed the centrality of mission throughout the Bible in *The Contemporary Christian*, Stott concludes:

> Do we profess to believe in God? He's a missionary God. Do we say we are committed to Christ? He's a missionary Christ. Do we claim to be filled with the Spirit? He's a missionary Spirit. Do we delight in belonging to the church? It's a missionary society. Do we hope to go to heaven when we die? It's a heaven filled with the fruits of the missionary enterprise. . . . The authentic Christianity of the Bible is not a safe, smug, cosy, selfish, escapist little religion. On the contrary, it is deeply disturbing to our sheltered security. It is an explosive, centrifugal force, which pulls us out from our narrow self-centredness and flings us into God's world to witness and to serve.[43]

[42] Wright, in Stott with Wright, *Christian Mission* (2015), 79.
[43] Stott, *The Contemporary Christian*, 335; see also Stott, *The Incomparable Christ*, 16.

CHAPTER 9

LOVING A NEEDY WORLD

Evangelicals in the nineteenth century had a fine record of social involvement. William Wilberforce and John Newton campaigned against slavery. George Muller and Charles Spurgeon established orphanages in Bristol and London respectively. William Carey, the pioneer missionary to India, did a bit of everything: he campaigned for women's rights and the humane treatment of lepers, started savings banks to combat loan sharks, founded schools for both boys and girls from all castes, pioneered lending libraries, introduced new systems of gardening, reformed agriculture, and published the classics of Indian literature.[1]

But for various reasons, evangelicals lost their social conscience over the first two-thirds of the twentieth century. A growing welfare system created the impression that the care of the needy could be left to the state. The "social gospel," a movement in the early twentieth century that redefined the church's task as building the kingdom of God predominantly within history, meant social action became tainted by association. Perhaps most significantly, liberal theology put evangelicals on the back foot, turning them into a beleaguered minority within the wider church. As a result, it felt easier to hunker down in a ghetto than to get out into the big, bad world with an agenda for reform. The historian Timothy Smith called this retreat "the great reversal."[2] Evangelical Christians, once in the vanguard of social reform, had shifted into reverse and retreated from the world.

---

1 Ruth and Vishal Mangalwadi, *Carey, Christ and Cultural Transformation: The Life and Influence of William Carey* (Carlisle: OM, 1993), 1–8.

2 David O. Moberg, *The Great Reversal: Reconciling Evangelism and Social Concern*, 2nd ed. (Eugene, OR: Wipf & Stock, 2006), 11.

Things began to change in the second half of the twentieth century—evangelicals began to reverse the great reversal.[3] Social engagement was a concern of the "new evangelicals." Carl Henry, their leading spokesman, published *The Uneasy Conscience of Modern Fundamentalism*, which, in an allusion to the parable of Good Samaritan, described fundamentalism as "the modern priest and Levite, bypassing suffering humanity."[4] In 1966 a thousand evangelicals met in Berlin for a congress on world evangelization.[5] Although the official focus was on evangelism, a significant minority maintained that evangelism would be effective only if accompanied by social action. The condemnation of racism in the final declaration was unprecedented.

Social action was also on the agenda of the first National Evangelical Anglican Congress in Keele in 1967. "We believe that our evangelical doctrines have important ethical implications," the final report said, and "evangelism and compassionate service belong together in the mission of God." Michael Saward sees Keele as the turning point in evangelical social responsibility in Britain.[6] The following year George Hoffman joined the UK Evangelical Alliance as a part-time assistant to its general secretary, Morgan Derham. On Hoffman's arrival, Derham handed him a number of files and told him to make what he could of them. One of them, which bore the rather odd name "EAR Fund" (Evangelical Alliance Relief Fund), contained details of small amounts of money received and paid out for work among refugees. Within three years Hoffman had dropped all his other responsibilities to concentrate on the fund, now called Tearfund. Today, Tearfund is one of Britain's largest development charities and has a prominent place in the life of British evangelicalism.[7] Then in 1971, Britain witnessed the Nationwide Festival of Light, which aimed to make "a positive stand for purity, love and family life" in an increasingly permissive culture.[8] Although not exclusively evangelical, the majority of its supporters were from the evangelical constituency.

A common factor behind this evangelical reengagement in social issues was the involvement of John Stott. He aligned himself with the new

[3] See Tim Chester, *Awakening to a World of Need: The Recovery of Evangelical Social Concern* (Leicester: Inter-Varsity Press, 1993).
[4] Carl F. H. Henry, *The Uneasy Conscience of Modern Fundamentalism* (Grand Rapids, MI: Eerdmans, 1947), 17.
[5] See Chester, *Awakening to a World of Need*, 27–30.
[6] Michael Saward, *The Anglican Church Today: Evangelicals on the Move* (Oxford: Mowbray, 1987), 63.
[7] See Chester, *Awakening to a World of Need*, 41–43.
[8] John Capon, *And There Was Light: The Story of the Nationwide Festival of Light* (London: Lutterworth, 1972).

evangelicals and cooperated with Carl Henry and Billy Graham to organize the Berlin Congress, where he was also one of the main speakers. He chaired the organizing committee of the Keele Congress and drafted its final declaration. He became president of Tearfund and was on the Festival of Light's council of reference. "John Stott," says Kenneth Hylson-Smith, "was foremost in demonstrating the evangelical concern to remain loyal to the revelation of God and yet relevant to the needs of and demands of the modern world."[9]

The Case for Social Involvement

Stott made the case for Christian social involvement repeatedly through his ministry. In *The Contemporary Christian* he identifies three main arguments. The first is the character of God.

> The God of the biblical revelation, being both Creator and Redeemer, is a God who cares about the total well-being (spiritual and material) of all the human beings he has made. . . . God cares for the poor and the hungry, the alien, the widow and the orphan. He denounces oppression and tyranny, and calls for justice. He tells his people to be the voice of the voiceless and the defender of the powerless, and so to express their love for them.[10]

Stott then shows how these characteristics are reflected in both the Law and the Prophets. God's people are commanded to care for the poor, and the prophets hold them to this obligation. It is not just that the commandments of the Mosaic law commend justice and care; they are explicitly presented as the way in which God's people will "walk in all his ways." The people are to do justice because God himself "executes justice for the fatherless and the widow, and loves the sojourner, giving him food and clothing" (Deut. 10:12–20).

Stott's second reason for social involvement is the ministry and teaching of Jesus. "There can be no question that words and works went together in his public ministry. . . . His words explained his works, and his works dramatized his words."[11] Stott particularly highlights the emotions of

[9] Kenneth Hylson-Smith, *Evangelicals in the Church of England 1734–1984* (Edinburgh: T&T Clark, 1989), 320.
[10] John Stott, *The Contemporary Christian: An Urgent Plea for Double Listening* (Leicester: Inter-Varsity Press, 1992), 343.
[11] Stott, *The Contemporary Christian*, 345.

Jesus. If we are to be Christlike, we too should feel anger at injustice and compassion for its victims.[12]

Stott compares the parables of the prodigal son and the good Samaritan. Although both involve victims, the prodigal is a victim of his own sin, while the man whom the Samaritan meets is the victim of other people's sin. Both involve rescues that are acts of love. Each includes a sub-plot in which the alternative to obedience is exemplified. Stott concludes:

> Thus each parable emphasizes a vital aspect of Christian discipleship—its beginning when like the prodigal son we come home for salvation, and its continuing when like the good Samaritan we go out in mission. Each of us resembles the prodigal; each of us *should* resemble the Samaritan. First we face our own sins, and then we face the world's sufferings. First we come in and receive mercy, and then we go out and show mercy. Mercy cannot be shown until it has been received; but once it has been received it must be shown to others. Let us not divorce what Christ has married. We have all been prodigals; God wants us all to be Samaritans too.[13]

Third, Stott argues for Christian social action because it assists "the communication of the gospel."[14] "To begin with, [the gospel] must be verbalized." Christians cannot give up on words. "There is a precision in verbal communication, whether the words are spoken or written, which is absent from all other media."[15] Nevertheless, it is also true that "we cannot announce God's love with credibility unless we also exhibit it in action. So we cannot stand aloof from those to whom we speak the gospel, or ignore their situation, their context."[16]

In *Issues Facing Christians Today*, Stott structures his argument in a slightly different way. He speaks, first, of "a fuller doctrine of God" in which we recognize that God is not confined to the religious dimensions of life or concerned only with his covenant people. Citing prophetic oracles against the nations, Stott comments, "It is clear from these Old Testament passages that God hates injustice and oppression *everywhere*, and that he loves and promotes justice *everywhere*."[17]

---

12 Stott, *The Contemporary Christian*, 347.
13 Stott, *The Contemporary Christian*, 347.
14 Stott, *The Contemporary Christian*, 348.
15 Stott, *The Contemporary Christian*, 348–49.
16 Stott, *The Contemporary Christian*, 349.
17 John Stott, *Issues Facing Christians Today*, 2nd ed. (London: Marshall Pickering, 1990), 17.

Second, Stott speaks of "a fuller doctrine of human beings." It is the image of God, marred but remaining, in all human beings which "accounts for their unique worth and which has always inspired Christian philanthropy."[18]

Third, Stott calls for "a fuller doctrine of Christ." Here, as in *The Contemporary Christian*, he refers to the model given to us in Christ's incarnation and ministry. "Jesus of Nazareth was moved with compassion by the sight of needy human beings, whether sick or bereaved, hungry, harassed or helpless; should not his people's compassion be aroused by the same sights?"[19]

Fourth, Stott talks of "a fuller doctrine of salvation." "We must not separate Jesus the Saviour," he says, "from Jesus the Lord." He draws on the Reformation emphasis on love and faith belonging together. "Although justification is by faith alone, this faith cannot remain alone. If it is living and authentic, it will inevitably issue in good works."[20]

Finally, Stott speaks of "a fuller doctrine of the Church." Here he refers to a common theme in his teaching on the church: the need for holy worldliness—that is, a godly involvement in the world for the world.

The Lausanne Covenant

In August 1960, Billy Graham and Carl Henry met, along with other evangelical leaders, in Switzerland to discuss the possibility of bringing evangelicals from across the world together for "fellowship, study and challenge." Nothing happened immediately, but in early 1964, Graham telephoned Henry in Washington. Graham was about to take a taxi from the White House to the airport. Could he pick Henry up in order to talk with him? In the back of the taxi Graham again shared his vision of an international congress on evangelism.[21] So it was that the vision for the Berlin Congress was born. On October 25, 1966, more than a thousand evangelicals gathered in Berlin under the title "One Race, One Gospel, One Task."

Although it was a congress on evangelism, there were signs that social involvement was creeping up the evangelical agenda. The closing statement included a condemnation of racism and confessed the failure to love

18 Stott, *Issues Facing Christians Today*, 18.
19 Stott, *Issues Facing Christians Today*, 22.
20 Stott, *Issues Facing Christians Today*, 23.
21 The story is told by Carl Henry in *Confessions of a Theologian: An Autobiography* (Waco, TX: Word, 1986), 252.

with "a love that transcends every human barrier and prejudice." In particular, it was becoming clear that many felt that the task of evangelizing the world could not be adequately met without also facing the issue of social involvement. John Stott, one of the main speakers, spoke of the need to identify with people and to demonstrate God's love to them. We must, he argued, "win the right to share with them the good news of Christ."[22] Nevertheless, the financial backers of the congress ensured that social action did not feature greatly on the official agenda, despite the wishes of Henry. Instead, the spirit of the congress was typified by a thirty-foot-high population clock that clocked up a 1,764,216 increase in the world's population during the congress. The goal of the congress "was nothing short of the evangelization of the human race in this generation," and it viewed this task with an almost apocalyptic urgency.

Stott himself said our task is "not to reform society, but to preach the gospel."[23] But his views were changing. Looking back on what he had said at Berlin, he would later comment, "I now consider that I was unbalanced to assert that the risen Lord's commission was entirely evangelistic, not social."[24] In a 1989 interview with *World Christian*, he expands on this further. "Gradually, and I don't think it was through anybody's particular influence but through my own reflection on the New Testament, I came to see that this view was very narrow and unbiblical."[25]

In 1962, Stott had visited Africa for a second time, leading university missions across the continent, and in the summer of 1963 he was in Asia. Many further visits around the Global South followed over the years. Stott's visits were significant for an emerging generation of evangelical leaders, offering a model of intellectually robust and evangelistically oriented expository ministry. But these visits were also formative in Stott's own development. "In the early 1960s," said Stott in the *World Christian* interview, "I began to travel in the Third World, and I saw poverty in Latin America, Africa, and Asia as I had not seen it before." It became clear to him, he said, that mission could not ignore social needs.[26]

---

[22] John Stott, "The Great Commission (John 20:19–23)," in *One Race, One Gospel, One Task: The World Congress on Evangelism, Berlin 1966*, ed. C. F. H. Henry and W. Stanley Mooneyham, vol. 1 (Minneapolis: World Wide Publications, 1967), 41.

[23] John Stott, "The Great Commission (Luke 24:44–49)," in Henry and Mooneyham, *One Race, One Gospel, One Task*, 50.

[24] John Stott, memorandum to Timothy Dudley-Smith, May 12, 1997, cited in Dudley-Smith, *John Stott*, vol. 2, *A Global Ministry* (Leicester: Inter-Varsity Press, 2001), 123.

[25] John Stott, "Learning to Fly Kites: World Christian Interviews John Stott," *World Christian*, October 1989, cited in Dudley-Smith, *John Stott*, 2:127.

[26] Stott, "Learning to Fly Kites," cited in Dudley-Smith, *John Stott*, 2:127.

Berlin was followed by a series of regional conferences. At the last of these, the 1971 European Congress on Evangelism, Stott again argued that the Spirit of God can use the non-verbal witness of the Christian community to communicate the gospel. Christians, he said, need to communicate the love of God in actions even if this then needs to be interpreted by words.

But it was the Lausanne Congress and its covenant that marked the major turning point in evangelical attitudes toward social action. And Stott was very much at the fore of this movement. Conferences are not always as significant at the grassroots level as the organizers and participants like to think. More often they are signs of changes already underway. The Lausanne Congress was certainly such a sign—the clearest indication yet that social action was being accepted as a legitimate concern among evangelicals. Yet it was also an exception to the rule, for it in turn was a significant influence on the thinking of others. No previous conference could have claimed to speak for evangelicals in such a way, and it spoke in favor of social action, providing "international sanction for evangelical social commitment."[27] For many, it was a challenge to rethink their position; for others, it gave them confidence in their convictions.

The Lausanne Congress met in July 1974. If the Berlin Congress met during the heady optimism of the 1960s, the Lausanne gathered during more troubled times. The United States was in the midst of its greatest political crisis in years, with President Nixon resigning just two weeks after the end of the congress. In September and October 1973, the Organization of Petroleum Exporting Countries (OPEC) raised the price of oil by 70 percent. Dominated as it was by Middle Eastern countries, OPEC also used the price of oil as a political weapon against Western support of Israel in the war of October 1973. This led to a further 130 percent rise in December. The oil crisis severely affected economies throughout the world. Meanwhile, many of the radicals of the 1960s were turning their attention to environmental issues, highlighting for the first time the ecological problems facing the planet. And the needs of the poor were as great as ever. During the year before the Lausanne Congress, twenty million people had faced starvation in India as a result of drought—a fact made immediate in Western homes as never before via the growing medium of television.

[27] D. W. Bebbington, *Evangelicalism in Modern Britain: A History from the 1730s to the 1980s* (London: Unwin Hyman, 1989), 266.

Thus it was that Lausanne met in a more somber atmosphere. There was a realism about the needs of the world and about what could be achieved as a result of the congress. There was perhaps also less triumphalism. Stott told the conference, "I hope in my paper to strike a note of evangelical repentance, and indeed I hope we shall continue to hear this note throughout the Congress."[28] Those professing to live under the authority of Scripture, he explained, have very often been selective in their submission to what it teaches, and their traditions have often owed more to culture than to Scripture.

It was the younger Global South theologians René Padilla and Samuel Escobar who really "set the cat among the pigeons," according to Stott,[29] by placing the issue of social action and its relationship to the gospel at the center of congress discussion. Stott was friends with Padilla, then the IFES associate general secretary for Latin America, having traveled on two visits to the Continent with Padilla acting as his translator (Stott had even managed to convert Padilla to ornithology). At the heart of Padilla's and Escobar's concern was the fear that the congress would endorse an evangelistic strategy in which, for the sake of numerical success, the claims of the gospel would be replaced by a gospel of "cheap grace." They firmly maintained that any true proclamation of the gospel must include the call to repentance in its social as well as individual dimensions. Escobar said:

> The temptation for evangelicals today is to reduce the Gospel, to mutilate it, to eliminate any demands for the fruit of repentance and any aspect that would make it unpalatable. . . . [The church] must stress the need for the whole Gospel of Jesus Christ as Savior and Lord whose demands cannot be cheapened. No eagerness for the quantitative growth of the church should render us silent about the whole counsel of God.[30]

What emerged from the contributions of Padilla and Escobar was not simply a concern that social action should be given a place alongside evangelism. Rather, the issue as they saw it was whether repentance in all its facets was to have a primary place in evangelism. Their protest was against an easy gospel or cheap grace that was prepared to sacrifice the kind of

---

[28] John Stott, "The Biblical Basis of Evangelism," in *Let the Earth Hear His Voice*, ed. J. D. Douglas (Minneapolis: World Wide Publications, 1975), 65.
[29] John Stott, "The Significance of Lausanne," *International Review of Mission* 64, no. 255 (1975): 289.
[30] Samuel Escobar, "Evangelism and Man's Search for Freedom, Justice and Fulfilment," in Douglas, *Let the Earth Hear His Voice*, 310.

discipleship demanded by the cross for the sake of numerical results. The need, they believed, was for the church to be faithful to the ethical demands of the gospel, in particular in its social dimensions. The affluence of the West in contrast to the poverty of the Global South, coupled with a culturally conditioned view of the gospel, threatened to undermine the very cause their detractors sought to espouse—the evangelization of the world. The issue was not simply whether social action was part of mission but whether the church would proclaim a gospel that included the call to repent and to produce the fruit of good works, particularly action against poverty, racism, and injustice. At Lausanne, Padilla concluded: "The future of the church does not depend on our ability to persuade people to give intellectual assent to a truncated gospel but on our faithfulness to the full gospel of our Lord Jesus Christ."[31]

Instead of such fears being realized, Lausanne in fact proved significant for its note of repentance and its endorsement of social action. Under the chairmanship of John Stott, the drafting committee of the congress's covenant strengthened its position on social involvement as the congress developed. The term "social action" was replaced by "socio-political involvement," and a call to denounce injustice was added. These changes made it clear that the covenant was affirming not only social care or philanthropy but also social reform. Paragraph 5 of the Lausanne Covenant on "Christian Social Responsibility" is worth reading in full to understand Stott's thinking, not only because he was the primary drafter of the declaration but also because he often referred to it subsequently as a marker for evangelical social involvement:

> We affirm that God is both the Creator and the Judge of all men. We therefore should share his concern for justice and reconciliation throughout human society and for the liberation of men from every kind of oppression. Because mankind is made in the image of God, every person, regardless of race, religion, colour, culture, class, sex, or age, has an intrinsic dignity because of which he should be respected and served, not exploited. Here too we express penitence both for our neglect and for having sometimes regarded evangelism and social concern as mutually exclusive. Although reconciliation with man is not reconciliation with God, nor is social action evangelism, nor is political liberation salvation, nevertheless we affirm that evangelism and socio-political involvement

31 C. René Padilla, *Mission between the Times* (Grand Rapids, MI: Eerdmans, 1985), 37.

> are both part of our Christian duty. For both are necessary expressions of our doctrine of God and man, our love for our neighbour and our obedience to Jesus Christ. The message of salvation implies also a message of judgment upon every form of alienation, oppression and discrimination, and we should not be afraid to denounce evil and injustice wherever they exist. When people receive Christ they are born again into his kingdom and must seek not only to exhibit but also to spread its righteousness in the midst of an unrighteous world. The salvation we claim should be transforming us in the totality of our personal and social responsibilities. Faith without works is dead.[32]

The covenant has had a tremendous impact. As Padilla puts it, "Social involvement had finally been granted full citizenship in evangelical missiology."[33] With Lausanne, evangelical social concern became official. The congress has been variously described as "a turning point in evangelical thinking" (both Athol Gill and John Stott), "a definitive step" (René Padilla), "a watershed" (both Edward Dayton and coauthors Vinay Samuel and Chris Sugden), and "a catalyst for a whole movement" (Vinay Samuel and Chris Sugden).[34] Chris Wright captures the post-Lausanne mood among many younger evangelicals:

> Those were the days of exciting ferment in the wake of the Lausanne Congress of 1974. Younger evangelical like myself were keen to see a re-engagement of our biblical faith with the surrounding culture in all its social, economic and political dimensions. John Stott was our hero in that flush of activity.[35]

After the congress, a Continuation Committee was formed. The issue of social action was center stage at its first meeting in Mexico City. On the first evening, Billy Graham described how the letters he had received were divided between those who wanted the Lausanne movement to have a broad vision that reflected its covenant (in other words, to in-

[32] The Lausanne Covenant is printed in John Stott, *Explaining the Lausanne Covenant* (Lausanne Occasional Papers, 1975); Douglas, *Let the Earth Hear His Voice*, 3–9; *Christianity Today* 18, no. 22 (1974): 22–24; *International Review of Mission* 63, no. 252 (1974): 579–74; Arthur Johnston, *The Battle for World Evangelism* (Wheaton, IL: Tyndale, 1978), 369–78; Chris Sugden, *Radical Discipleship* (London: Marshall, Morgan and Scott, 1981), 176–84; C. René Padilla and Chris Sugden, eds., *Texts on Evangelical Social Ethics 1974–1983* (Nottingham: Grove, 1985), 5–7; and John Stott, ed., *Making Christ Known: Historic Missions Documents from the Lausanne Movement, 1974–1989* (Carlisle: Paternoster/LCWE, 1996), 1–55.
[33] C. René Padilla, "How Evangelicals Endorsed Social Responsibility," *Transformation* 2, no. 3 (1985): 29.
[34] Chester, *Awakening to a World of Need*, 76.
[35] Chris Wright, in *John Stott: A Portrait by His Friends*, ed. Chris Wright (Nottingham: Inter-Varsity Press, 2011), 144.

clude social action) and those who wanted a narrow focus on evangelism alone. He declared himself in favor of a narrow objective. The following morning Stott took upon himself the "unenviable task" of disagreeing with Billy Graham,[36] arguing that anything other than a broad purview would be a betrayal of the Lausanne Covenant. In addition to his own convictions, he was aware that the Global South delegates (who were already underrepresented) would feel diffident about defying the esteemed Dr. Graham. This public rebuttal provoked tearful accusations of a power grab, accusations that in turn produced tears in Stott. A heated debate followed, and in the end the broad vision was accepted with an affirmation of the priority of evangelism.

Social Action and the Kingdom of God

For some, though, the Lausanne Covenant did not go far enough. On the Sunday night of the congress, around two hundred participants met together. They agreed that a small group should draw up a response to Lausanne, which the group entitled "Theology and Implications of Radical Discipleship."[37] This statement, largely made up of quotations from various congress papers, went significantly further than the first drafts of the Lausanne Covenant. The Christian community, the response stated, must make known this gospel not only through proclamation but also through its life as the new society, through the prophetic denouncement of evil, through the pursuit of justice, and through the care of creation. While affirming that salvation is by grace alone, they emphasized the need for radical repentance in every area of a person's life. The statement, eventually signed by over five hundred people, also confessed that often evangelicals have confused the gospel with a particular culture and have failed properly to proclaim the gospel, to emphasize repentance, and to seek justice.

Stott tried to persuade a delegation of their leaders, led by John Howard Yoder, that their concerns could be, and indeed were being, expressed within the covenant itself. He urged them at least not to style it as an "alternative covenant," but to produce a statement that could be included in the "compendium" of the congress. The leaders agreed, but later that night one of them came to Stott in "considerable distress," because it was proving

36 John Stott, cited in Dudley-Smith, *John Stott*, 2:221.
37 The statement on radical discipleship is printed in Douglas, *Let the Earth Hear His Voice*, 1294–96; *International Review of Mission* 63, no. 252 (1974): 574–76; Sugden, *Radical Discipleship*, 173–76; and Padilla and Sugden, *Texts an Evangelical Social Ethics*, 7–11.

impossible to "sell" the idea to the "rank and file." So Stott himself went immediately and spoke with the wider group for over an hour.

> They were very grateful with the revised official document and with the Planning Committee's willingness to include the report in the compendium, and they agreed to withdraw their document as an alternative Covenant, but they still wanted to issue a statement which they believed would add important emphases.

Stott received confirmation of their intent minutes before he was due to present the official covenant to the congress—too late to consult the planning group. "I then had a very difficult decision to make," Stott wrote later. He felt "the only way to take the heat out of the situation" was publicly to welcome the statement on radical discipleship as an addendum to the Lausanne Covenant. He also said he himself would be the first to sign it. He recognized this was a big risk on his part but added, in hindsight, "I believe and hope that this had the desired effect in that the Congress ended in unity nor division, and certainly the radical groups were happy and did not feel that they had been supressed."[38] Commenting on it yet later, Stott says: "I felt so much in sympathy . . . and in agreement with what they were saying that I begged them not to produce an alternative. . . . I didn't want there to be an unnecessary polarization."[39]

The "Theology and Implications of Radical Discipleship" statement at Lausanne had made the kingdom of God central to social action. This inclined Christian social action toward radical change (shaped by the radical transformation of the coming kingdom), as opposed to a focus on the doctrine of creation, which created a more politically conservative approach (oriented toward the preservation of the created order). The "Radical Discipleship" statement defined the gospel as "Good News of liberation, of restoration, of wholeness, and of salvation that is personal, social, global and cosmic." This made social change not only part of mission but part of the gospel. This factor above all others distinguishes the social thinking of the radical evangelicals from that of the evangelical social activists of the nineteenth century.

If the Lausanne Covenant made social action "official" within evangelicalism, it was Ron Sider's 1977 book *Rich Christians in an Age of Hun-*

---

[38] John Stott, letter to Paul Little, August 13, 1974, Church of England Record Centre, STOTT/4/2/4/1/3.
[39] John Stott, interview by Tim Chester, November 26, 1992.

ger that brought it to popular attention. Two years before its publication, Sider had published an article that was later republished in booklet form as *Evangelism, Salvation and Social Justice*, with a response by John Stott.[40] The debate between them was not whether evangelicals should be involved in social action, for they were both happy to affirm that. Instead it concerned the theological basis for social action and the extent of the kingdom prior to the return of Christ.

In *Evangelism, Salvation and Social Justice*, Sider wrote, "The kingdom comes wherever Jesus overcomes the power of evil. That happens most visibly in the church. But it also happens in society at large because Jesus is Lord of the world as well as the church."[41] This argument has proved influential,[42] although Sider himself later distanced himself from it.[43] In response, Stott insisted that the kingdom of God in the New Testament is always centered on Christ: "It may be said to exist only where Jesus Christ is consciously acknowledged as Lord."[44] Still, Stott added, the righteous standards of the kingdom "will spill over into the world."[45]

Social Action and Evangelism

In contrast to those who thought Lausanne had not gone far enough, some believed it had gone far too far. The most notable critic was Arthur P. Johnston, professor of mission at Trinity Evangelical Divinity School, Deerfield, Illinois. Initially Johnston welcomed Lausanne, comparing it favorably with Edinburgh 1910, the first great ecumenical missionary conference.[46]

In 1978, however, he published *The Battle for World Evangelism*. The book charts the developments within the WCC and evangelicalism. The clear implication is that, by including social action within mission,

---

40 Ronald J. Sider, with a response by John R. W. Stott, *Evangelism, Salvation and Social Justice* (Nottingham: Grove, 1977). Sider's article was published separately under the same title in the *International Review of Mission* 64, no. 255 (1975): 251–67, and the *Evangelical Review of Theology* 2, no. 1 (April 1970): 70–88.

41 Sider and Stott, *Evangelism, Salvation and Social Justice*, 9.

42 See Vinay Samuel and Chris Sugden, "Evangelism and Social Responsibility—A Biblical Study in Priorities," in *In Word and Deed: Evangelism and Social Responsibility*, ed. Bruce Nicholls (Exeter: Paternoster, 1985), 210; and Samuel and Sugden, "God's Intention for the World," in *The Church in Response to Human Need*, ed. Vinay Samuel and Chris Sugden (Oxford: Regnum, 1987), 154.

43 In Ronald Sider and James Parker, "How Broad Is Salvation in Scripture?," in Nicholls, *In Word and Deed*, 104, esp. note 32, Sider acknowledged that none of the references to the kingdom in the New Testament speak of its presence outside the confession of Christ. See Tim Chester, *Mission and the Coming of God: Eschatology, the Trinity and Mission in the Theology of Jürgen Moltmann and Contemporary Evangelicalism* (Carlisle: Paternoster, 2006), 136–40.

44 Sider and Stott, *Evangelism, Salvation and Social Justice*, 23.

45 Sider and Stott, *Evangelism, Salvation and Social Justice*, 23. A similar phrase is used in *The Grand Rapids Report: Evangelism and Social Responsibility*, which Stott drafted (Exeter: Paternoster, 1982), 34.

46 Arthur P. Johnston, "The Unanswered Prayer of Edinburgh," *Christianity Today* 19, no. 4 (1974): 10–14.

evangelicalism is in danger of heading in the same direction as the WCC. Although Johnston did not necessarily oppose social action itself,[47] he argued that too much emphasis on it inevitably leads to an abandonment of evangelism.[48] Johnston decried Lausanne's "holistic" view of mission. Mission, for Johnston, is evangelism and evangelism alone.[49] It was not enough, he thought, for the Lausanne Covenant to maintain that "evangelism is primary" (sec. 6); it should "have retained not only its priority and primacy, but also the unique status it held from the nineteenth century to Berlin" (that is, the 1966 Berlin Congress).[50] If sociopolitical action is included as part of mission, Johnston argued, evangelism will inevitably be edged out. Indeed, Johnston contended that Christian social action will not be possible if evangelism is not accorded this unique status, since there will be no Christians.

Johnston was particularly critical of the position taken by Stott, accusing him of having "dethroned evangelism as the only historical aim of mission."[51] As Johnston saw it, Stott was saying mission must include social action, and this Johnston could not accept. "The principle of the complete self-authentication of the word of the gospel in mission through the ministry of the Holy Spirit in evangelism," Johnston argued, "is modified by the necessity of some incarnational sociopolitical actions."[52] He also attacked Stott's acceptance of the response to Lausanne as an addendum to the covenant, accusing Stott, Padilla, and Escobar of supporting an unrepresentative and "ecumenical theology of evangelism."[53]

Christianity Today allowed Stott to write an open letter in reply to Johnston's criticism.[54] In it Stott points out that the distinction between evangelism and social action is often artificial. The words and works of Jesus "belonged indissolubly to one another," the works making the words visible. In this way service cannot only precede and follow evangelism, as Johnston acknowledges, but must also be in partnership with evangelism. Individual Christians may have specialist ministries, but "the Christian

47 Johnston, *The Battle for World Evangelism*, 55, 68, 138.
48 Johnston, *The Battle for World Evangelism*, 19.
49 Johnston, *The Battle for World Evangelism*, 18.
50 Johnston, *The Battle for World Evangelism*, 329.
51 Johnston, *The Battle for World Evangelism*, 302–3.
52 Johnston, *The Battle for World Evangelism*, 303.
53 Johnston, *The Battle for World Evangelism*, 331.
54 John Stott, "The Battle for World Evangelism: An Open Response to Arthur Johnston," *Christianity Today* 23, no. 7 (1979): 34–35. See also Stott, "The Biblical Scope of the Christian Mission," *Christianity Today* 24, no. 1 (1980): 34–35.

community as a whole should not have to choose, any more than Jesus did." He agrees with Johnston that the gospel is self-authenticating, but asks, "Does not the gospel lack credibility whenever Christians contradict it by their lives?" Citing 1 John 3:17, Stott concludes by claiming that, rather than dethroning evangelism as the only historical aim of mission, he has sought to "enthrone love as the essential historical motivation for mission."

Stott defines mission as "everything the church is sent into the world to do," including "Christian service in the world comprising both evangelism and social action."[55] In *The Contemporary Christian* he recognizes that some evangelicals believe this broad definition of mission will deflect missionaries from their priority tasks of evangelizing, discipling, and church planting. Noting that "mission" is not a biblical term, and sharing the concern that people should not be deflected from evangelism, Stott nevertheless insists that what Christ sends his people into the world to do "cannot be limited to proclamation evangelism, even though . . . this has primacy in the church. . . . We are sent into the world both to witness and to serve."[56] This conviction is based on the model of Christ. "His sending us into the world is like his Father's sending him into the world [John 17:18; 20:21]. If words and works went together in his ministry, they should also in ours."[57] As for the danger of missionaries being sidetracked, Stott says, "The best way to avoid this, in my view, is not to deny that 'mission' is broader than evangelism, but rather to insist that each 'missionary' must be true to his or her particular calling."[58]

Stott also wrote a private letter to Johnston suggesting that they meet face-to-face to discuss the issues further. He hoped that the Lausanne Committee for World Evangelization (LCWE) would organize a consultation to look specifically at the relationship between evangelism and social responsibility. Johnston agreed and they both served on the organizing committee. The committee invited people from across the evangelical spectrum so that the full range of views was represented. The LCWE and the World Evangelical Fellowship jointly sponsored it, although not without a measure of hesitation on the part of the LCWE. Some felt that it would only be divisive and stir up controversy. The committee also imposed certain

[55] John Stott, *Christian Mission in the Modern World* (London: Falcon, 1975), 30, 34.
[56] Stott, *The Contemporary Christian*, 342.
[57] Stott, *The Contemporary Christian*, 342.
[58] Stott, *The Contemporary Christian*, 342.

limits upon the gathering: the question of the primacy of evangelism, for example, would not be open to discussion.[59]

The Consultation on the Relationship between Evangelism and Social Responsibility (CRESR) met in June 1982 at Grand Rapids, Michigan.[60] The conference was potentially a very difficult one. The papers and responses to them that circulated in advance had been sharply critical of one another. "Before we met," says Stott, "I was almost in despair." He confessed to arriving at it "with a considerable degree of apprehension."[61] At times relationships were pretty tense, especially during the first day or two. In one discussion group, one of the participants accused another of advocating that other gospel which was anathema to Paul (a reference to Gal. 1:6–9). As the consultation progressed, however, the participants rejoiced at the unity and fellowship God brought to them. Bong Rim Ro and Gottfried Osei-Mensah were able to call it "a model of how Christians should approach a potentially divisive issue."[62] Stott comments, "Adjusting one's position demands a high degree of integrity and humility. Yet this is exactly what I witnessed in brothers and sisters at CRESR."[63] In fact, when most of the conference participants thought an agreed statement would be impossible, Stott went away and overnight produced the report essentially in its final form. Some who went to the consultation with an almost McCarthyite suspicion for evangelical social action had their fears dispelled.

The Grand Rapids report, *Evangelism and Social Responsibility: An Evangelical Commitment*, explains the relationship between evangelism and social responsibility in three ways: (1) social activity is the *consequence* of evangelism, indeed it is one of its aims; (2) social activity can be a *bridge* to evangelism, although it should not be a bribe; (3) social activity is the *partner* of evangelism, and the report described this partnership in terms of a marriage.[64] Social action, then, can precede, accompany, and follow evangelism.

Given this relationship, evangelism, according to the report, has priority only in two senses. First, it has a logical priority, since "Christian social

59 See Valdir Steuernagel, "Social Responsibility within the Lausanne Movement" (DTh diss., Lutheran School of Theology, Chicago, 1988), 201. Steuernagel gives a full description of the tensions within the Lausanne movement in the run-up to the Grand Rapids Consultation.

60 The Grand Rapids report was entitled *Evangelism and Social Responsibility: An Evangelical Commitment* (Exeter: Paternoster, 1982), and the conference papers were published in Nicholls, *In Word and Deed*. I cite it hereafter as "The Grand Rapids Report."

61 John Stott, interview by Tim Chester, November 26, 1992; and John Stott, "Seeking Theological Agreement," *Transformation* 1, no. 1 (1984): 22.

62 Preface to Nicholls, *In Word and Deed*, 7.

63 Stott, "Seeking Theological Agreement," 22.

64 The Grand Rapids Report, 21–24.

responsibility presupposes socially responsible Christians."[65] This, however, need not imply a temporal priority. Second, evangelism has a priority stemming from the unique nature of the gospel, for it "relates to people's eternal destiny, and in bringing them Good News of salvation Christians are doing what nobody else can do."[66] The report goes on to conclude that, in reality, the choice is largely conceptual. In practice the ministry of Jesus, in which the two were inseparable, is to be our model.[67] "It is the churches," the report concludes, "which visibly demonstrate the righteousness and peace of the kingdom which will make the greatest evangelistic and social impact on the world."[68]

In fact, at points the report seems to go further. It says that "evangelism and social responsibility, while distinct from one another, are integrally related in our proclamation of and obedience to the gospel."[69] It also speaks of both evangelism and service as forms of witness to Christ: "To give food to the hungry (social responsibility) has evangelistic implications, since good works of love, if done in the name of Christ, are a demonstration and commendation of the gospel."[70]

The Second Lausanne Congress was held in Manila in 1989. Stott was again the drafter of its final statement, which includes the following:

> While we acknowledge the diversity of spiritual gifts, callings and contexts, we also affirm that good news and good works are inseparable. It has been said, therefore, that evangelism, even when it does not have a primarily social intention, nevertheless has a social dimension, while social responsibility, even when it does not have a primarily evangelistic intention, nevertheless has an evangelistic dimension.[71]

The distinction between "dimension" and "intention" is one that Stott drew from Lesslie Newbigin. "Everything the church does has a missional dimension," comments Chris Wright, "since the church exists for the sake of God's mission, but some things the church does have specific missional intention." This reflects the breadth of the church's calling while protecting

[65] The Grand Rapids Report, 24.
[66] The Grand Rapids Report, 25.
[67] The Grand Rapids Report, 25.
[68] The Grand Rapids Report, 46.
[69] The Grand Rapids Report, 24.
[70] The Grand Rapids Report, 24, 44.
[71] "The Gospel and Social Responsibility," paragraph 4 of *The Manila Manifesto* (1989), Lausanne Movement (website), https://www.lausanne.org/content/manifesto/the-manila-manifesto.

its mission from the outcome of which Stephen Neill famously warned: that if everything is mission then nothing is mission.[72]

After the Manila Congress, Stott wrote in his diary:

> The radicals could see that the Manila Manifesto went considerably further than the Lausanne Covenant in declaring the indispensability of social action, "good works" making the "good news" visible. But conservatives were pleased too, especially (I suspect) with the strong theological statements on the human predicament and the uniqueness of Christ.[73]

The strength of the Manila Manifesto, he believed, was that it brought evangelical and social action together rather than dealing with them as separate topics.

At Lausanne, Stott had acknowledged that he had once limited the focus of mission to preaching, converting, and teaching. In his 1975 Chavasse Lectures, he says, "Today, however, I would express myself differently."[74] In part, this is because the Matthean Great Commission includes the duty of teaching people to obey all that Jesus commanded, which must include the social aspects of discipleship. But Stott goes further: "I now see more clearly that not only the consequences of the commission but the actual commission itself must be understood to include social as well as evangelistic responsibility."[75] At this point he turns to the Johannine commission: "As the Father has sent me, even so I am sending you" (John 20:21). Clearly aspects of Jesus's own sending are unique—we are not called to be saviors of the world. So, what does it mean to be sent as Jesus is sent? Stott cites Mark 10:45: "For even the Son of Man came not to be served but to serve, and to give his life as a ransom for many." The ransoming sin offering was unique to Jesus; but the service is not (as the context of Mark 10:40–45 makes clear). "Therefore our mission, like his, is to be one of service."[76] "It is in our servant role that we can find the right synthesis of evangelism and social action. For both should be for us, as they undoubtedly were for Christ, authentic expressions of the love that serves."[77]

---

[72] Chris Wright in John Stott with Christopher J. H. Wright, *Christian Mission in the Modern World*, 2nd ed. (London: Inter-Varsity Press, 2015), 46.
[73] John Stott, Travel Diary 1980, Church of England Record Centre, STOTT 6/1/18.
[74] Stott, *Christian Mission in the Modern World*, 23.
[75] Stott, *Christian Mission in the Modern World*, 23.
[76] Stott, *Christian Mission in the Modern World*, 24.
[77] Stott, *Christian Mission in the Modern World*, 24.

Social action, argues Stott, is more than a means to evangelism (merely creating opportunities to preach) and more than a manifestation of evangelism (an enacted illustration of our message). Instead, "social action is a partner of evangelism": "As partners the two belong to each other and yet are independent of each other. Each stands on its own feet in its own right alongside the other. Neither is a means to the other, or even a manifestation of the other. For each is an end in itself. Both are expressions of unfeigned love."[78] This does not mean Christians must engage in both of them all the time. Each situation requires a different emphasis, and there is a diversity of Christian callings.

Stott then takes another tack. "I venture to say that sometimes, perhaps because it was the last instruction Jesus gave us before returning to the Father, we give the Great Commission too prominent a place in our Christian thinking." He is quick to reaffirm his commitment to take the gospel to all nations. But he reminds us that this was not the only command Jesus left us; Jesus also called us to love our neighbors in fulfillment of the Old Testament law. "The Great Commission neither explains, nor exhausts, nor supersedes the Great Commandment."[79] Clearly, we cannot claim to love someone if we withhold from that person the words of life. "Equally, however, if we truly love our neighbour we shall not stop with evangelism."[80] People are not disembodied souls but embodied, social beings; so love must include a concern for their physical well-being and their sociopolitical context. Stott says: "If pressed . . . if one has to choose, eternal salvation is more important than temporal welfare. This seems to me indisputable. But I want immediately to add that one should not normally have to choose."[81] I, in turn, would add that it remains vital to keep the eternal perspective in view; otherwise proclamation all too easily ceases to be central in our mission as we become preoccupied by immediate and visible temporal needs.

Stott's focus on the Johannine commission—a consistent feature of his writing on mission[82]—is open to critique. He concedes that the other four versions of the commission (Matt. 28:19–20; Mark 16:15; Luke 24:47; Acts 1:8) focus on preaching, but he emphasizes the Johannine commission to

---

78 Stott, *Christian Mission in the Modern World*, 27.
79 Stott, *Christian Mission in the Modern World*, 29.
80 Stott, *Christian Mission in the Modern World*, 29.
81 John Stott, in *The Gospel and Culture*, ed. John Stott and Robert Coote (Pasadena, CA: William Carey Library, 1979), 21.
82 See, for example, Stott, *The Contemporary Christian*, 244n2, 265, 342n2, 358n2.

justify a wider definition of mission. But this ignores both its immediate and broader contexts. In its immediate context the focus is on proclaiming the forgiveness of sins (John 20:23). In its broader context John structures his Gospel around a number of miraculous signs that point to the identity of Jesus. Each of these signs must be interpreted. John relates the feeding of the five thousand, for example, and then recounts Jesus's explanation of how he is the bread of life. The same is true of the works we do—they need interpretation if they are to point to Jesus. Otherwise we are like signposts pointing nowhere. Or worse, we point the wrong way—to ourselves and our good works. People will assume we care for the poor or campaign for justice because we believe this life is all that really matters or because we believe we are saved by our good works. Social action without proclamation is misleading. Stott himself says, "Works are ambiguous, they need to be interpreted by the proclamation of the gospel."[83]

Social Action in Practice

The demise of Christendom, the decline of the church in the West, and the rise of pluralism mean Christians face a new political situation. Stott recognized this in 1972 when he first wrote *Issues Facing Christians Today*, and the situation has only intensified since. By what process should Christians seek to shape society?

Typically, Stott identifies two false extremes before charting a mediating option. He rejects imposition (citing the Inquisition in Europe and Prohibition in the United States as examples), but he also rejects a laissez-faire attitude (citing the failure of churches to oppose Hitler as an example). Instead, our strategy should be "persuasion by argument."[84] God's concern for justice rules out the laissez-faire option, while a respect of human consciences rules out imposition. "Because God is who he is, we cannot be indifferent when his truth and law are flouted, but because man is who he is, we cannot try to impose them by force."[85] Stott draws a parallel at this point between evangelism and social action. In evangelism, neither imposition nor laissez-faire is an option; instead we try to persuade. The same is true for social action. "We therefore need doctrinal apologetic in evangelism (arguing the truth of the gospel) and ethical apologetic in so-

[83] John Stott, *Authentic Christianity: From the Writings of John Stott*, ed. Timothy Dudley-Smith (Downers Grove, IL: InterVarsity Press, 1995), 343.
[84] Stott, *Issues Facing Christians Today*, 50.
[85] Stott, *Issues Facing Christians Today*, 51.

cial action (arguing the goodness of the moral law)."[86] Persuasion is possible because "the same moral law, which God has revealed in Scripture, he has also stamped (even if not so legibly) on human nature. . . . In every human community, therefore, there is a basic recognition of the difference between right and wrong."[87] In *The Living Church*, Stott lists six "weapons" of our social engagement: prayer, evangelism, example, argument, action, and suffering.[88]

Citing Archbishop William Temple (1881–1944), Stott argues that the church cannot and should not expect to agree on specific policies. The church is not to become involved in direct, specific political action. Instead, its role is to focus on principles. Working out principles together will not be easy, and Stott warns against oversimplification. Nevertheless, he is optimistic. "True humility will lead us to sit patiently under the revelation of God and to affirm by faith that he can bring us to a substantially common mind."[89] Meanwhile, some Christians are called to apply those principles within the political process as politicians and reformers. And all Christians should be socially responsible as conscientious citizens through the way they vote and by being informed, lobbying those in power, and engaging in debate.[90]

Anticipating the objection that social change is impossible unless people are converted, Stott lists a number of examples of change brought about through Christian social action. "Of course we long for people to be converted. But Jesus Christ through his people has had an enormous influence for good on society as a whole."[91] Legislative reform can bring about social reform, and Christians can bring about legislative reform because "even fallen human beings retain sufficient vestiges of the divine image to prefer justice to injustice, freedom to oppression, and peace to violence."[92] The paradox of humanity shapes our expectation of change. We cannot be unduly optimistic, since people are also fallen; so we will never build Utopia. But neither should we be wholly pessimistic, because people retain

---

86 Stott, *Issues Facing Christians Today*, 52.
87 John Stott, *The Message of Romans: God's Good News for the World* (Leicester: Inter-Varsity Press; Downers Grove, IL: InterVarsity Press, 1994), 89.
88 John Stott, *The Living Church: Convictions of a Lifelong Pastor* (Leicester: Inter-Varsity Press, 2007), 144. See also Stott, "Making a Christian Impact on Society," London Institute for Contemporary Christianity Lecture, Church of England Record Centre, STOTT/2/3; Stott, *Issues Facing Christians Today*, 63–79; and Stott, *Students of the Word: Engaging with Scripture to Impact Our World* (Oxford: IFES, 2013), 46.
89 Stott, *Issues Facing Christians Today*, 30.
90 Stott, *Issues Facing Christians Today*, 13.
91 Stott, *The Contemporary Christian*, 351.
92 Stott, *The Contemporary Christian*, 351.

the image of God and people are therefore still capable of compassion and generally prefer justice to injustice. Reform is possible. Stott notes the tendency of evangelical Christians to lament the deterioration of standards in our society. But, he asks, who is to blame? "If the house is dark at night, there is no sense in blaming the house for its darkness. That is what happens when the sun goes down. The question to us is: where is the light?"[93]

[93] Stott, *The Living Church*, 143.

CHAPTER 10

ALL OF LIFE UNDER THE LORD OF ALL

At a Scripture Union camp in his undergraduate days, Stott was urged to sing a light-hearted song during the "Late Night entertainment." With what he later saw as mistaken piety, he replied by quoting a hymn:

> Take my voice, and let me sing
> always, only, for my King.[1]

Stott himself describes how a fellow camp leader "justly retorted" by asking who Stott thought the other performers had been singing for! Stott comments, "I clearly hadn't yet got the dualism of sacred and secular sorted out."[2]

Sorting out that dualism became one of the abiding themes of his ministry. He was concerned to demonstrate how all of life can and should be lived under the lordship of Christ. "If we are Christians, everything we do, however 'secular' it may seem (like shopping, cooking, totting up figures in the office etc.) is 'religious' in the sense that it is done in God's presence and according to God's will."[3]

Handing over the reins of All Souls in 1970 freed up Stott to pursue a project he had had in mind for some years. Back in 1960, when he had been

1 Frances Ridley Havergal, "Take My Life and Let It Be" (1874).
2 John Stott, memorandum to Timothy Dudley-Smith, June 8, 1995, cited in Dudley-Smith, *John Stott*, vol. 1, *The Making of a Leader* (Leicester: Inter-Varsity Press, 1999), 129.
3 John Stott, *The Message of the Sermon on the Mount: Christian Counter-Culture* (Leicester: Inter-Varsity Press; Downers Grove, IL: InterVarsity Press, 1978), 153; see also 170.

asked to give the Payton Lectures at Fuller Seminary, he had been struck by the usefulness of an endowed lectureship. So in 1974 he launched an annual series of lectures "to encourage biblical thinking on contemporary issues."[4] J. I. Packer was enthusiastic, and Latimer House agreed to handle the finances. Introducing the lectures to All Souls, Stott said:

> The Christianity which most of us prefer is more ancient than modern, more biblical than contemporary. . . . What Scripture plainly teaches we gladly receive and hold fast, but it is not congenial to us to develop a Christian mind, informed with Christian presuppositions, and with this mind of Christ to grapple with the great problems of the day, so as to develop a Christian worldview.[5]

In a bold move, the first lecturer for the London Lectures in Contemporary Christianity was José Míguez Bonino, an Argentinian Methodist whose lectures on Christianity and Marxism highlighted the links between the two as well as the differences.[6] The following year the lectures were given by Sir Norman Anderson, who looked at a number of key issues surrounding birth (genetic engineering, birth control, abortion) and death (euthanasia, suicide, capital punishment, war).[7]

From the London Lectures arose the London Institute for Contemporary Christianity (LICC).[8] When James Houston, the principal of Regent College in Vancouver, failed to tempt Stott to join its faculty, he instead urged Stott to set up an equivalent in London. Missiologist Andrew Kirk, then based in Buenos Aires, was thinking along similar lines. The LICC was launched in 1982. The centerpiece was its ten-week course aiming to integrate "Christian faith, life and mission." John Stott was its director, a post he held for a five-year period. In one of the planning papers, Stott said, "Our goal would be to help students become more complete Christians in their personal and home life, and more effective Christians in their professional and public life." Though he hoped it would prepare them to be better church members, he stressed, "Our eyes will be mainly on the world rather than the church as the arena in which the Christian lives and serves." The aim was not preparing people to be pastors or mis-

[4] See "John Stott London Lecture," www.johnstottlondonlecture.org.uk.
[5] John Stott, *All Souls Newsletter*, May 1974, cited in Timothy Dudley-Smith, *John Stott*, vol. 2, *A Global Ministry* (Leicester: Inter-Varsity Press, 2001), 168.
[6] José Míguez Bonino, *Christians and Marxists: The Mutual Challenge to Revolution* (London: Hodder, 1975).
[7] Sir Norman Anderson, *Issues of Life and Death* (London: Hodder, 1976).
[8] See www.licc.org.uk.

sionaries in the traditional sense but preparing them to be witnesses to Christ and agents of change in business, politics, the professions, and the wider community.[9]

Throughout the 1970s, Stott contributed articles to the All Souls parish newsletter on current issues. A number of these were adapted into a monthly series of "cornerstone" articles in *Christianity Today*, which ran between 1977 and 1981. Michael Baughen also asked Stott to preach a sermon each quarter at All Souls under the title "Issues Facing Britain Today." Before each one, Stott organized a study group that included those directly involved in each issue. All these sources came together in Stott's book *Issues Facing Christians Today*. It covered nuclear weapons, environmental issues, global inequality, human rights, unemployment, industrial relations, racism, feminism, divorce, abortion, and homosexuality. Subsequent revisions have added further chapters with the help of Roy McCloughry and John Wyatt. It was an ambitious undertaking, requiring a knowledge of economics, politics, and sociology, along with biblical exegesis and moral theology. It is therefore no surprise that in the preface, Stott confesses to being tempted more than once to give up.[10] But he was determined to help Christians develop a Christian mind on these issues.

The Lordship of Christ

What drove this commitment to develop a Christian perspective on all of life was a big view of Christ. Christ is not simply our ticket to heaven. He is the one to whom the Father has given all authority. Jesus is, in a passage often quoted by Stott, the one before whom "every knee should bow, in heaven and on earth and under the earth" (Phil. 2:10).

In *The Contemporary Christian*, Stott speaks of Christ's lordship over our lives having a "vocational dimension." He starts with 1 Corinthians 7:20: "Each one should remain in the condition [literally "the calling"] in which he was called." The word "calling," argues Stott, is being used in two senses. There is the general call to follow Christ, which all Christians experience at conversion ("in which he was called"). This is not person-specific, for it is true for everyone. But there is also a call particular to each person ("in the condition" or "calling"). Paul elaborates, says Stott, with three examples: "our domestic situation (married or single), cultural situation

[9] John Stott, "Memorandum No. 4," August 14, 1980, cited in Dudley-Smith, *John Stott*, 2:288.
[10] John Stott, *Issues Facing Christians Today*, 2nd ed. (London: Marshall Pickering, 1990), xi.

(Jewish or Gentile) and social situation (slaves or free)."[11] In contrast to the Corinthians' tendency to think everything from their old life could be repudiated, Paul urges them to transform, rather than leave, their current circumstances.

This does not mean we can never change our situations. Stott gives the example of Paul himself doing this when he allows for a slave to gain his or her freedom (1 Cor. 7:21). "What Paul was opposing was thoughtless and reckless actions, change for change's sake, and especially the notion that nothing before conversion and nothing outside religion has any value to God."[12] In other words, it is not that we *cannot* change our situation but that we *need not*. We do not need to be ascetics to be truly spiritual.

If, as Stott has argued, "Paul was opposing . . . the notion that . . . nothing outside religion has any value to God," then, conversely, we can assert that life outside of religion is of value to God. "The whole of our life belongs to God and is part of his calling, both before conversion and outside religion."[13] Our pre-conversion responsibilities, obligations, and abilities do not become irrelevant.

> For these things were not accidental aspects of our life. They were part of God's providence to which he had called us and which he had assigned to us. God's sovereignty extends over both halves of our life. He did not begin to work in and for us at our conversion, but at our birth, even before our birth in our genetic inheritance, as later in our temperament, personality, education and skills. And what God made us and gave us before we became Christians, he redeems, sanctifies and transforms afterwards.[14]

Stott himself testified to this: "Even before my conversion, I believe God gave me a social conscience."[15] At school he formed a society to give baths to tramps or hobos. "It was extremely naïve," he acknowledges, and it came to an end when the treasurer lent the fund to his brother, who promptly spent it.[16] Nevertheless, Stott saw this as an indication of God's work in his early life. In *Baptism and Fullness* he emphasizes the link that often exists between natural talents and spiritual gifts (*charismata*). "The

---

11 John Stott, *The Contemporary Christian: An Urgent Plea for Double Listening* (Leicester: Inter-Varsity Press, 1992), 135.
12 Stott, *The Contemporary Christian*, 136.
13 Stott, *The Contemporary Christian*, 136, 139.
14 Stott, *The Contemporary Christian*, 139.
15 John Stott, *Balanced Christianity: A Call to Avoid Unnecessary Polarisation*, 2nd ed. (Nottingham: Inter-Varsity Press, 2014), 70.
16 Stott, *Balanced Christianity*, 70.

same God is God of creation and of new creation, working out through both his perfect will."[17] Both Jeremiah and Paul could trace God's hand in their lives before conversion, preparing them for service after conversion (Jer. 1:5; Gal. 1:15–16). Stott takes the gift of giving as an example (Rom. 12:8). Does this involve a post-conversion windfall? No, says Stott. The money is already there. What the Spirit does after conversion is to transform the *motives* of the giver. The same, argues Stott, could be true of teaching and exhorting. A natural ability is given new purpose and driven by new motives.

Vocation

Stott applies the same whole-life perspective to ministry. He refuses to define "ministry" as something that takes place simply within the orbit of the church. "All Christians without exception are called to ministry."[18] "We do a great disservice to the Christian cause whenever we refer to the pastorate as 'the ministry.'"[19] The use of the definite article implies that pastoral ministry is the only ministry there is or the only ministry that matters. From this it follows that "there is a wide variety of Christian ministries."[20] Stott refers to Acts 6, where the word "ministry" is used of both the ministry of the word conducted by the twelve apostles and the "ministry of tables" conducted by the seven.

> I was myself brought up as a young Christian to think of different vocations or ministries as forming a hierarchy or pyramid. Perched precariously at the top of the pyramid was the cross-cultural missionary. He was our hero, she our heroine. I was taught that if I was really out and out for Christ I would undoubtedly join their ranks overseas. If I was not as keen as that, I would stay at home and be a pastor. If I did not aspire even to that, I would probably become a doctor or a teacher, whereas, if I were to go into business, politics or the media, I would not be far from backsliding![21]

Stott in no way decries the need for missionaries and pastors. "At the same time, there is a crying need for Christian men and women who see their daily

17 John Stott, *Baptism and Fullness: The Work of the Holy Spirit Today*, 2nd ed. (Leicester: Inter-Varsity Press, 1975), 90.
18 Stott, *The Contemporary Christian*, 140; see also Stott, *Christian Mission in the Modern World* (London: Falcon, 1975), 31–32.
19 Stott, *The Contemporary Christian*, 140.
20 Stott, *The Contemporary Christian*, 141.
21 Stott, *The Contemporary Christian*, 142; see also Stott, *The Living Church: Convictions of a Lifelong Pastor* (Leicester: Inter-Varsity Press, 2007), 141–42.

work as their primary Christian ministry and who determine to penetrate their secular environment for Christ."[22] The founding of LICC was an attempt to put this into practice by equipping Christians for "ministry" in all walks of life.

David Turner describes how Stott dissuaded him from leaving his legal career for ordination. "We need Christian lawyers," Stott told Turner. Turner comments, "The seriousness with which he took so-called 'secular' work was wonderfully affirming. There was no message that such work would be 'second best,' there was no arena in which God's people were not needed."[23] Turner went on to become a circuit judge as well as a reader (lay preacher) at All Souls. Nigel Goodwin, founder of Genesis Arts Trust, writes in a similar vein about Stott's impact on him and other artists. He describes how involvement in the church and involvement in the arts were often seen by Christians as incompatible:

> You can imagine the pain and confusion this dichotomy created for many. John Stott, however, did not make such a division. On the contrary, he saw the arts as any other profession. If it was your gift, your calling, then you should remain within the situation in which you were called (1 Corinthians 7:24); because it is there that you will be both salt and light. That was his hugely encouraging message to people like me. All Souls Church became a haven, a shelter, for many in the media and arts.[24]

"It's no use," Stott would say, "just singing pretty songs: 'Jesus I love you.' They don't prove anything. It's only in daily life that you prove, through obedience, whether or not you love Jesus."[25]

We began this chapter with the young Stott refusing to sing a "secular" song. In contrast, fifty years later the mature Stott wrote:

> We should determine to recognize and acknowledge, appreciate and celebrate, all the gifts of the Creator:
>
> - the glory of the heavens and of the earth, of mountain, river and sea, of forest and flowers, of birds, beasts and butterflies, and of the intricate balance of the natural environment;

[22] Stott, *The Contemporary Christian*, 140. See also Stott, *Focus on Christ: An Enquiry into the Theology of Prepositions* (Eastbourne: Kingsway, 1979), 108–12; and Stott, *Christian Basics: An Invitation to Discipleship* (London: Hodder, 1991), 157–59.
[23] David Turner, in *John Stott: A Portrait by His Friends*, ed. Chris Wright (Nottingham: Inter-Varsity Press, 2011), 84–85.
[24] Nigel Goodwin, in Wright, *John Stott*, 170.
[25] Cited in Wright, *John Stott*, 217.

- the unique privileges of our humanness (rational, moral, social and spiritual), as we were created in God's image and appointed his stewards;
- the joys of gender, marriage, sex, children, parenthood and family life, and of our extended family and friends;
- the rhythm of work and rest, of daily work as a means to cooperate with God and serve the common good, and of the Lord's day when we exchange work for worship;
- the blessings of peace, freedom, justice and good environment, and of food and drink, clothing and shelter; and
- our human creativity expressed in music, literature, painting, sculpture and drama, and in the skills and strengths displayed in sport.

To reject these things is to abandon the faith, since it insults the Creator. To receive them thankfully and celebrate them joyfully is to glorify God, "who richly provides us with everything for our enjoyment" (1 Tim. 6:17 [NIV]).[26]

Nuclear Weapons

One of the more controversial issues on which Stott spoke out was that of nuclear weapons. In *The Contemporary Christian* he laments the failure of evangelicals "to condemn as immoral and indefensible all indiscriminate weaponry—both the use of atomic, biological and chemical weapons as being indiscriminate by nature, and the indiscriminate use of conventional weapons."[27] Stott had moved from his early pacifism to adopt a just-war position, the long-standing rationale for a moral approach to war. Two recognized principles of the just-war theory are (1) non-combatants should never be directly or deliberately attacked (the principle of discrimination); and (2) the human, financial, and environmental costs of military action should not outweigh the likely gains (the principle of proportion). On both counts, Stott finds nuclear weapons immoral. "A nuclear war could never be a just war."[28] Stott does qualify this by arguing (in the context of the then Soviet threat) that, since unilateral disarmament might destabilize the status quo, we should retain nuclear weapons as a temporary measure (recognizing the ambiguities involved in holding weapons whose use you consider immoral).[29]

---

[26] John Stott, *The Message of 1 Timothy and Titus: The Life of the Local Church* (Leicester: Inter-Varsity Press; Downers Grove, IL: InterVarsity Press, 1996), 115; bullet points added.
[27] Stott, *The Contemporary Christian*, 193.
[28] Stott, *Issues Facing Christians Today*, 95.
[29] John Stott, "Nuclear Weapons Change the Possibility of War," in *Handling Problems of Peace and War*, ed. Andrew Kirk (London: Marshall Pickering, 1988), 46; and Stott, *Issues Facing Christians Today*, 99–102.

What is striking, however, about this condemnation in *The Contemporary Christian* is that it comes in the context of a call to avoid cultural blind spots as we read God's word. It is not a section on ethics but a section on hermeneutics. In other words, what is driving Stott's attitude toward nuclear weapons is a concern to read the Bible aright. He concludes:

> The first step towards the recovery of our Christian integrity will be the humble recognition that our culture blinds, deafens and dopes us. We neither see what we ought to see in Scripture, nor hear God's Word as we should, nor feel the anger of God against evil. We need to allow God's Word to confront us, disturbing our security, undermining our complacency, penetrating our protective patterns of thought and behaviour, and overthrowing our resistance.[30]

Creation Care

The Radical Disciple was the last book John Stott wrote. In it he highlights eight aspects of discipleship he fears are neglected. They include themes one might expect, like maturity and Christlikeness. But among the eight are also "simplicity" and what Stott calls "creation-care." They represent two consistent concerns in Stott's ministry.

"Of all the global threats which face our planet," he says, "[climate change] is the most serious."[31] Stott highlights the threefold relationship in which God placed humanity: with God, with others, and with creation. All three relationships were corrupted by sin at the fall. "It stands to reason therefore that God's plan of restoration includes not only our reconciliation to God and to each other, but in some way the liberation of the groaning creation as well."[32] The climax of salvation is a new creation (2 Pet. 3:13; Rev. 21:1).

Yet, many evangelicals remain nervous about environmental concerns and environmentalism. In part, this is a kind of guilt by association, for many environmentalists have views of God (or "god") and nature that Christians cannot share. Stott acknowledges this concern and therefore emphasizes the need to avoid "the deification of nature." But he also adds that Christians are partly to blame. Having abandoned the field, we cannot complain that it has been taken over by others with different

[30] Stott, *The Contemporary Christian*, 193.
[31] John Stott, *The Radical Disciple: Wholehearted Christian Living* (Leicester: Inter-Varsity Press, 2010), 62.
[32] Stott, *The Radical Disciple*, 56.

worldviews. It is certainly no justification for going to the opposite extreme: "the exploitation of nature."[33]

Simple Lifestyle

The Lausanne Covenant committed those who signed it to "develop a simple lifestyle." Although it was not originally his suggestion, Stott insisted on its inclusion despite opposition from some quarters. Indeed, Ruth Graham, Billy Graham's wife, refused to sign the covenant because of it, arguing that it was too confining and too vague.[34] Through his travels in the Global South, Stott was already convinced of the need for a simple lifestyle. The problem was that "simple lifestyle" meant very little in practice to most people. What is it? How does one live it? What is its biblical basis?

Those moved by the description of socioeconomic injustice in Ron Sider's book *Rich Christians in an Age of Hunger* and challenged by the biblical teaching on poverty inevitably wanted some guidance on how they as individuals could respond. At the end of *Rich Christians*, Sider outlined his vision of a simpler lifestyle. He spoke of how we in the West persuade ourselves that we "need" our relatively high incomes to live "comfortably." The sin of materialism is reason enough to commit ourselves to a simpler lifestyle quite apart from the needs of the poor. Sider suggested as one, admittedly rather modest, possible model a graduated tithe in which a person gives a higher percentage of income the more he or she earns.[35]

Meanwhile, as Stott met with Global South Christians, they repeatedly asked him whether Western Christians were really serious about the commitment they had made to a simple lifestyle in the Lausanne Covenant. He and Sider agreed on the need for a consultation that would be cosponsored by the Lausanne Theology and Education Group, of which Stott was chair, and by the Unit on Ethics and Society of the Theological Commission of the World Evangelical Fellowship, of which Sider was the convener. The Lausanne Committee agreed, with some hesitation, and only if simple lifestyle were looked at in relation to evangelization.

The Consultation on Simple Lifestyle was held in March 1980 at Hoddesdon, England, the culmination of a two-year process involving local

[33] Stott, *The Radical Disciple*, 58.
[34] See William Martin, *A Prophet with Honor: The Billy Graham Story*, 2nd ed. (Grand Rapids, MI: Zondervan, 2018), 457–58.
[35] Ronald Sider, *Rich Christians in an Age of Hunger* (London: Hodder, 1978), 157–59; see also *Living More Simply: Biblical Principles and Practical Models*, ed. Ronald Sider (London: Hodder, 1980).

groups in fifteen countries and regional conferences in India, Ireland, and the United States.[36] The resulting Evangelical Commitment to Simple Lifestyle, steered through by Stott, placed simple lifestyle in its wider context so that it was not divorced from issues of justice. At its heart, however, was a commitment "to develop a just and simple lifestyle." "Our Christian obedience demands a simple lifestyle," the statement says, "irrespective of the needs of others. Nevertheless, the facts that 800 million people are destitute and that about 10,000 die of starvation every day make any other lifestyle indefensible."

> [Jesus] calls all his followers to an inner freedom from the seduction of riches (for it is important not to serve God and money) and to sacrificial generosity ("to be rich in good works, to be generous and ready to share," 1 Timothy 6:18). Indeed the motivation and model for Christian generosity are nothing less than the example of Jesus Christ himself who, though rich, became poor that through his poverty we might become rich (2 Cor. 8:9). . . .
>
> All of us are determined to develop a simpler lifestyle. We intend to re-examine our income and expenditure, in order to manage on less and give away more. We lay down no rules or regulations for either ourselves or others. Yet we resolve to renounce waste and oppose extravagance in personal living, clothing and housing, travel and church building. We also accept the distinction between necessities and luxuries, creative hobbies and empty status symbols, modesty and vanity, occasional celebrations and normal routine, between service of God and slavery to fashion.[37]

The declaration goes on to commend releasing money to care for the poor and reach the lost.

For a while, simple lifestyle was very much part of the evangelical agenda. After *Rich Christians* was published, for example, both *Crusade* magazine and *Third Way* produced supplements called, respectively, "That's the Style" and "Hard Questions for Rich Christians." During the 1980s it declined as an issue, but it has resurfaced, this time in response to environmental issues. It certainly remained an important issue for Stott himself. Speaking of the Consultation on Simple Lifestyle in *The Radical Disciple*, he says somewhat mournfully, "It made a little impact at the time

[36] The conference papers and the resulting statement were published in *Lifestyle in the Eighties: An Evangelical Commitment to Simple Lifestyle*, ed. Ronald Sider (Exeter: Paternoster, 1982).
[37] Cited in Stott, *The Radical Disciple*, 77.

but in my view has received insufficient attention either then or since."[38] He took the opportunity to republish the Evangelical Commitment to Simple Lifestyle in its entirety.

For Stott the issue was linked with his own experience of seeing poverty around the world and meeting those involved in serving the poor. These experiences clearly moved him personally, and out of this compassion and anger (which he speaks about eloquently as Christlike virtues in *The Contemporary Christian*)[39] arose a concern that Western Christians needed to respond with changed lifestyles. There is perhaps something of a sense of tokenism in his response. In *The Living Church* he says, "Those of us who live in affluent circumstances must simplify our economic lifestyle—not because we imagine this will solve the world's macro-economic problems, but out of solidarity with the poor."[40] There is a tacit recognition here that the problem is not Western affluence per se, but the global economic structures that have created and continue to maintain stark imbalances of wealth from slavery through colonialism to unjust terms of trade. Nevertheless, Stott never loses sight of the real drivers of a simple lifestyle: the dangers of materialism, the call to generosity, and the needs of gospel ministry.

What is striking about these radical concerns of Stott is that they are simultaneously both unexpected for a man in his background and totally in keeping with his character. He grew up in privileged circumstances and was schooled in elite institutions. In many ways he was a figure of the establishment, becoming a chaplain to the queen. Yet he was also a listener who approached people and issues with humility. His travels took him across the world, where he saw poverty firsthand and was influenced by Global South Christians. The 1960s and 1970s were times of political ferment, and Stott's commitment to double listening meant he heard the challenges of the radical movements to which he was instinctively sympathetic. His focus in the early 1960s was on issues of morality. But at a point when he might easily have become a relic of a passing generation, harking after a lost golden era, he instead heard in the younger generation's cry of protest an echo of the biblical concern for social justice. His commitment to Scripture meant he was never going to buy into a liberal ideology; but his commitment to Scripture also meant he would never be a slavish defender

38 Stott, *The Radical Disciple*, 67.
39 Stott, *The Contemporary Christian*, 123–24.
40 Stott, *The Living Church*, 29.

of the status quo. Each issue was considered on its biblical merits, with an empathy for those involved and a humble willingness to follow where Scripture led. He recognized that, given the current nomenclature of the Christian world, he was a conservative evangelical. But the label "conservative" irked him. Instinctively, he wanted to be a radical—not in the sense of pushing theology to its limits but in the sense of wanting to pursue alternatives to both the ecclesiastical and political status quo.

CHAPTER 11

A VISION OF CHRIST

In 2007, John Stott stood up to speak at the Keswick Convention.[1] It was forty-five years since his first address, and he had spoken there many times in the intervening years. He was eighty-six years old and a few weeks previously had called an end to his public speaking. But he decided to honor this final engagement. It took him some time to reach the lectern with assistance, and a chair had been provided in case he needed to sit down. But he managed to stand throughout his address. Though there were occasional pauses as Stott took a moment to gather his thoughts, his delivery was clear and articulate.

As he stood to speak, he knew it was for the last time. What would he take as the topic for his final sermon? The sufficiency of the cross? The authority of the Bible? The importance of the mind? The urgency of mission? The place for social action? All might have formed a fitting conclusion to his ministry. But Stott ended with Jesus Christ. He began by asking his hearers what they thought God's primary purpose for his people is. He suggested a number of possible answers before saying, "I want to share with you where my mind has come to rest as I approach the end of my pilgrimage on earth. It is this: God wants his people to become like Christ, for Christlikeness is the will of God for the people of God."[2]

---

[1] The address was published as chap. 2 of John Stott, *The Radical Disciple: Wholehearted Christian Living* (Leicester: Inter-Varsity Press, 2010), 31–41, and in Stott, *The Last Word: Reflections on a Lifetime of Preaching* (Milton Keynes: Authentic Media, 2008). See also Stott, *Focus on Christ: An Enquiry into the Theology of Prepositions* (Eastbourne: Kingsway, 1979), 139–54.
[2] Stott, *The Radical Disciple*, 32.

Citing Romans 8:29, 2 Corinthians 3:18, and 1 John 3:2, Stott spoke of the three tenses of Christlikeness: we were predestined in the past by the Father for Christlikeness; we are being transformed in the present by the Holy Spirit; and we will be like the Son in the future. Stott then said we are to be like Christ in his incarnation—not in the sense in which God took on human flesh, which was a unique act, but, as Paul indicates in Philippians 2:5–9, we are to be like him in his humility. We are to be like Christ in his *service*, taking the role of a slave as Jesus did when he washed the disciples' feet. We are to be like Christ in his *love*, living a life of love patterned on the cross. We are to be like Christ in his *patient endurance*, an increasingly relevant call as persecution increases in many cultures today. And we are to be like Christ in his *mission* (John 20:21). Just as Christ entered our world, we are to enter other people's worlds—seeing the world as they see it and empathizing with them in their doubts, questions, and loneliness.

Stott ended with three practical consequences of this vision of Christlike formation. The first is that it explains suffering: God is using suffering to shape us into the image of his Son (Rom. 8:28–29). Second, Stott asked why our evangelism so often ends in failure. Though several reasons could be given, "one main reason is that we don't look like the Christ we proclaim."[3] Finally, Stott asked whether this vision of Christlikeness is possible. Not, he answered, in our own strength, but God has given us the Holy Spirit. And so Stott concluded, "God's purpose is to make us like Christ, and God's way is to fill us with his Holy Spirit."[4]

What the transcripts do not reveal is that Stott ended his talk by inviting the congregation to join him in reciting a children's song. And it was with these words that he ended his public preaching ministry:

> Like Jesus, like Jesus,
> I want to be like Jesus.
> I love him so;
> I want to grow
> like Jesus every day.

A TV reporter once asked Stott, "You've had a brilliant academic career; firsts at Cambridge, Rector at twenty-nine, Chaplain to the Queen; what is

---
[3] Stott, *The Radical Disciple*, 39.
[4] Stott, *The Radical Disciple*, 41.

your ambition *now*?" Stott replied, "To be more like Jesus."[5] In an LICC lecture on John 15, Stott said Christian fruitfulness is "not soul-winning but Christlikeness."[6] It is striking, too, that Stott's classic presentation of the gospel in *Basic Christianity* starts not with humanity's need (which forms part 2) or with Christ's saving work (which forms part 3) but with the person of Christ. Stott explains:

> Take Christ from Christianity, and you disembowel it; there is practically nothing left. Christ is the centre of Christianity; all else is circumference. We are not concerned primarily to discuss the nature of his philosophy, the value of his system, or the quality of his ethic. Our concern is fundamentally with the character of his person.[7]

This is in contrast to evangelistic approaches that start with creation or the plight of humanity or the mechanics of the atonement. What Stott found compelling about Christianity was Christ. What follows in *Basic Christianity* is a portrait of Christ: the audacity of his claims, the beauty of his character, and the reality of his resurrection. "We are concerned to show that Jesus stands in a moral category by himself. To concede that he was 'the greatest man who ever lived' does not begin to satisfy us. We cannot talk of Jesus in comparative, or even superlative terms. To us it is a question not of comparison, but of contrast." Jesus is not "even the best of men"; he is "good with the absolute goodness of God."[8] Jesus is central to not only the gospel *message* but also the gospel *motive*: "The strongest evangelistic incentive," says Stott in *Our Guilty Silence*, is "the pre-eminent name of Jesus."[9]

Submitting to Christ Our Teacher—A Humble Mind

Christians do not read books on Jesus. It is one of the truisms of Christian publishing. No one is sure why, but it is probably because people want books that meet a felt need. It is remarkable, then, how many of Stott's books are essentially about Jesus. Even in books that are not explicitly on Christology, the fingerprints of Jesus are everywhere. Christian life, Stott

5 Dr. D. H. Trapnell, interview by Timothy Dudley-Smith, February 18, 1993, in Dudley-Smith, *John Stott*, vol. 2, *A Global Ministry* (Leicester: Inter-Varsity Press, 2001), 452.
6 John Stott, "He Left a Secret (John 15): Exploring Our Christian Heritage—Studies in John 13–17," LICC, August 1993, Church of England Record Centre, STOTT/2/3.
7 John Stott, *Basic Christianity*, rev. ed. (Leicester: Inter-Varsity Press, 1971), 21.
8 Stott, *Basic Christianity*, 36.
9 John Stott, *Our Guilty Silence: The Church, the Gospel and the World* (London: Hodder & Stoughton, 1967), 20.

says in *Focus on Christ*, is life "through, on, in, under, for, with, unto and like" Christ.[10]

Stott concludes his book *Christ the Controversialist* with a meditation on John 13:13–14: "You call me Teacher and Lord, and you are right, for so I am. If I then, your Lord and Teacher, have washed your feet, you also ought to wash one another's feet." This, Stott says, tells us something important about Jesus: he is the teacher and Lord who humbled himself to be a servant. But it also tells us something important about Christians. Christians are those who are willing to learn from Jesus as our teacher and submit to Jesus as our Lord. We cannot claim to follow him while we pick and choose what we will believe or obey. This involves "a greater commitment to humility. . . . Christians are not free to disagree with Christ or to disobey Christ."[11] For all Stott's emphasis on the mind, he always pursued a mind in submission to Christ our teacher.

If the formal principle of Stott's theology was often a dialectic approach, then the material principle of his theological method was Christ. Why did Stott place so much emphasis on the authority of Scripture? Because Christ did so. What was the starting point for Stott's soteriology? The person of Christ. What was central to Stott's understanding of the Christian life? A process of becoming more like Christ. Why was Stott committed to mission? Many reasons can be given, but primarily it was to bring glory to Christ. What governed his commitment to vocation and discipleship in all of life? The universal lordship of Christ.

Consider his treatment of the authority of Scripture. Stott founded this on Christ's example and made it an issue of Christ's lordship. We submit to Scripture because Christ endorsed the authority of the Old Testament and provided for the writing of the New Testament through the apostolic testimony.

> If we would submit to the authority of Christ, we must submit to the authority of scripture. If we wish to hear the voice of Christ, we must listen to scripture through which he speaks. For the authority of scripture and the authority of Christ go together. The ultimate question before the church in every age is: Who is the Lord? Is the church the lord of Jesus Christ, so that it has liberty to edit and manipulate his teaching? Or is

[10] Stott, *Focus on Christ*, 14.
[11] John Stott, *But I Say to You: Christ the Controversialist* (Nottingham: Inter-Varsity Press, 2013), 208; see also Stott, *Understanding the Bible* (London: Scripture Union, 1972), 203.

> Jesus Christ the Lord of the church, so that it must believe and obey him? Since Jesus Christ is Lord, there should be no hesitation about our answer to that question. We must accept the authority of scripture.[12]

Christ is not only the foundation of our commitment to Scripture; he is also the end or goal of Scripture. "Where then shall we find the authentic Jesus? The answer is that he is to be found in the Bible—the book which could be described as the Father's portrait of the Son painted by the Holy Spirit."[13] In *Christ the Controversialist*, Stott warns against bibliolatry, "behaving as if Scripture rather than Christ were the object of . . . devotion."[14] This is a common accusation leveled against evangelicals. But rather than defending evangelicals against the accusation, Stott recognizes it as a danger. It is the danger of making the Bible the end rather than the means. Stott illustrates this by imagining a family going to a local beauty spot, and he picks, as an example, Box Hill on the North Downs in Surrey. Imagine, he says, seeing a signpost marked "Box Hill." "Do we immediately stop the car, get out and have our picnic round the signpost?" Of course not, we follow the sign and reach our destination. In the same way, the Bible is the signpost that points us to Jesus. It is ridiculous to linger round the signpost without following its lead to Christ, "Christ, not the Bible, is the object of our faith and the centre of our fellowship."[15]

Submitting to Christ Our Lord—A Humble Life

In John 13, Jesus not only shows that he is our teacher; he also describes himself as our Lord. For Stott, the Christian life was always lived under the lordship of Christ. But, as he points out in *Christ the Controversialist*, the one who calls himself Lord in John 13 is the one who has just sat down after washing the feet of his disciples. "He who said he was their teacher and lord humbled himself to be their servant."[16] Again and again in his writings Stott returns to this nexus of Christ's lordship, humility, and service. For us, as followers of Christ, it means submission to his lordship in every area of life, and imitation of his humility and service.

---

[12] John Stott, *Students of the Word: Engaging with Scripture to Impact Our World* (Oxford: IFES, 2013), 24.
[13] Stott, *The Radical Disciple*, 49.
[14] Stott, *But I Say to You*, 81.
[15] Stott, *But I Say to You*, 92–93. In Stott, *Fundamentalism and Evangelism* (London: Crusade, 1956; Grand Rapids, MI: Eerdmans, 1959), 22, Stott uses the image of a man treasuring his wife's photograph more than his wife.
[16] Stott, *But I Say to You*, 204.

Not only was this what Stott taught; it was also what he lived. René Padilla tells the story of traveling with Stott in Argentina. They arrived late at night in the pouring rain and had to splash through the mud to reach the place where they were staying. The next morning Padilla was woken by the sound of Stott cleaning the mud off Padilla's shoes. "John! What are you doing?" he cried. "My dear René," Stott replied, "Jesus told us to wash one another's feet. Today we do not wash feet the way people did in Jesus' day, but I can clean your shoes." Padilla comments, "Several times I heard John preach on humility; many times I saw him putting it into practice."[17] Frances Whitehead says, "It still amazes me that he emptied my office wastepaper basket every day for many, many years."[18] Ken Perez, who worked at LICC, says, "Some people are impressive in public, but disappointing in private. John is the opposite. He is even more impressive in private than in public. His Christlikeness, gentleness, personal kindness and authenticity are unforgettable."[19] Flattery, Stott would say, is like cigarette smoke; it does you no harm so long as you do not inhale.[20] Daniel Bourdanné, IFES general secretary, writes: "Every time I met him personally . . . I was struck by his humility, and by the love and servant-heartedness he demonstrated."[21]

Commenting on Colossians 3:17 and 23 ("Whatever you do, in word or deed, do everything in the name of the Lord Jesus" and "Whatever you do, work heartily, as for the Lord and not for men"), Stott says:

> Firstly, I have got to learn . . . to treat other people *as if I were Jesus Christ*. That is what it means to do everything in the name of the Lord Jesus. . . . I have got to learn, if I am a Christian, to treat other people with the respect and the consideration, the thoughtfulness and the graciousness with which Jesus Christ himself would treat them. The second principle is . . . to treat people *as if they were Jesus Christ*. I must learn to do everything as unto the Lord. . . . I must learn to treat every person with the graciousness, the humility, the understanding, and the courtesy . . . I would give to him. . . . These two principles, to treat other people as if they were Christ and as if I were Christ, are as realistic as they are revolutionary. This is not idealistic rubbish. This is practical advice about personal relationships.[22]

---

[17] René Padilla, in *John Stott: A Portrait by His Friends*, ed. Chris Wright (Nottingham: Inter-Varsity Press, 2011), 121.
[18] Frances Whitehead, in Wright, *John Stott*, 55.
[19] Cited in Roger Steer, *Inside Story: The Life of John Stott* (Nottingham: Inter-Varsity Press, 2009), 214–15.
[20] Cited in Wright, *John Stott*, 151.
[21] Daniel Bourdanné, foreword to Stott, *Students of the Word*, 9.
[22] John Stott, *Authentic Christianity: From the Writings of John Stott*, ed. Timothy Dudley-Smith (Downers Grove, IL: InterVarsity Press, 1995), 221–22; emphasis added.

We should not imagine that this humble service of others was easy or automatic for Stott. In his younger days he could be very task-oriented and this, combined with the formality of his upbringing, meant people often found him forbidding. This is what Ted Schroder found when he came to All Souls as a curate in the 1960s.

> He wouldn't even come out of his study to eat. He would put "do not disturb" on his study door. I would have to go in and drag him down to eat. I violated his privacy because I felt somebody had to do it. He was intimidating to a lot of people and nobody would ever confront him. When he did come down for a meal, and we were all round the table, everybody would fall silent. They were frightened of doing or saying the wrong thing. It was unnatural.[23]

Schroder was a New Zealander with no time for English upper-class aloofness, and he challenged the starchy atmosphere of English reserve that was part of the culture of the All Souls staff team. Frances Whitehead, too, says, "In those early years John Stott may have seemed distant and unapproachable—living to a strict timetable with an endless list of tasks to be accomplished each day. . . . But he wonderfully mellowed over the years."[24] What is striking about these words is how closely they resemble Stott's own description of his hero Charles Simeon. In his appreciation of Simeon, Stott concedes that in his early years Simeon could be "awkward, even brusque." Stott describes the daughters of Henry Venn, Simeon's early mentor, finding Simeon's clumsy manner amusing. So Venn told them to pick a peach, knowing it would be unripe. "Well, my dears," he commented, "it is green now, and we must wait; but a little more sun and a few more showers, and the peach will be ripe and sweet. So it is with Mr Simeon." To this Stott adds: "He was right. Simeon mellowed with age, and the fruit of the Spirit grew ever riper within him."[25] For twenty years Frances called him "Mr Stott" or "Rector." Only when he became rector emeritus—which she refused to call him—did they agree she could call him "John." In many ways, being in the Global South gave Stott permission to throw off the reserve of his upbringing and be himself.

---

23 Ted Schroder, cited in Steer, *Inside Story*, 141.
24 Frances Whitehead, in Wright, *John Stott*, 55.
25 John Stott, "Charles Simeon: A Personal Appreciation," in *Evangelical Preaching: An Anthology of Sermons by Charles Simeon*, ed. James M. Houston (Portland, OR: Multnomah, 1986), xxxix.

What fueled Stott's humility and service was a sense of the grace, beauty, and love of Christ.

The Grace of Christ

Corey Widmer, one of his study assistants, would bring Stott coffee at 11:00 a.m. sharp each morning. With Stott deep in concentration, Widmer would quietly set the cup down on his desk. "I'm not worthy," Stott would mumble. At first Widmer found this amusing, but after a few months it started to bother him. Eventually he replied, "Oh, sure you are." At this, Stott stopped what he was doing and gave Widmer his undivided attention. "You haven't got your theology of grace right," he said with a combination of playfulness and earnestness. "It's only a cup of coffee," said Widmer defensively as he retreated from the room. "It's just the thin end of the wedge," Stott shouted after him as he left.[26]

In his postscript to *Evangelical Truth*, Stott begins, "I make so bold as to claim . . . that the supreme quality which the evangelical faith engenders (or should do) is humility."[27] He explains:

> The more the three persons of the Trinity are glorified, the more completely human pride is excluded. To magnify the self-revelation of God is to confess our complete ignorance without it. To magnify the cross of Christ is to confess our utter lostness without it. To magnify the regenerating, indwelling and sanctifying role of the Holy Spirit is to confess our abiding self-centredness without it.[28]

Stott says, "Pride is the greatest hindrance to spiritual progress."[29] In this he echoes Simeon, who, when asked what he considered the principal mark of regeneration, replied: "self-loathing and abhorrence. . . . I want to see more of this humble, contrite, broken spirit among us."[30] Schroder remembers Saturday night prayer meetings for staff in Stott's office.

> What left a lasting impression on me was the way in which this great man, who inspired such admiration and, indeed, not a little awe, began

---

[26] Corey Widmer, in Wright, *John Stott*, 196.

[27] John Stott, *Evangelical Truth: A Personal Plea for Unity, Integrity and Faithfulness*, rev. ed. (Nottingham: Inter-Varsity Press, 2015), 143.

[28] Stott, *Evangelical Truth*, 144.

[29] John Stott, *Favourite Psalms: Growing Closer to God* (London: Monarch, 2003), 122.

[30] William Carus, ed., *Memoirs of the Life of the Rev. Charles Simeon* (New York: Robert Carter, 1847), 352, cited in Stott, "Charles Simeon," xxxix–xl.

his prayer. He would echo the words of Abraham: "Now that I have been so bold as to speak to the Lord, though I am nothing but dust and ashes" (Genesis 18:27, NIV).[31]

The Beauty of Christ

Above all, what drives this commitment to Christlike humble service is a vision of Christ. As we see Christ's glory, we want to serve him; as we see his beauty, we want to imitate him. This is the repeated refrain of Stott's final book, *The Radical Disciple*:

> If Christian maturity is maturity in our relationship with God, in which we worship, trust and obey him, then the clearer *our vision of Christ*, the more convinced we become that he is worthy of our commitment.
>
> So if we want to develop truly Christian maturity, we need above all *a fresh and true vision of Jesus Christ.*
>
> If only we could *see Jesus in the fullness of who he is and what he has done*! Why then surely we should see how worthy he is of our wholehearted allegiance, and faith, love and obedience would be drawn out from us and we would grow into maturity. Nothing is more important for mature Christian discipleship than *a fresh, clear, true vision of the authentic Jesus.*
>
> For the discipleship principle is clear: the poorer *our vision of Christ*, the poorer out discipleship will be, whereas the richer *our vision of Christ*, the richer our discipleship will be.[32]

The reason Stott was Christlike is simple: he wanted to be like Christ. He found the person of Christ utterly compelling and wanted to be like him. Here is Stott speaking of the fruit of the Spirit in Galatians 5:22–23:

> The mere recital of these Christian graces should be enough to make the mouth water and the heart beat faster. For this is a portrait of Jesus Christ. No man or woman has ever exhibited these qualities in such balance or to such perfection as the man Christ Jesus. Yet this is the kind of person that every Christian longs to be.[33]

---

31 Ted Schroder, in Wright, *John Stott*, 60.
32 Stott, *The Radical Disciple*, 47, 48, 50, 51; emphasis added. See also Stott, *Understanding the Bible*, 8.
33 John Stott, *Baptism and Fullness: The Work of the Holy Spirit Today*, 2nd ed. (Leicester: Inter-Varsity Press, 1975), 76.

The Love of Christ

Stott notes a variety of ways in which people have identified the key mark of genuine Christianity: truth, faith, religious experience, service. All these, he says, are essential. But Stott himself says love has precedence. "Love is the greatest thing in the world."[34] God is love in his innermost being (1 John 4:8, 16), existing in self-giving triune love. And this God of love calls us to love. "Love is the principal, the paramount, the preeminent, the distinguishing characteristic of the people of God. Nothing can dislodge or replace it. Love is supreme."[35] "The Christian life is essentially a love-relationship to Jesus Christ. . . . Without this love, the Church's work is lifeless. . . . toil becomes drudgery if it is not a labour of love."[36]

Only love brings true joy and peace. Indeed, Stott argues that the pursuit of happiness in and of itself is elusive. "For joy and peace are not suitable goals to pursue; they are by-products of love. God gives them to us, not when we pursue *them*, but when we pursue *him* and *others* in love."[37] There is a place for self-affirmation, but it cannot be uncritical and unqualified, because we are sinners. Sin has corrupted our lives. So aspects of our selves need to repudiated rather than affirmed. After all, in the Bible self-love is a synonym for sin. "The self-conscious pursuit of happiness will always end in failure. But when we forget ourselves in the self-giving service of love, then joy and peace come flooding into our lives as incidental, unlooked-for blessings."[38]

This is a healthy counterbalance to distorted versions of Christian hedonism. Even joy in Christ can become a selfish and therefore futile pursuit. It is more biblical and more Christlike to pursue the joy *of others* in Christ. Those others may be Christians whose joy we pursue through pointing them to Christ in pastoral care and discipleship, or they may be unbelievers whose joy we pursue by pointing them to Christ in evangelism.

> This utter disregard of self in the service of God and man is what the Bible calls love. There is no self-interest in love. The essence of love is self-sacrifice. The worst of men is adorned by an occasional flash of such nobility. But the life of Jesus irradiated it with a never-fading incandes-

---

[34] John Stott, *The Contemporary Christian: An Urgent Plea for Double Listening* (Leicester: Inter-Varsity Press, 1992), 148.
[35] John Stott, *The Contemporary Christian*, 148.
[36] John Stott, *What Christ Thinks of the Church: Expository Addresses on the First Three Chapters of the Book of Revelation* (London: Lutterworth, 1958), 28.
[37] Stott, *The Contemporary Christian*, 149.
[38] Stott, *The Contemporary Christian*, 150–51.

> cent glow. Jesus was sinless because he was selfless. Such selflessness is love. And God is love.[39]

As might be expected, Stott is keen that a focus on love does not become disconnected from the wider witness of Scripture. He describes John 14:21 as "one of my favourite verses":[40] "Whoever has my commandments and keeps them, he it is who loves me. And he who loves me will be loved by my Father, and I will love him and manifest myself to him." Stott concludes, "The test of love is obedience, and the reward of love is a self-manifestation of Christ."[41] So love is not to be treated independently of law; instead it is informed by law. Responding to advocates of situational ethics, especially those who argue that in the New Testament love trumps law, Stott says, "The life and teaching of Jesus do not demonstrate such a neat distinction between law and love."[42] "He did not reject law. What he rejected were *misinterpretations* of the law, not the law itself."[43] It is a mistake to assume that an emphasis on law automatically equates to legalism. Love and law are not incompatible, for love is guided by law. To think love can be self-directing is naïve. Human beings are fallen and love can therefore be blind. Stott thereby affirms, explicitly so in *The Message of 1 Timothy and Titus*,[44] what the Reformers called "the third use of the law." The first use is to restrain evil in society; the second is to expose our need of Christ; and the third is to guide the lifestyle of justified believers.

What, then, of the times when Paul says Christians are not under law? "It is true that he uses this expression several times, but never on its own. He always supplies (or at least implies) a contrast." In other words, statements intended to provide a contrast are ambiguous on their own. They are clear only when you know to what they are being contrasted. Stott gives as an example the phrase "he does not behave like a man." On its own it is unclear whether this is good or bad. But suppose it is paired with the phrase "he is more like an angel." Now we know this statement means that the person in question behaves *better* than a man typically behaves. This is how we are to understand Paul's statements that we are not under the law.

---

39 Stott, *Basic Christianity*, 44–45.
40 Stott, *Focus on Christ*, 125; and Stott, *The Living Church: Convictions of a Lifelong Pastor* (Leicester: Inter-Varsity Press, 2007), 185.
41 Stott, *The Living Church*, 185.
42 Stott, *But I Say to You*, 124.
43 Stott, *But I Say to You*, 124.
44 John Stott, *The Message of 1 Timothy and Titus: The Life of the Local Church* (Leicester: Inter-Varsity Press; Downers Grove, IL: InterVarsity Press, 1996), 46–48.

"He never meant that the category of law has been altogether abolished, but rather that we do not look to the law for either our justification or our sanctification."[45] The law cannot achieve justification or sanctification, because of its inherent weakness (Rom. 8:3). This is another way of saying we cannot achieve justification or sanctification through the law, because we are fatally weakened by sin. "The problem is not with the law but with us. . . . Because we cannot keep the law, it can neither justify nor sanctify us."[46] Instead, it is God who justifies us through the Son and sanctifies us through the Spirit. This is where the contrasts come in. We are not under law, because we are now under grace for our justification (Rom. 6:14), and we are not under law, because we are now led by the Spirit for our sanctification (Gal. 5:18). This, then, is what is meant by being free from the law. This is the freedom Paul urges us not to lose by going back to thinking we can be justified or sanctified through our obedience to the law.

But this does not mean we can dispense with the law. "We still need it as a guide to how we should behave." We are justified so that the righteous requirements of the law might be met in us (Rom. 8:3). And, though we are sanctified by the Spirit rather than by the law, one of the ways the Spirit does this is by writing the demands of the law on our hearts. "Keeping God's law is not the *basis* on which we are put right with God—but it is the *result* of it. Again, keeping God's law is not the *means* of sanctification—but it is the *essence* of it."[47]

Freedom

"True freedom is freedom to be our true selves, as God made us and meant us to be," Stott says.[48] He starts with God. God's freedom does not include the freedom to choose sin, yet God is the most free being. From this it is clear that freedom is not having a multiplicity of choices, even though that is what it has come to mean in much of our political and economic discourse. Instead, true freedom is the ability to be true to yourself. That,

---

[45] Stott, *But I Say to You*, 144.
[46] Stott, *But I Say to You*, 144–45.
[47] Stott, *But I Say to You*, 145–46. See also Stott, *Men Made New: An Exposition of Romans 5–8* (London: Inter-Varsity Press, 1966), 58–83; Stott, *The Message of Galatians: Only One Way* (Leicester: Inter-Varsity Press; Downers Grove, IL: InterVarsity Press, 1968), 142–43; Stott, *The Message of the Sermon on the Mount: Christian Counter-Culture* (Leicester: Inter-Varsity Press; Downers Grove, IL: InterVarsity Press, 1978), 69–81; Stott, *The Bible: Book for Today* (Leicester: Inter-Varsity Press, 1982), 73–74; Stott, *Christian Basics: An Invitation to Discipleship* (London: Hodder, 1991),102–3; and Stott, *The Message of Romans: God's Good News for the World* (Leicester: Inter-Varsity Press; Downers Grove, IL: InterVarsity Press, 1994), 189–215, 221–22.
[48] Stott, *The Contemporary Christian*, 53.

though, requires that we understand what it means for human beings to be true to themselves. And the answer, seen in Christ, is counterintuitive. Let me give Stott himself the final word with an extended quotation from one of the most beautiful passages in his writing:

> What, then, about human beings? If fish were made for water, what are human beings made for? I think we have to answer that, if water is the element in which fish find their fishiness, then the element in which humans find their humanness is love, the relationships of love. . . .
>
> It is in love that we find and fulfil ourselves. Moreover, the reason for this is not far to seek. It is that God is love in his essential being, so that when he made us in his own image, he gave us a capacity to love as he loves. It is not a random thing, therefore, that God's two great commandments are to love him and each other, for this is our destiny. A truly human existence is impossible without love. Living is loving, and without love we wither and die. As Robert Southwell, the sixteenth-century Roman Catholic poet, expressed it: "Not when I breathe, but when I love, I live." He was probably echoing Augustine's remark that the soul lives where it loves, not where it exists.
>
> True love, however, places constraints on the lover, for love is essentially self-giving. And this brings us to a startling Christian paradox. True freedom is freedom to be my true self, as God made me and meant me to be. And God made me for loving. But loving is giving, self-giving. Therefore, in order to be myself, I have to deny myself and give myself. In order to be free, I have to serve. In order to live, I have to die to my own self-centredness. In order to find myself, I have to lose myself in loving.
>
> True freedom is, then, the exact opposite of what many people think. It is not freedom from all responsibility to God and others, in order to live for myself. That is bondage to my own self-centredness. Instead, true freedom is freedom from my silly little self, in order to live responsibly in love for God and others. . . .
>
> One could, then, perhaps paraphrase Jesus' epigram in these terms: "If you insist on holding on to yourself, and on living for yourself, and refuse to let yourself go, you will lose yourself. But if you are willing to give yourself away in love, then, at the moment of complete abandon, when you imagine that everything is lost, the miracle takes place and you find yourself and your freedom." It is only sacrificial service, the giving of the self in love to God and others, which is perfect freedom.[49]

[49] Stott, *The Contemporary Christian*, 54–56.

BIBLIOGRAPHY

If you want to read Stott for yourself, then I suggest you start with *The Cross of Christ* and *The Contemporary Christian. The Cross of Christ* is often cited as Stott's magnum opus, while *The Contemporary Christian* brings together many of the key themes of his thought. Indeed, the archive of his lecture outlines suggests that *The Contemporary Christian* largely reflects the material Stott taught around the world throughout the course of his global ministry.[1] *The Contemporary Christian* is being reissued in an updated form in five small volumes with the titles *The Gospel, The Disciple, The Bible, The Church*, and *The World* (London: Inter-Varsity Press).

Stott was an expositor, and another good way to get a feel for both his thought and his methodology would be read his contributions to the Bible Speaks Today series. I recommend starting with *The Message of Romans* and *The Message of Ephesians*.

Primary Sources

For a fuller list of John Stott's writing, see Timothy Dudley-Smith, *John Stott: A Comprehensive Bibliography* (Leicester: Inter-Varsity Press, 1995).

Authentic Christianity: From the Writings of John Stott. Edited by Timothy Dudley-Smith. Downers Grove, IL: InterVarsity Press, 1995.

The Authentic Jesus: A Response to Current Scepticism in the Church. Basingstoke: Marshall, Morgan and Scott, 1985.

Balanced Christianity: A Call to Avoid Unnecessary Polarisation. 2nd ed. Nottingham: Inter-Varsity Press, 2014.

[1] John Stott, "Lecture Outlines," Church of England Record Centre, STOTT/2/3.

Baptism and Fullness: The Work of the Holy Spirit Today. 2nd ed. Leicester: Inter-Varsity Press, 1975.

Basic Christianity. Rev. ed. Leicester: Inter-Varsity Press, 1971.

Between Two Worlds: The Art of Preaching in the Twentieth Century. Grand Rapids, MI: Eerdmans, 1982. UK edition entitled *I Believe in Preaching.* London: Hodder, 1982.

The Bible: Book for Today. Leicester: Inter-Varsity Press, 1982.

"The Bible in World Evangelization." In *Perspectives on the World Christian Movement: A Reader,* edited by Ralph D. Winter and Steven C. Hawthorne, 3–9. Pasadena, CA: William Carey Library, 1981.

"The Biblical Basis of Evangelism." In *Let the Earth Hear His Voice,* edited by J. D. Douglas, 65–78. Minneapolis: World Wide Publications, 1975.

"Biblical Teaching on Divorce." *Churchman* 85, no. 3 (1971): 165–74.

But I Say to You: Christ the Controversialist. Nottingham: Inter-Varsity Press, 2013. Originally published as *Christ the Controversialist: A Study in Some Essentials of Evangelical Religion.* London: Tyndale Press; Downers Grove, IL: InterVarsity Press, 1970.

Calling Christian Leaders: Biblical Models of Church, Gospel and Ministry. Leicester: Inter-Varsity Press, 2002. US edition entitled *Basic Christian Leadership: Biblical Models of Church, Gospel and Ministry.* Downers Grove, IL: InterVarsity Press, 2002.

"Charles Simeon: A Personal Appreciation." In *Evangelical Preaching: An Anthology of Sermons by Charles Simeon,* edited by James M. Houston, xxvii–xli. Portland OR: Multnomah, 1986.

"The Christian and the Poor." *All Souls Papers,* February 16, 1981.

Christian Basics: An Invitation to Discipleship. London: Hodder, 1991. Originally published as *Your Confirmation.* London: Hodder, 1958.

Christian Mission in the Modern World. London: Falcon, 1975.

(and Christopher J. H. Wright.) *Christian Mission in the Modern World.* 2nd ed. London: Inter-Varsity Press, 2015. Updated and expanded.

Christ the Controversialist. See *But I Say to You.*

Confess Your Sins: The Way of Reconciliation. London: Hodder, 1964.

The Contemporary Christian: An Urgent Plea for Double Listening. Leicester: Inter-Varsity Press, 1992.

The Cross of Christ. 2nd ed. Leicester: Inter-Varsity Press, 1989.

Culture and the Bible. Downers Grove, IL: InterVarsity Press, 1979.

The Epistles of John: An Introduction and Commentary. London: Tyndale Press, 1964.

(and David L. Edwards.) *Essentials: A Liberal-Evangelical Dialogue.* London: Hodder & Stoughton, 1988.

"The Evangelical Doctrine of Baptism." *Churchman* 112, no. 1 (1998): 47–59.

Evangelical Truth: A Personal Plea for Unity, Integrity and Faithfulness. Rev. ed. Nottingham: Inter-Varsity Press, 2015.

(and Ron Sider.) *Evangelism, Salvation and Social Justice.* 2nd ed. Grove Booklets on Ethics. Bramcote: Grove, 1979.

Explaining the Lausanne Covenant. Lausanne Occasional Papers, 1975.

Favourite Psalms: Growing Closer to God. London: Monarch, 2003. First published as *The Canticles and Selected Psalms.* London: Hodder & Stoughton, 1966.

Focus on Christ: An Enquiry into the Theology of Prepositions. Eastbourne: Kingsway 1979.

(and Coote, Robert, eds.) *The Gospel and Culture.* Pasadena, CA: William Carey Library, 1979. Papers of the 1978 Willowbank International Consultation on Gospel and Culture. Published in the UK as *Down to Earth: Studies in Christianity and Culture.* London: Hodder & Stoughton, 1980.

The Incomparable Christ. Leicester: Inter-Varsity Press, 2001. London Lectures in Contemporary Christianity, 2000.

Issues Facing Christians Today. 2nd ed. London: Marshall Pickering, 1990. Fourth edition with contributions from Roy McCloughry and John Wyatt. *Issues Facing Christians Today.* Rev. ed. Grand Rapids, MI: Zondervan, 2006.

"Is the Incarnation a Myth?" *Christianity Today* 22, no. 3 (1977).

"Jesus Christ, the Life of the World." *Churchman* 97, no. 1 (1983): 6–15.

John Stott at Keswick: A Lifetime of Preaching. Milton Keynes: Authentic Media, 2008.

The Last Word: Reflections on a Lifetime of Preaching. Milton Keynes: Authentic Media, 2008. Includes John Stott's 2007 Keswick address entitled "Becoming Like Christ."

The Lausanne Covenant: An Exposition and Commentary. Minneapolis: World Wide Publications, 1975.

The Living Church: Convictions of a Lifelong Pastor. Leicester: Inter-Varsity Press, 2007.

"The Living God Is a Missionary God." In *Perspectives on the World Christian Movement: A Reader,* edited by Ralph D. Winter and Steven C. Hawthorne, 10–18. Pasadena, CA: William Carey Library, 1981.

(ed.) *Making Christ Known: Historic Missions Documents from the Lausanne Movement, 1974–1989*. Carlisle: Paternoster/LCWE, 1996.

Men Made New: An Exposition of Romans 5–8. London: Inter-Varsity Press, 1966.

Men with a Message: An Introduction to the New Testament and Its Writers. London: Longmans, 1954.

The Message of 1 Timothy and Titus: The Life of the Local Church. Bible Speaks Today. Leicester: Inter-Varsity Press; Downers Grove, IL: InterVarsity Press, 1996.

The Message of 2 Timothy: Guard the Gospel. Bible Speaks Today. Leicester: Inter-Varsity Press; Downers Grove, IL: InterVarsity Press, 1973.

The Message of Acts: To the Ends of the Earth. Bible Speaks Today. Leicester: Inter-Varsity Press; Downers Grove, IL: InterVarsity Press, 1990.

The Message of Ephesians: God's New Society. Bible Speaks Today. Leicester: Inter-Varsity Press, 1979.

The Message of Galatians: Only One Way. Bible Speaks Today. Leicester: Inter-Varsity Press; Downers Grove, IL: InterVarsity Press, 1968.

The Message of Romans: God's Good News for the World. Bible Speaks Today. Leicester: Inter-Varsity Press; Downers Grove, IL: InterVarsity Press, 1994.

The Message of the Sermon on the Mount: Christian Counter-Culture. Bible Speaks Today. Leicester: Inter-Varsity Press; Downers Grove, IL: InterVarsity Press, 1978.

The Message of Thessalonians: Preparing for the Coming King. Bible Speaks Today. Leicester: Inter-Varsity Press; Downers Grove, IL: InterVarsity Press, 1991.

One People: Clergy and Laity in God's Church. London: Falcon, 1969.

Our Guilty Silence: The Church, the Gospel and the World. London: Hodder & Stoughton, 1967.

Parochial Evangelism by the Laity. Westminster: Church Information Board/London Diocese, 1952.

The Preacher's Portrait. London: Tyndale Press; Grand Rapids, MI: Eerdmans, 1961.

The Radical Disciple: Wholehearted Christian Living. Leicester: Inter-Varsity Press, 2010.

"Reconciliation," *Churchman* 68, no. 2 (1954): 79–83.

"Seeking Theological Agreement." *Transformation* 1, no. 1 (1984): 21–22.

Students of the Word: Engaging with Scripture to Impact Our World. Oxford: IFES, 2013.

Understanding the Bible. London: Scripture Union, 1972.

What Christ Thinks of the Church: Expository Addresses on the First Three Chapters of the Book of Revelation. London: Lutterworth, 1958.

Why I Am a Christian. Leicester: Inter-Varsity Press, 2003.

Your Mind Matters: The Place of the Mind in the Christian Life. Leicester: Inter-Varsity Press, 1972; Downers Grove, IL: InterVarsity Press, 2006.

Secondary Sources

Anderson, G. H., and T. F. Stransky, eds. *Mission Trends: Third World Theologies*. New York: Paulist; Grand Rapids, MI: Eerdmans, 1976.

Adeyemo, Tokunboh, Vinay Samuel, and Ronald J. Sider. "Editorial: Christian Faith and Politics." *Transformation* 2, no. 3 (1985).

Atherstone, Andrew. *An Anglican Evangelical Identity Crisis: The Churchman—Anvil Affair of 1981–1984*. London: Latimer Trust, 2008.

Atherstone, Andrew. "The Keele Congress of 1967: A Paradigm Shift in Anglican Evangelical Attitudes." *Journal of Anglican Studies* 9 (2011): 175–97.

Atherstone, Andrew, and David Ceri Jones, eds. *Engaging with Martyn Lloyd-Jones: The Life and Legacy of "the Doctor."* Nottingham: Apollos, 2011.

Atherstone, Andrew, and John Maiden. *Evangelicalism and the Church of England in the Twentieth Century: Reform, Resistance and Renewal*. Woodbridge: Boydell, 2014.

Barclay, Oliver R. *Charles Simeon and the Evangelical Tradition*. Lewes: Focus Christian, 1986.

Barclay, Oliver. *Evangelicalism in Britain 1935–1995: A Personal Sketch*. Leicester, Inter-Varsity Press, 1997.

Barclay, Oliver. "The Theology of Social Ethics: A Survey of Current Positions." *Evangelical Quarterly* 62, no. 1 (1990): 63–86.

Barclay, Oliver R. *Whatever Happened to the Jesus Lane Lot?* Leicester: Inter-Varsity Press, 1977.

Barclay, Oliver R. *Whose World?* Leicester: Inter-Varsity Press, 1970. Published under the pseudonym A. N. Triton.

Barclay, Oliver R., and Robert M. Horn. *From Cambridge to the World: 125 Years of Student Witness*. Leicester: Inter-Varsity Press, 2002.

Barrett, Matthew. *None Greater: The Undomesticated Attributes of God*. Grand Rapids, MI: Baker, 2019.

Beasley-Murray, George R. *Jesus and the Kingdom of God*. Grand Rapids, MI: Eerdmans; Exeter: Paternoster, 1986.

Bebbington, David W. *The Dominance of Evangelicalism: The Age of Spurgeon and Moody.* Leicester: Inter-Varsity Press, 2005.

Bebbington, David W. *Evangelicalism in Modern Britain: A History from the 1730s to the 1980s*. London: Unwin Hyman, 1989.

Bebbington, David W. *Holiness in Nineteenth-Century England*. Carlisle: Paternoster, 2000.

Bediako, Kwame. "World Evangelisation, Institutional Evangelicalism and the Future of the Christian World Mission." In *Proclaiming Christ in Christ's Way: Studies in Integral Evangelism*, edited by Vinay Samuel and Albrecht Hauser, 52–68. Oxford: Regnum, 1989.

Beisner, Calvin. "Justice and Poverty: Two Views Contrasted." *Transformation* 10, no. 1 (1993): 16–22.

Bennett, Arthur. "Charles Simeon: Prince of Evangelicals," *Churchman* 102, no. 2 (1988): 122–42.

Bennett, John C. "The Legacy of Charles Simeon," *International Bulletin of Missionary Research* 18, no. 2 (1994): 72–77.

Beyerhaus, Peter. "A Biblical Encounter with Some Contemporary Philosophical and Theological Systems." In *In Word and Deed: Evangelism and Social Responsibility*, edited by Bruce Nicholls, 165–88. Exeter: Paternoster, 1985.

Beyerhaus, Peter. *Missions: Which Way? Humanization and Redemption*. Grand Rapids, MI: Zondervan, 1971.

Blamires, Harry. *The Christian Mind: How Should a Christian Think?* London: SPCK, 1963.

Blanch, Allen, M. *From Strength to Strength: A Life of Marcus Loane*. Melbourne: Australian Scholarly, 2015.

Bloesch, Donald G. *The Future of Evangelical Christianity: A Call for Unity amid Diversity.* New York: Doubleday, 1983.

Bonino, José Miguez. *Revolutionary Theology Comes of Age: Doing Theology in a Revolutionary Situation*. London: SPCK, 1975.

Bosch, David. "In Search of a New Evangelical Understanding." In *In Word and Deed: Evangelism and Social Responsibility*, edited by Bruce Nicholls, 63–83. Exeter: Paternoster, 1985.

Bosch, David. "Towards Evangelism in Context." In *The Church in Response to Human Need*, edited by Vinay Samuel and Chris Sugden, 180–92. Oxford: Regnum, 1987.

Bosch, David. *Transforming Mission: Paradigm Shifts in Theology of Mission*. Maryknoll, NY: Orbis, 1997.

Bosch, David. *Witness to the World: The Christian Mission in Theological Perspective*. London: Marshall, Morgan and Scott, 1980.

Bradshaw, Bruce. *Bridging the Gap: Evangelism, Development and* Shalom. Monrovia, CA: MARC, 1993.

Branson, Mark Lau, and C. René Padilla, eds. *Conflict and Context: Hermeneutics in the Americas*. Grand Rapids, MI: Eerdmans, 1986.

Brencher, John. *Martyn Lloyd-Jones (1899–1981) and Twentieth Century Evangelicalism*. Milton Keynes: Paternoster, 2002.

Budziszewski, J., ed. *Evangelicals in the Public Square: Four Formative Voices on Political Thought and Action*. Grand Rapids, MI: Baker, 2006.

Cameron, Julia. "John Stott and the Lausanne Movement." *Anvil* 27, no. 2 (2010): 40–49.

Cameron, Julia. *John Stott's Right Hand: The Untold Story of Frances Whitehead*. Eugene, OR: Cascade, 2018.

Capon, John. *And There Was Light: The Story of the Nationwide Festival of Light*. London: Lutterworth, 1972.

Carr, Paul A. "Are the Priorities and Concerns of Charles Simeon Relevant for Today?" *Churchman* 114, no. 2 (2000): 153–66.

Catherwood, Christopher. *Five Evangelical Leaders*. London: Hodder & Stoughton, 1984.

Chapman, Alister. *Godly Ambition: John Stott and the Evangelical Movement*. New York, Oxford University Press, 2012.

Chapman, Ian. "Charles Simeon of Cambridge." *Churchman* 109, no. 4 (1995): 333–60.

Chester, Tim. *Awakening to a World of Need: The Recovery of Evangelical Social Concern*. Leicester: Inter-Varsity Press, 1993.

Chester, Tim. *Good News to the Poor*. Leicester: Inter-Varsity Press, 2004; Wheaton, IL: Crossway, 2013.

Chester, Tim, ed. *Justice, Mercy and Humility: Integral Mission and the Poor*. Carlisle: Paternoster, 2002.

Chester, Tim. *Mission and the Coming of God: Eschatology, the Trinity and Mission in the Theology of Jürgen Moltmann and Contemporary Evangelicalism*. Paternoster Theological Monographs. Carlisle: Paternoster, 2006.

Chester, Tim. *Mission Matters: Love Says So*. London: Inter-Varsity Press, 2015.

Cho, J. Chongnahm. "The Mission of the Church: Theology and Practice." In *In Word and Deed: Evangelism and Social Responsibility*, edited by Bruce Nicholls, 215–38. Exeter: Paternoster, 1985.

Church of England Evangelical Council. *Truth, Error and Discipline in the Church*. London: Vine, 1978.

Clowney, Edmund P. *The Church*. Leicester: Inter-Varsity Press; Downers Grove, IL: InterVarsity Press, 1995.

Cook, William. "Reflections on Wheaton '83." *Evangelical Review of Theology* 9, no. 1 (1985): 27–31.

Cope, Christopher. "The Relationship between Evangelism and Social Responsibility in Evangelical Thought from the Wheaton Conference of 1966 to the Wheaton Conference of 1983." MPhil thesis, University of Manchester, 1990.

Costas, Orlando. *Christ outside the Gate: Mission beyond Christendom*. Maryknoll, NY: Orbis, 1984.

Costas, Orlando. *The Church and Its Mission: A Shattering Critique from the Third World*. Wheaton, IL: Tyndale, 1982.

Costas, Orlando. "Proclaiming Christ in the Two Thirds World." In *Sharing Jesus in the Two Thirds World: Evangelical Christologies from the Contexts of Poverty, Powerlessness and Religious Pluralism*, edited by Vinay Samuel and Chris Sugden, 1–15. Bangalore: PIM, 1983.

Crowe, Philip. *Keele '67: The National Evangelical Anglican Congress*. London: Falcon, 1967.

Davies, Gaius. *Genius, Grief and Grace: A Doctor Looks at Suffering and Success*. Fearn, Ross-shire: Christians Focus, 2011.

Demarest, Bruce. *The Cross and Salvation: The Doctrine of Salvation*. Wheaton, IL: Crossway, 1997.

DeYoung, Kevin, and Greg Gilbert. *What Is the Mission of the Church? Making Sense of Social Justice, Shalom, and the Great Commission*. Wheaton, IL: Crossway, 2011.

Dolezal, James E. *All That Is in God: Evangelical Theology and the Challenge of Classical Christian Theism*. Grand Rapids, MI: Reformation Heritage, 2017.

Dolezal, James E. *God without Parts: Divine Simplicity and the Metaphysics of God's Absoluteness*. Eugene, OR: Pickwick, 2011.

Douglas, J. D., ed. *Let the Earth Hear His Voice*. Minneapolis: World Wide Publications, 1975. Papers of Lausanne, 1974.

Douglas, J. D., ed. *Proclaim Christ Until He Comes: Calling the Whole Church to Take the Whole Gospel to the Whole World*. Minneapolis: World Wide Publications, 1990. Papers of the International Congress of World Evangelism, 1989 (Lausanne II).

Dudley-Smith, Timothy. *John Stott: A Comprehensive Bibliography*. Leicester: Inter-Varsity Press, 1995.

Dudley-Smith, Timothy. *John Stott*. Vol. 1, *The Making of a Leader*. Leicester: Inter-Varsity Press, 1999.

Dudley-Smith, Timothy. *John Stott*. Vol. 2, *A Global Ministry*. Leicester: Inter-Varsity Press, 2001.

Dudley-Smith, Timothy. "Stott, John Robert Walmsley." In *The SPCK Handbook of Anglican Theologians*, edited by Alister E. McGrath, 203–5. London: SPCK, 1998.

Eden, Martyn, and David Wells, eds. *The Gospel in the Modern World: A Tribute to John Stott*. Leicester: Inter-Varsity Press; Downers Grove, IL: InterVarsity Press, 1991.

Escobar, Samuel. "Evangelism and Man's Search for Freedom, Justice and Fulfilment." In *Let the Earth Hear His Voice*, edited by J. D. Douglas, 303–26. Minneapolis: World Wide Publications, 1975. Also published in *Mission Trends: Third World Theologies*, edited by G. H. Anderson and T. F. Stransky, 104–10. New York: Paulist; Grand Rapids, MI: Eerdmans, 1976.

Escobar, Samuel. "The Social Responsibility of the Church." In *Is Revolution Change?*, edited by Brian Griffiths, 84–111. Leicester: Inter-Varsity Press, 1972.

Fountain Trust and the Church of England Evangelical Council. *Gospel and Spirit: A Joint Statement*. Esher: Fountain Trust; London: The Church of England Evangelical Council, 1977.

Frame, John M. *The Doctrine of God*. Phillipsburg, NJ: P&R, 2002.

Frame, John M. *Systematic Theology: An Introduction to Christian Belief*. Phillipsburg, NJ: P&R, 2013.

George, Timothy, ed. *J. I. Packer and the Evangelical Future: The Impact of His Life and Thought*. Grand Rapids, MI: Baker, 2009.

Gill, Athol. "Christian Social Responsibility." In *The New Face of Evangelicals*, edited by C. René Padilla, 87–102. London: Hodder & Stoughton, 1976.

Gladwin, John. "Politics, Providence and the Kingdom." *Churchman* 91 (1977): 47–57.

Goodhew, David. "The Rise of the Cambridge Inter-Collegiate Christian Union, 1910–1971." *Journal of Ecclesiastical History* 54, no. 1 (2003): 62–88.

Gordon, James M. *Evangelical Spirituality: From the Wesleys to John Stott*. London: SPCK, 1991.

The Grand Rapids Report: Evangelism and Social Responsibility. Exeter: Paternoster, 1982. The conference report of the Consultation on the Relationship between Evangelism and Social Responsibility, Grand Rapids, 1982.

Grant, Jamie A., and Dewi A. Hughes. *Transforming the World? The Gospel and Social Responsibility*. Nottingham: Apollos, 2009.

Greene, Mark. *Thank God It's Monday: Ministry in the Workplace*. 2nd ed. London: Scripture Union, 1997.

Greenman, J. P. "Stott, John Robert Walmsley," *Biographical Dictionary of Evangelicals*, edited by T. Larsen, 638–41. Leicester: Inter-Varsity Press, 2003.

Grigg, Viv. *Companion to the Poor.* Sydney: Albatross; Oxford: Lion, 1984.

Grogan, Geoffrey W. *The Faith Once Entrusted to the Saints? Engaging with Issues and Trends in Evangelical Theology.* Nottingham, Inter-Varsity Press, 2010.

Hambrick-Stowe, Charles E. *The Practice of Piety: Puritan Devotional Principles in Puritan New England.* Chapel Hill: University of North Carolina Press, 1982.

Harrison, Glynn. *The Big Ego Trip: Finding True Significance in a Culture of Self-Esteem.* Nottingham: Inter-Varsity Press, 2013.

Harvey, Thomas. "Baptism as a Means of Grace: A Response to John Stott's 'The Evangelical Doctrine of Baptism.'" *Churchman* 113, no. 2 (1999): 103–12.

Hathaway, Brian. *Beyond Renewal: The Kingdom of God.* Milton Keynes: Word, 1999.

Hathaway, Brian. "The Kingdom Manifesto." *Transformation* 7, no. 3 (1990): 6–11.

Haugen, Gary. *Good News about Injustice: A Witness of Courage in a Hurting World.* Nottingham: Inter-Varsity Press, 1999.

Henry, Carl. *Confessions of a Theologian: An Autobiography.* Waco, TX: Word, 1986.

Henry, Carl F. H. *The Uneasy Conscience of Modern Fundamentalism.* Grand Rapids, MI: Eerdmans, 1947.

Henry, Carl F. H., and Stanley Mooneyham, eds. *One Race, One Gospel, One Task.* 2 vols. Minneapolis: World Wide Publications, 1967. The official reference volumes of Berlin, 1966.

Hoekema, A. A. *The Bible and the Future.* Exeter: Paternoster, 1978.

Hoekendijk, J. C. *The Church Inside Out.* Philadelphia: Westminster, 1964.

Hoekstra, Harvey T. *Evangelism in Eclipse: World Mission and the World Council of Churches.* Exeter: Paternoster, 1979.

Hopkins, Evan. *The Law of Liberty in the Spiritual Life.* London: Marshall, 1884.

Hopkins, Hugh Evan. *Charles Simeon of Cambridge.* London: Hodder & Stoughton, 1977.

Hudson, Neil. *Imagine Church: Releasing Whole-Life Disciples.* Nottingham: Inter-Varsity Press, 2012.

Hughes, Philip E. "Editorial." *Churchman* 76, no. 3 (1962): 131–35.

Hustler, Jonathan. "The Late Greats: John Stott." *Preach* 14 (2018): 26–27.

Hylson-Smith, Kenneth. *The Churches in England from Elizabeth I to Elizabeth II.* Vol. 3, *1833–1998.* London, SCM, 1998.

Hylson-Smith, Kenneth. *Evangelicals in the Church of England 1734–1984*. Edinburgh: T&T Clark, 1989.

Jeffery, Steve, Michael Ovey, and Andrew Sach. *Pierced for Our Transgressions: Rediscovering the Glory of Penal Substitution*. Nottingham, Leicester, 2007.

Jenkins, Gary. *A Tale of Two Preachers: Preaching in the Simeon-Stott Tradition*. Cambridge: Grove, 2012.

Jensen, Michael P. *Sydney Anglicanism: An Apology*. Eugene, OR: Wipf & Stock, 2012.

Johnson, Douglas. *Contending for the Faith: A History of the Evangelical Movement in the Universities and Colleges*. Leicester: Inter-Varsity Press, 1979.

Johnston, Arthur P. *The Battle for World Evangelism*. Wheaton, IL: Tyndale, 1978.

Johnston, Arthur P. "The Kingdom in Relation to the Church and the World." In *In Word and Deed: Evangelism and Social Responsibility*, edited by Bruce Nicholls, 109–34. Exeter: Paternoster, 1985.

Kirk, J. Andrew, ed. *Handling Problems of Peace and War: An Evangelical Debate*. London: Marshall Pickering, 1988.

Kirk, J. Andrew. *A New World Coming: Looking Afresh at the Gospel for Today*. Basingstoke: Marshalls, 1983.

Kirk, J. Andrew. *What Is Mission? Theological Explorations*. London: Darton, Longman & Todd, 1999.

Kuzmic, Peter. "History and Eschatology: Evangelical Views." In *In Word and Deed: Evangelism and Social Responsibility*, edited by Bruce Nicholls, 135–64. Exeter: Paternoster, 1985.

Ladd, George Eldon. *The Presence of the Future*. London: SPCK, 1974.

Lamb, Jonathan, with Ian Randall. *Knowing God Better: The Vision of the Keswick Movement*. Nottingham: Inter-Varsity Press, 2015.

The Lausanne Covenant. The statement of Lausanne 1974, published with the conference documents in *Let the Earth Hear His Voice*, edited by J. D. Douglas. Minneapolis: World Wide Publications, 1975.

Lister, Rob. *God Is Impassible and Impassioned: Toward a Theology of Divine Emotion*. Wheaton, IL: Crossway, 2013.

Lloyd-Jones, D. Martyn. *Christ Our Sanctification*. London: Inter-Varsity Press, 1948.

Lloyd-Jones, D. Martyn. *Knowing the Times: Addresses Delivered on Various Occasions*. Edinburgh: Banner of Truth, 1989.

Lloyd-Jones, D. Martyn. *Romans 6: The New Man*. Edinburgh: Banner of Truth, 1992.

Maggay, Melba. *Transforming Society.* Oxford: Regnum, 1994.

Manwaring, Randle, *From Controversy to Co-existence: Evangelicals in the Church of England 1914–1980.* Cambridge: Cambridge University Press, 1985.

Marsden, George M. *Reforming Fundamentalism: Fuller Seminary and the New Evangelicalism.* Grand Rapids, MI: Eerdmans, 1987.

Martin, William. *A Prophet with Honor: The Billy Graham Story.* 2nd ed. Grand Rapids, MI: Zondervan, 2018. First edition, *The Billy Graham Story: A Prophet with Honour.* London: Hutchinson, 1991.

McCloughry, Roy. *The Eye of the Needle.* Nottingham: Inter-Varsity Press, 1990.

McGavran, Donald A. "Will Uppsala Betray the Two Billion?" *Church Growth Bulletin* 4, no. 5 (1968).

McGrath, Alister. *C. S. Lewis: A Life.* London: Hodder & Stoughton, 2013.

McGrath, Alister. *To Know and Serve God: A Biography of James Packer.* London: Hodder & Stoughton, 1977.

Meyer, Jason. *Lloyd-Jones on the Christian Life: Doctrine and Life as Fuel and Fire.* Wheaton, IL: Crossway, 2018.

Moberg, David O. *The Great Reversal: Reconciling Evangelism and Social Concern.* 2nd ed. Eugene, OR: Wipf & Stock, 2006.

Mott, Stephen Charles. *Biblical Ethics and Social Change.* Oxford: Oxford University Press, 1982.

Mott, Stephen Charles. *A Christian Perspective on Political Thought.* Oxford: Oxford University Press, 1993.

Mott, Stephen Charles. "The Contribution of the Bible to Economic Thought." *Transformation* 4, no. 3–4 (1987): 25–33.

Mott, Stephen Charles. "The Partiality of Biblical Justice." *Transformation* 10, no. 1 (1993): 23–29.

Mountain, James, comp. *Hymns of Consecration and Faith.* 2nd ed. London: Marshall, 1902. Revised by Evan Hopkins.

Mouw, Richard. *Political Evangelism.* Grand Rapids, MI: Eerdmans, 1973.

Mouw, Richard. *Politics and the Biblical Drama.* Grand Rapids, MI: Baker, 1976.

Mouw, Richard. *When the Kings Come Marching In: Israel and the New Jerusalem.* Grand Rapids, MI: Eerdmans, 1983.

Munden, Alan F. "Umbrellas, Great-Coats and Polished Shoes, and the Spirituality of Charles Simeon." *Churchman* 113, no. 2 (1999): 113–24.

Murray, Iain H. *David Martyn Lloyd-Jones: The Fight of Faith 1939–1981.* Edinburgh: Banner of Truth, 1990.

Murray, Iain H. *Evangelicalism Divided: A Record of the Crucial Change in the Years 1950 to 2000*. Edinburgh: Banner of Truth, 2000.

Murray, Iain H. *The Forgotten Spurgeon*. Edinburgh: Banner of Truth, 1966.

Myers, Bryant L. *Walking with the Poor: Principles and Practices of Transformational Development*. Maryknoll, NY: Orbis, 1999.

Naselli, Andrew David. "Keswick Theology: A Survey and Analysis of the Doctrine of Sanctification in the Early Keswick Movement." *Detroit Baptist Seminary Journal* 13, no. 1 (2008): 17–67.

Naselli, Andrew David. *No Quick Fix: Where Higher Life Theology Came From, What It Is, and Why It's Harmful*. Bellingham, WA: Lexham, 2017.

Nazir-Ali, Michael. *From Everywhere to Everywhere: A World View of Christian Mission*. London: Collins, 1991.

Newbigin, Lesslie. *The Gospel in a Pluralistic Society*. London: SPCK, 1989.

Nicholls, Bruce, ed. *In Word and Deed: Evangelism and Social Responsibility*. Exeter: Paternoster, 1985. Conference papers of the Consultation on the Relationship between Evangelism and Social Responsibility, Grand Rapids, 1982.

Noll, Mark A. *A History of Christianity in the United States and Canada*. Grand Rapids, MI: Eerdmans; London: SPCK, 1992.

O'Donovan, Oliver. *The Desire of the Nations: Rediscovering the Roots of Political Theology*. Cambridge: Cambridge University Press, 1996.

O'Donovan, Oliver. *Resurrection and Moral Order: An Outline for Evangelical Ethics*. Leicester: Inter-Varsity Press, 1986.

Packer, J. I. "Evangelical Annihilationism in Review." *Reformation and Revival Journal* 6, no. 2 (1997): 37–49.

Packer, J. I. "Expository Preaching: Charles Simeon and Ourselves." *Churchman* 74, no. 2 (1960): 94–100.

Packer, J. I. *Keep in Step with the Spirit*. Leicester: Inter-Varsity Press, 1984.

Packer, J. I. "'Keswick' and the Reformed Doctrine of Sanctification." *The Evangelical Quarterly* 27, no. 3 (1955): 153–67.

Padilla, C. René. "Evangelism and the World." In *Let the Earth Hear His Voice*, edited by J. D. Douglas, 116–46. Minneapolis: World Wide Publications, 1975. Also published in C. René Padilla, *Mission between the Times*, 1–44. Grand Rapids, MI: Eerdmans, 1985.

Padilla, C. René. "Hermeneutics and Culture—A Theological Perspective." In *Down to Earth: Studies in Christianity and Culture*, edited by John Stott and Robert Coote, 63–78. London: Hodder & Stoughton, 1980.

Padilla, C. René. "How Evangelicals Endorsed Social Responsibility 1966–1983." *Transformation* 2, no. 3 (1985): 28–32. Also published by Grove Booklets, Nottingham, 1985.

Padilla, C. René. *Mission between the Times*. Grand Rapids, MI: Eerdmans, 1985.

Padilla, C. René, ed. *The New Face of Evangelicals: An International Symposium on the Lausanne Covenant*. London: Hodder & Stoughton, 1976.

Padilla, C. René. "The Politics of the Kingdom of God and the Political Mission of the Church." In *Proclaiming Christ in Christ's Way: Studies in Integral Evangelism*, edited by Vinay Samuel and Albrecht Hauser, 180–98. Oxford: Regnum, 1985.

Padilla, C. René, and Chris Sugden, eds. *Texts on Evangelical Social Ethics, 1974–1983*. Nottingham: Grove, 1985.

Peterson, Robert A. "A Traditionalist Response to John Stott's Arguments for Annihilationism." *Journal of the Evangelical Theological Society* 37, no. 4 (1994): 553–68.

Price, Charles, and Ian Randall. *Transforming Keswick: The Keswick Convention Past, Present and Future*. Carlisle: OM, 2000.

Prime, Derek. *Charles Simeon: An Ordinary Pastor of Extraordinary Influence*. Leominster: Day One, 2011.

Randall, Ian. "'To Be Occupied with God': John Stott on Worship." *Anvil* 23, no. 4 (2006): 247–57.

Rogers, Katherin A. *Perfect Being Theology*. Reason and Religion. Edinburgh: Edinburgh University Press, 2000.

Ryken, Leland. *J. I. Packer: An Evangelical Life*. Wheaton, IL: Crossway, 2015.

Ryle, J. C. *Holiness*. Edinburgh: Banner of Truth, 2014. Originally published in 1877 and enlarged in 1879.

Samuel, Vinay, and Chris Sugden, eds. *The Church in Response to Human Need*. Oxford: Regnum, 1987.

Samuel, Vinay, and Chris Sugden. "Evangelism and Social Responsibility—A Biblical Study on Priorities." In *In Word and Deed: Evangelism and Social Responsibility*, edited by Bruce Nicholls, 189–214. Exeter: Paternoster, 1985.

Samuel, Vinay, and Chris Sugden, eds. *Evangelism and the Poor*. Oxford: Regnum, 1983.

Samuel, Vinay, and Chris Sugden, eds. *Sharing Jesus in the Two Thirds World: Evangelical Christologies from the Contexts of Poverty, Powerlessness and Religious Pluralism*. Bangalore: PIM, 1983.

Samuel, Vinay, and Chris Sugden. "Toward a Theology of Social Change." In *Evangelicals and Development*, edited by Ronald Sider, 45–68. Exeter: Paternoster, 1981.

Sanlon, Peter. *Simply God: Recovering the Classical Trinity.* Nottingham: Inter-Varsity Press, 2014.

Saward, Michael. *The Anglican Church Today: Evangelicals on the Move.* Oxford: Mowbray, 1987.

Sider, Ronald, ed. *Evangelicals and Development.* Exeter: Paternoster, 1981. Papers of the Consultation on the Theology of Development, Hoddesdon, 1980.

Sider, Ronald. *Evangelism and Social Action: Uniting the Church to Heal the Lost and Broken.* London: Hodder & Stoughton, 1993.

Sider, Ronald, ed. *Lifestyle in the Eighties.* Exeter: Paternoster, 1982. The papers of the Consultation on Simple Lifestyle, Hoddesdon, 1980.

Sider, Ronald, ed. *Living More Simply: Biblical Principles and Practical Models.* London: Hodder, 1980.

Sider, Ronald. *Rich Christians in an Age of Hunger.* London: Hodder & Stoughton, 1977.

Sider, Ronald J., with a response by John R. W. Stott. *Evangelism, Salvation and Social Justice.* Nottingham: Grove, 1977. Sider's contribution was first published under the same title in *International Review of Mission* 64, no. 255 (1975): 251–67, and later published in *Evangelical Review of Theology* 2, no. 1 (1978): 70–88.

Sider, Ronald, et al. "Editorial: Christian Faith and Politics." See Adeyemo, Tokunboh, Vinay Samuel, and Ronald J. Sider. "Editorial: Christian Faith and Politics."

Sider, Ronald, with James Parker. "How Broad Is Salvation in Scripture?" In *In Word and Deed: Evangelism and Social Responsibility,* edited by Bruce Nicholls, 85–108. Exeter: Paternoster, 1985.

Simeon, Charles. *Evangelical Preaching: An Anthology of Sermons by Charles Simeon.* Edited by James M. Houston. Portland, OR: Multnomah, 1986.

Simeon, Charles. *Horae Homileticae.* London: Richard Watts, 1819. Second edition published by London: Holdsworth & Ball, 1832.

Sine, Tom. *Mustard Seed vs. McWorld: Reinventing Life and Faith for the Future.* Oxford: Monarch, 1999.

Sire, James W. *Discipleship of the Mind: Learning to Love God in the Ways We Think.* Nottingham: Inter-Varsity Press, 1990.

Smith, David W. *Mission after Christendom.* London: Darton, Longman & Todd, 2003.

Smith, David W. *Transforming the World? The Social Impact of British Evangelicalism.* Carlisle: Paternoster, 1998.

Smyth, Charles. *The Art of Preaching: A Practical Survey of Preaching in the Church of England 747–1939.* London: SPCK, 1940.

Stanley, Brian. *Christianity in the Twentieth Century: A World History*. Princeton, NJ: Princeton University Press, 2018.

Stanley, Brian. *The Global Diffusion of Evangelicalism: The Age of Billy Graham and John Stott*. Nottingham: Inter-Varsity Press, 2013.

Steer, Roger. *Inside Story: The Life of John Stott*. Nottingham: Inter-Varsity Press, 2009.

Steuernagel, Valdir R. "Social Concern and Evangelisation." *Transformation* 7, no. 1 (1990): 12–16.

Steuernagel, Valdir R. "The Theology of Mission in Its Relation to Social Responsibility within the Lausanne Movement." DTh thesis, Lutheran School of Theology, Chicago, 1988.

Sugden, Chris. "Evangelicals and Wholistic Evangelism." In *Proclaiming Christ in Christ's Way*, edited by Vinay Samuel and Albrecht Hauser, 29–51. Oxford: Regnum, 1989. A shorter version of this article was published in *Transformation* 7, no. 1 (1989): 9–12, under the title "Theological Developments since Lausanne I."

Sugden, Chris. *Radical Discipleship*. Basingstoke: Marshall, Morgan and Scott, 1981.

Taylor, John V. *Enough Is Enough*. London: SCM, 1975.

Taylor, Justin. "50 Years Ago Today: The Split between John Stott and Martyn Lloyd-Jones." An interview with Andrew Atherstone. The Gospel Coalition. October 18, 2016. https://www.thegospelcoalition.org/blogs/evangelical-history/50-years-ago-today.

Thompson, David M. *Same Difference? Liberals and Conservatives in the Student Movement*. Birmingham: Student Christian Movement, 1990.

Tinker, Melvin. *Evangelical Concerns: Rediscovering the Christian Mind on Issues Facing the Church Today*. Fearn, Ross-shire: Mentor, 2001.

"Transformation—The Church in Response to Human Need." The statement of Wheaton '83, published in *Transformation* 1, no. 1 (1984): 23–28. Also published under the same title, Grove Booklets on Ethics. Bramcote: Nottingham, 1986. And published with the conference papers in *The Church in Response to Human Need*, edited by Vinay Samuel and Chris Sugden, 254–65. Oxford: Regnum, 1987.

Treloar, Geoffrey R. *The Disruption of Evangelicalism: The Age of Torrey, Mott, McPherson and Hammond*. London: Inter-Varsity Press, 2016.

Volf, Miroslav. "On Loving with Hope: Eschatology and Social Responsibility." *Transformation* 7, no. 3 (1990): 28–31.

Wallis, Jim. *The New Radical*. Tring: Lion, 1993.

Wallis, Jim. *The Soul of Politics*. New York: Fount, 1994.

Warren, Max. "Charles Simeon: His Methods in the Local Church, the Church of England and the Nation." *Churchman* 92, no. 2 (1978): 112–24.

Weinandy, Thomas G. *Does God Suffer? The Mystery of God's Love.* Notre Dame, IN: Notre Dame University Press, 2000.

Welsby, Paul A. *A History of the Church of England 1945–1980.* Oxford, Oxford University Press, 1984.

Wolffe, John. *Evangelical Faith and Public Zeal: Evangelicals and Society in Britain 1780–1980.* London: SPCK, 1995.

Woodhouse, John. "Evangelism and Social Responsibility." In *Christians in Society,* edited by B. G. Webb, 3–26. Explorations. Homebush West, NSW, Australia: Lancer / Moore Theological College, 1988.

World Council of Churches. "Evangelism 1974: A Symposium." *International Review of Mission* 63, no. 249 (1974): 96–123.

Wright, Chris, ed. *John Stott: A Portrait by His Friends.* Nottingham: Inter-Varsity Press, 2011.

Wright, Christopher J. H. *Living as the People of God: The Relevance of Old Testament Ethics.* Nottingham: Inter-Varsity Press, 1983.

Wright, Christopher J. H. *The Mission of God: Unlocking the Bible's Grand Narrative.* Nottingham: Inter-Varsity Press, 2006.

Wright, Christopher J. H. *The Mission of God's People: A Biblical Theology of the Church's Mission.* Grand Rapids, MI: Zondervan, 2010.

Yoder, John Howard. *The Politics of Jesus.* Grand Rapids, MI: Eerdmans, 1972.

GENERAL INDEX

SCRIPTURE INDEX